Value, Historicity, and Economic Epistemology

Alain Herscovici

Value, Historicity, and Economic Epistemology

An Archaeology of Economic Science

palgrave
macmillan

Alain Herscovici
Vitoria, Espírito Santo, Brazil

ISBN 978-3-031-21156-0 ISBN 978-3-031-21157-7 (eBook)
https://doi.org/10.1007/978-3-031-21157-7

This Palgrave Macmillan imprint is published by the registered company Springer Nature Switzerland AG
The registered company address is: Gewerbestrasse 11, 6330 Cham, Switzerland

This research demonstrates the significance of ontology for methodology and seeks to identify the ontology implicit in any type of methodology. A particular contrast is drawn by critical realists between an open-system ontology, which requires some kind of open-system methodology, and the closed-system ontology identified as implicit in orthodox methodology.

(Dow, 2020)

Perhaps as important as what these definitions say is what they do not say.

(Backhouse, 2002)

The evolutionary point of view, therefore, leaves no place for a formulation of natural laws in terms of definitive normality, whether in economics or in any other branch of inquiry.

(Veblen, 1898)

Escrever um livro, um poema, ou compor uma música, é uma aventura, uma viagem, cujo destino é incerto. Dedico este livro à Denise, minha mulher, minha companheira que, durante mais de vinte anos, me acompanhou durante estas minhas inúmeras viagens.

Écrire un livre, un poème, ou composer une musique, est un aventure, un voyage dont la destination est inconnue. Je dédie ce livre à Denise, ma femme, ma compagne qui, durant plus de vingt ans, m'a accompagné dans mes multiples voyages.

Writing books, poems, or composing music is an adventure, a journey, whose end is uncertain. I dedicate this book to Denise, my wife, my partner, who, for more than twenty years, has accompanied me during my innumerous journeys.

In memory of my parents, Pincu Herscovici and Hélène Herscovici.

Foreword

This volume appears at a time when we are seeing an unprecedented degree of reflection on the discipline of economics. Economic and financial crises have sparked off periods of reflection in the past, but this time feels different. Mainstream economics has evolved somewhat to reflect the changing environment. At the same time, the policy discourse has been drawing increasingly on a wider range of ideas from other schools of thought in order to address crises in the economy, in finance, in climate, in health and in state provision of physical and social infrastructure. We are beginning to see signs of these changes being embedded in economics education, ensuring a more lasting set of changes to economic theorizing in the future. A key factor has been the organization and activities of the international student movement (notably in the form of Rethinking Economics and INET's Young Scholars Initiative) seeking a more pluralist education from a wider philosophical and historical perspective. Although it has been a focus of heterodox schools of thought for a long time, reflection on the discipline is being given new life.

The differences between heterodox economics and the mainstream stem from a deeper level than theorizing as such, but there is a reluctance within the mainstream to contemplate any other level, inhibiting debate. Addressing the basis of our thought is certainly challenging. Not only does it require economic communities to have philosophical self-awareness but it also requires a capacity to contemplate fundamentally different ways of understanding. If different understandings persist as they do in economics, then any meaningful discourse, far less any resolution of difference, requires the willingness and the capacity to dig deep.

Such efforts are now supported by an ever-expanding body of research on the philosophy and methodology of economics. We are better equipped now to address a range of important questions. Does economic thought inevitably progress (and what does that mean)? If not how do we account for the history of economic thought? Is there a framework outside of economics by which to judge theoretical developments? How do we understand and deal with a range of different schools of thought in economics? How far are such differences ultimately philosophical?

Alain Herscovici takes a deep dive into these questions and how we might attempt to address them. He does so by drawing on Michel Foucault's concept of episteme and Thomas Kuhn's concept of paradigm. Both thinkers have influenced the way in which we reflect on economic discourse. Foucault's influence is less evident than that of Kuhn. Fortunately, we have in Iara Vigo de Lima's important 2010 volume *Foucault's Archaeology of Political Economy* a detailed critical account of Foucault's archaeology of knowledge in relation to political economy. It is a pioneering exercise in carefully articulating Foucault's ideas on historiography and methodology in relation to the history of economic thought, demonstrating the scope for Foucault's ideas to illuminate our understanding of modern economics. Like Vigo de Lima, Herscovici compares Foucault's ideas to those of Kuhn. While Kuhn's work is more accessible than Foucault's and accordingly has been applied more widely to economics, his ideas have often been misunderstood. But drawing on both Foucault and Kuhn we can better appreciate how different understandings of epistemology, like economics, have emerged and what to make of them. The nature and source of understandings in economics, how they evolve, and how they are ruptured, is the focus of Alain Herscovici's book.

The first part of the book sets out a detailed and insightful analysis of epistemological issues for economics. Epistemology is understood in Foucauldian terms as proceeding through a series of epistemes. This periodization charts how the subject matter of science is successively understood and the way in which scientific enquiry successively proceeds. Difficult issues with Foucault's framework are explored: the exclusivity of epistemes for Foucault within and between periods and how to understand the process of rupture and transition from one to another. Also further questions arise from the fact that what Foucault termed the "modern" episteme did not incorporate changes in economics which had already occurred by the 1960s. A notable omission which Alain Herscovici makes good is the process behind the rise to dominance of neoclassical economics. Did Foucault regard it as too challenging to step back from current thought in order to locate it in a historical meta-epistemic framework? Yet in our own time we inevitably start from a contemporary episteme. Does this in turn limit our capacity to understand preceding epistemes?

By drawing on Kuhn to address these issues, Alain Herscovici adapts Foucault's concept of epistemes, treating them as "ideal types" and setting out a more flexible framework allowing, for example for "hybrid types." He employs his flexible framework to offer a rich and impressively detailed account of different sets of ideas in economics in relation key figures and to schools of thought. He demonstrates how such accounts can clarify understanding by highlighting where problems of inconsistency arise. A particular focus is put on understanding ruptures in economic thought, distinguishing between the internal history and the external history of ideas. The former corresponds to Kuhn's normal science within which the paradigmatic framework is taken as given. The latter corresponds to extraordinary science whereby an alternative paradigm is put forward, with its success or failure depending on external circumstances which may challenge the prevailing episteme but also those which might impede rupture, such as the distribution of power.

The whole point of the exercise is to direct inquiry to the philosophical level, to the ontology and epistemology which underpin particular approaches to economics. Then the history of economic thought can be told in a way which makes more sense, addressing different sequential or concurrent understandings. Similarly, the different approaches to historiography can themselves be better understood by exploring their philosophical foundations. Of course, it is impossible to step outside one episteme (or paradigm) or another. The best we can do is to be self-aware and aware of our intellectual environment, be able to articulate the episteme of our own community, and to strive to understand that of others. Understanding differences does not necessarily mean resolving them—indeed where there are different concurrent epistemes or paradigms there is no scope for resolution. But there is scope for enlightenment. A deeper understanding should mean that philosophical differences and, importantly, inconsistencies are brought to the surface such that debate can be much more productive.

Alain Herscovici's volume makes an important contribution to such understanding, spelling out the philosophical issues in an innovative way and applying them with a wealth of detailed analysis of episodes and themes in the history of economic thought up to the present day.

August 2022

Sheila Dow
University of Stirling
Stirling, UK

Contents

About the Author

Alain Herscovici is Full Professor, Department of Economics and Post-Graduation Program, Federal University of Espírito Santo (UFES), Brazil, leader of the Grupo de Estudo em Macroeconomia (GREM) and the Grupo de Estudo em Economia da Cultura, da Comunicação, da Informação e do Conhecimento (GEECICC), UFES, CNPq (National Council for Scientific and Technological Development). His research areas are the following ones: Macroeconomics, Economic Epistemology, History of Economic Thought, Cultural Economics, Information Economics, Law and Economics and Institutional Economics.

List of Figures

List of Tables

CHAPTER 1

Introduction

An Archeology

Archeology is defined by Larousse as "The study of ancient civilizations carried out from material remains, or from their context." The archeology of Science consists, therefore, in "digging" into the past to identify the elements that make it possible to explain the birth of Science; this concept is particularly suitable to implement an epistemological study, that is, to study the different epistemological trajectories followed by Science.

Nevertheless, this study makes necessary a genealogical analysis; as one can see throughout this work, the concept of episteme is static in the sense that it is not able to explain the evolutions and succession of different epistemes. An analysis of *genealogical* nature is thus complementary and necessary: it should allow the study of the dynamics of discontinuities and thus reveal the endogenous forces that guide the trajectories followed by Science. Genealogical analysis provides "(…) an investigation tool aimed at understanding the emergence of unique configurations of subjects, objects and meanings in power relations, associating the examination of discursive and non-discursive practices" (Malheiros and Vinicius 2018).

This approach is intrinsically historical:

(i) It refutes the hypothesis of the autonomy of Science and the existence of an absolute or suprahistorical truth to be discovered. On the contrary, it shows from what specific and historical conditions

A. Herscovici, *Value, Historicity, and Economic Epistemology*,
https://doi.org/10.1007/978-3-031-21157-7_1

different scientific discourses were born and developed. Objects and subject are not suprahistorical analytical categories whose function consists solely in revealing the intrinsic truth embedded in Nature: the object and the subject are equally historically determined.

Science does not develop from an autonomous logic, regardless of historical, social, political and economic contingencies. Thus, in this perspective, it is not possible to conceive the existence of long-term scientific progress; the evolutions are not cumulative, but are, in part, due to the epistemological ruptures that characterize the History of Science.

The dynamics of these evolutions can be explained by the incompatibilities that characterize the different schools of thought, which translate into radical epistemological ruptures, but also by the elements of continuity that appear within each of these schools. From a Kuhnian perspective, we can claim that continuity is related to normal science and discontinuity to the ruptures that correspond to anomalies. Thus, *history of economic thought is inseparable from epistemology*: "We use the term 'methodology' to encompass both the methods actually employed within a school of thought and the underlying world-view which generated them" (Dow 1985, p. 2). However, it is not possible to discern a long-term trend that would guide these evolutions.

(ii) This approach reveals the relationship between discursive practices and non-discursive ones (Malheiros and Vinicius 2018, op. cit.): while the former appear explicitly in scientific discourse, the latter can be defined as the "doxa" that prevails in the period studied. These non-discursive practices are, by nature, hidden, and are the product of the power relationships that operate in the field of scientific production: "The subjective representation of the social world as legitimate is part of the complete truth of this world" (Bourdieu, 1984).

At a time when the technicalization of economics is reaching a particularly high level, it is important to implement a methodological and epistemological reflection to define the explanatory value and limits of the paradigms within which these techniques are developed.

The different techniques used only make sense once the hypotheses that characterize the paradigm within which they operate have been accepted: these techniques are explanatory within the scope of normal science (Kuhn 1991), and cease to be so when normal science encounters anomalies that it cannot resolve. In the absence of such reflection, Economics will soon become an economic engineering, an instrumental science (Feyerabend 1975) in which social, political and historical dimensions will be totally ignored.

The present book does not work within what Kuhn qualifies as normal science, either orthodoxy or different heterodoxies; it does not fit within a particular paradigm but, on the contrary, it intends to highlight the characteristics and limits of each paradigm and explain how the main evolutions of Economic Science occurred. In this sense, this work is "*borderline*": it will not limit to methodology study, but it will explicit the main characteristics of the paradigm, or the episteme, within which the methodology was elaborated: this means "(….) to identify the ontology implicit in any type of methodology" (Dow 2020, p. 4).

Why Foucault?

The issue that guides this work was suggested to me by Foucault, more specifically in the books "*Les mots et les choses*" and "*L'archéologie du savoir*." In these two works, the author highlights the intrinsic historicity of Science, based on Grammar, Natural Sciences and Political Economy; I will limit myself to developments dealing with Political Economy.

It is interesting to note that, in these two books, Foucault starts his study from mercantilism, proceeds with the Physiocratic School and with Classical Economics. He only mentions, anecdotally, marginalism and contemporary developments of the Neoclassical School. The analysis is mainly centered on the concept of episteme: Foucault thus relates the different schools of economic thought mainly with the classical episteme and with the episteme represented by modernity.

In later writings related to biopolitics (Foucault 1979), he mainly studies the theses developed by Mises and Hayek, based on the concept of power structure, and seems to have abandoned the concept of episteme developed in the two books mentioned; contrary to Foucault, I will include in my analysis the Neoclassical School and the Austrian School, and I will emphasize the relationships they maintain with the different epistemes. I will study long-term evolutions from the concept of episteme.

One of the limitations of Foucault's analysis comes from *the static character of the concept of episteme*: as it is a question of drawing up a retrospective of the different schools of economic thought, based on the discontinuities proper to episteme shift, it would have been interesting to relate the Neoclassical School with a certain episteme, but Foucault did not elaborate such an analysis. This highlights the limits of Foucault's analysis (Birken 1990), without a doubt: either the concept of episteme is unable to explain the emergence of the Neoclassical School and, in this case, the study is partial, or the Neoclassical School is conceived as the product of the episteme linked to modernity (Vigo 2010). In this case, this implies that, for example, the (neo-)Ricardian school and the Neoclassical School are the product of the same episteme: I will demonstrate why such a conception is hardly sustainable.

On the other hand, these limits come from Foucault's definition of episteme: its periodization is particularly rigid because he considers that each period is characterized by a single episteme, which does not allow, among other things, analyzing the dynamics of succession of different epistemes over time. I propose to "flexibilize" the concept of episteme in such a way that it allows the study of historical dynamics, that is, the endogenous dynamics that explain the passage from one episteme to another. From this "revisited" concept of episteme, I will include both Neoclassical Economics and the contributions of the Austrian school, mainly Hayek's, in the analysis.

Epistemology, History of Economic Thought and History of Ideas

Epistemology and Historicity

If epistemology defines itself as a branch of philosophy that studies the methods to be used in Science, I can already say that the study elaborated in this book cannot be limited to this traditional conception: epistemology, as an autonomous science, starts from the hypothesis according to which evolutions can be studied based on criteria that are unique to Science: this presupposes the autonomy of Science and its developments.

This epistemological approach is based on the assumption that the evolution of Science can only be explained from its internal history, and that it is possible to reason in terms of the progress of Science; this Popperian approach is supported by a universalist view according to which all these evolutions necessarily lead to the constitution of current science, that is, to a more evolved and more complete form.[1]

According to this conception, the evolution of Science would be essentially autonomous and cumulative, towards a progressive improvement; this conception is translated by the fact that scientific laws are universal, as well as the demarcation criteria from which scientificity is defined. In this perspective, the scientific character of the different schools of thought will be evaluated using the same criteria.

In this book, from the Historicity of Science, and more specifically of Economic Science, I will refute this approach. I will try to reconstruct the *sinuous paths* that run through the different researches in Economics, highlighting its different points of bifurcation, its contradictions, as well as the compatibilities and incompatibilities that exist between the different schools of thought. I will examine the elements of continuity, but also of discontinuity, in order to portray the main evolutions of Economic Science, since its foundation with the Physiocratic School until today.

I propose to design a *historicized epistemology* from which evolutions will be explained based on the combined action of internal and external History. It is not possible to limit the analysis to external determinisms, nor to the internal logic of the field of scientific production. Consequently, as these evolutions are explained from these two dimensions (internal and external), the History of Economic Thought has to incorporate a "purely" epistemological, i.e., the internal dimension, and another historical one linked to external History; for this reason, it would be more accurate to speak of a *History of Economic Ideas*.

The History of Economic Ideas and the Historical Method

From an epistemological point of view, the problems encountered to define the method to be used by the History of Economic Thought are similar to those dealt with by Histography, in which different conceptions are opposed.

A first distinction is made by Braudel (1969) between History that deals with short-term movements, and another that analyzes long-term movements. The first is more "punctual": a so-called "*évènementielle*" History concerns short-term movements and the situation appears on the

[1] Popper and Hayek, for different reasons, formulate such conclusion.

"surface." The other, called structural History (Bourdé 1983, pp. 234, 235), studies long-term movements.

An analysis in terms of episteme reveals, by nature, the second conception, that is, of long-term movements: the medium and/or the short term can only be conceived as a surface mechanism whose full meaning only appears in function of the long-term movement in which it participates: this is what Foucault is saying, in other words, elaborating and using the concept of episteme.

This study, of course, will not be exhaustive; I will purposely stop dealing with several authors to limit myself to the main paradigms that marked these evolutions, and to the modalities through which these paradigms are embedded in a specific episteme.

On the other hand, it is important to note the similarities between the concept of episteme and the conception of the History of mentalities. First, the concept of episteme aims to reveal "(…) mental structures (…) halfway between social organization and ideological discourse (…)" (Idem, p. 243); it is only possible to evaluate a school of thought based on the criteria in force in the episteme to which that school belongs. In other words, it is not possible to evaluate a thought formulated in the past based on criteria proper to the present time.

Such a choice implies practicing historical relativism and refuting, in the long run, the concept of progress in Science; this *démarche* comes from anthropology and ethnology, disciplines with which economists are not familiar: several economists have studied schools of the past in the light of the Neoclassical School, which is dominant today: thus, for example, Ricardo's theory of differential income is conceived as the premises of the marginalist school (Marshall 1920; Blaug 1992), which constitutes a misinterpretation (Schefold 2017, p. 19; Herscovici 2019). Second, these mentalities are not randomic, but they are determined from the mechanisms that govern the epistemes to which they belong.

Historicity and Substantial Hypothesis

The substantial hypothesis, explicit for certain authors (Dumont 1985; Orléan 2011) and implicit for others (Foucault 1966), is associated with the birth of Economic Science[2]; it would be the common denominator

[2] At this respect, Orléan (2011) speaks in value empire.

between the different schools of thought. In a first approximation, it is defined based on the hypothesis according to which the commodities exchanged in the markets have intrinsic characteristics, that is, "natural" ones.

For example, in this regard, Marx states that utility, that is, the use value of a commodity, does not express any social relationship (1859, p. 25): the use value would be a characteristic of the commodity. From Physiocracy to the Neoclassical School, the quality of goods, that is, the determinants of use value, is conceived as an exogenous variable: for Classical Economics, it represents an intrinsic characteristic of goods—for Neoclassical Economics, within the scope of the subjective theory of value, individual preferences are exogenous and qualities are characteristics of the commodity (Lancaster 1966).

Stiglitz (1987) refutes this hypothesis and, in the context of the construction of a "relational" economy (Herscovici 2019), *he endogenizes the qualities*, which represents a historicization of the analysis.

On the other hand, the dichotomy between orthodoxy and heterodoxy, in Economics, is not defined from the theory of value adopted, or from the absence of such a theory: the Austrian school, for example, does not adopt any theory of value, but it reaches results very close to those formulated by Neoclassical Economics. Likewise, Schumpeter, despite being considered heterodox, does not adopt any theory of value.

Thus, the differentiation between orthodoxy and heterodoxy is not characterized by the fact that it adopts a certain theory of value: the labor theory of value, with regard to heterodoxy, the utility value theory, with regard to orthodoxy, but by incorporation or the refutation of the historicity embedded in the theoretical framework that constitutes the hardcore of the research program; economic methodology cannot be studied independently of the paradigm, or the episteme, within which it was conceived. Notwitstanding, such typology remains imperfect: I will show that certain authors who are considered heterodox use the substantial hypothesis (this position corresponding to the universalist thesis), as do most authors who belong to orthodoxy.

The General Problematic

The issue from which I conceived this book is twofold:

(i) What are the different schools of thought present in Economic Science, and from what conditions, internal and external, did they arise? This question implies associating these different schools with different epistemes.
(ii) What are the elements that determine long-term evolutions, that is, from which dynamics did these evolutions and episteme changes occur?

Depending on the elements of answers, it is possible to question the concept of progress in Science: are these evolutions ordered from an ascending trend, or are they characterized by ruptures and discontinuities? It should also be noted that, more specifically, Economics is characterized by the coexistence of various schools of thought. *This makes it necessary to study the nature of the ruptures between these schools*: are they superficial ruptures, within the same paradigm, or of the same episteme, or are they fundamental ruptures, due to the fact that these schools belong to different epistemes? It is necessary to assess the respective weight of internal history and external history, in determining these evolutions, and this is based on the following elements:

(a) Lakatos privileges the Internal History of Science: this Internal History is the main element that allows studying these evolutions. In this regard, I will examine how, and to what extent, these evolutions can be deduced from the compatibilities and incompatibilities between these different schools of thought. These relationships can manifest themselves within the same episteme (or epistemological field, according to Foucault 1966, p. 13) or, on the contrary, from two different epistemes; in the latter case, they are insurmountable incompatibilities.

An epistemological period is characterized by the fact that there is *tacit agreement* about the problems that are deemed relevant; an epistemological period is also characterized by consensus regarding the definition of the object of study itself. Within the same epistemological field, the incompatibility existing between the answers provided by each sub-school matters less than the agreement regarding the problems to be dealt with (Bourdieu 1984).

Nevertheless, these evolutions are the product of a double movement. *Internal History allows me to explain the evolutions within the same epistemological field, External History the changes of the epistemological fields themselves. The first is characterized by epistemological continuity, the second by discontinuity*, which corresponds respectively, in Kuhn's (1991) terminology, to normal science and scientific revolutions. This archeology of economic knowledge will be studied in terms of these two dimensions.

(b) With regard to the study of External History, I will start from the seminal works of Kuhn and Foucault. Kuhn defines scientific revolutions as the moments in which the elements that allow explaining the paradigm shift appear. This paradigm shift is not the result of the autonomous progress of Science, but of choice whose determinants are essentially social, political and historical: the definition of the epistemological field is not explained by a progress that would translate into greater objectivity, nor by a power greater explanatory, but simply "(…) because of its conditions of possibility (…)" (Foucault 1966, p. 13).

The General Structure of the Book

In the first part, I will carry out an "archeology" of Economic Science, and introduce elements to conceive a genealogy; the first two chapters consist of carrying out this archeology from a static analysis. The third chapter provides elements to implement a study in terms of genealogy, in the sense of explaining the dynamics of evolutions and changes in epistemes; this genealogy will be applied to different schools of thought, from the Physiocrats to the Austrian school.

- In Chapter 2, I will explain the different conceptions regarding epistemology, and the modalities from which Historicity can be integrated in the analysis. The discussion will be essentially epistemological, and related to the different hypotheses and the different tools used in epistemology. Particular attention will be paid to the definition of subject and object, and their interrelationships.

- In Chapter 3, under a static approach, I will classify the different schools chosen according to the different epistemes defined by Foucault, and I will emphasize the explanatory limits of this author, with regard to Economics. The epistemological characteristics of each school do not correspond to the characteristics of a single episteme: they contain elements from different epistemes.

Episteme is an "abstract" concept, as it was conceived as an ideal type, that is, a "pure" form: the epistemological characteristics of each school are concrete forms, as they use elements that come from various epistemes. I will emphasize this *hybrid character* present in the different schools studied.

- In Chapter 4, I will demonstrate why Economic Science is characterized by the incommensurability of the different paradigms, and why it is not possible to conceive, from a long-term perspective, scientific progress.

In the second part, I will study in detail three contemporary controversies in Economic Science, and I will examine to what extent they reflect epistemological continuities or ruptures; I will define the epistemological nature of these ruptures, for each of the controversial ones.

- In Chapter 5, I will emphasize the criticism that the neo-Ricardian school makes in relation to the neoclassical aggregate model; it is an internal criticism that allows me to refute the micro and macroeconomic foundations of Neoclassical Economics, its main theoretical results and its applications in terms of economic policy.

We can note that even one of the most brilliant representatives of this neoclassical matrix, notably Paul Samuelson, was unable to respond to this criticism. Nevertheless, despite this failure, Neoclassical Economics remains the dominant current; if this primacy is not explained by internal history, it must be explained from external history.

- In Chapter 6, I will make explicit the foundations of the criticisms formulated by Hayek, in relation to the neoclassical model. I will study the nature of this critique, and show to what extent, beyond appearances, beyond the fact that it refutes the mechanisms proper to General Equilibrium and maximization by economic agents, the Hayekian paradigm shares part of the basic hypotheses of the neoclassical model: the primacy of the real sector in relation to money and finance.

- In Chapter 7, I will demonstrate to what extent the (post-)Keynesian matrix allows refuting both neoclassical and Hayekian analysis, from a different conception of money and financial assets: while neoclassical and Hayekian analysis considers that money and finance are neutral, on the contrary, post-Keynesian analysis emphasizes the non-neutrality of money and finance, which implies refuting this primacy of the real sector.

The last chapter will be a synthesis of this second part: (a) I will emphasize the explanatory limits of the currents that claim that the microeconomic foundations allow the implementation of a global regulation, and (b) One can see why any collectivity is regulated by an order that, as an *emergent property*, transcends the purely individual microeconomic components. This concept of order should complement the concept of episteme, introducing dynamic elements that make it possible to explain the long-term evolutions of Economic Science, and should make it possible to classify the different schools of thought according to the type of concrete order that characterizes them.

References

Birken, Lawrence. 1990. Foucault, Marginalism, and the History of Economic Thought: A Rejoinder to Amariglio. *History of Political Economy* 22 (3): 557–569.

Blaug, Mark. 1992. *The Methodology of Economics or How Economists Explain*, 2nd ed. Cambridge: Cambridge University Press.

Bourdé, Guy. 1983. «L'école des «Annales»». In *Bourdé Guy et Hervé Martin, Les écoles historiques*, 215–244. Paris: Editions du Seuil.

Bourdieu, Pierre. 1984. *Questions de Sociologie*. Paris: Les Éditions de Minuit.

Braudel, Fernand. 1969. *Écrits sur l'hstoire*. Paris: Flammarion.

Dow, Sheila. 1985. *Macroeconomic Thought: A Methodological Approach*. Oxford: Basil Blackwell.

———. 2020. *Economic Methodology, the Philosophy of Economics and the Economy: Another Turn?* Division of Economics, Stirling Management School, University of Stirling, Stirling FK9 4LA, UK.

Dumont, Louis. 1985. *Homo aequalis. Genèse et épanouissement de l'idéologie économique*. Paris: NRF, Editions Gallimard.
Feyerabend, Paul. 1975. *Against Method*. London: New Left Books.
Foucault, Michel. 1966. *Les mots et les choses*. Paris: Tel Galimard.
———. 1969. *L'archéologie du savoir*. Paris: Gallimard.
———. 1979. Naissance de la Biopolitique. In *Michel Foucault, Dits et écrits: 1954-1988, tome II, 1976–1988*, ed. Daniel Defert and François Ewald, 818–826. Paris: Gallimard.
Herscovici, Alain. 2019. *Essays on the Historicity of Capital*. Cham: Palgrave Macmillan.
Kuhn, Thomas S. 1991 [1962]. *A estrutura das revoluções científicas*. São Paulo: Editora Perspectiva.
Lancaster, Kelvin. 1966. A New Approach to Consummer Theory. *Journal of Political Economy* 74 (2, April): 132–157.
Malheiros, Moraes, and Marcos Vinicius. 2018. Genealogia-Michel Foucault, Enciclopédida de Antropologia. https://ea.fflch.usp.br/conceito/genealogia-michel-foucault. Accessed 28 September 2021.
Marshall, Alfred. 1920. *Principles of Economics*, 8th ed. London: Macmillan and Co.
Marx, Karl. 1972 [1859]. *Contribution à la critique de l'économie politique*. Paris: Editions Sociales.
Marx, Karl. 1976 [1867, 1894]. *Le Capital*, *Critique de l'économie politique*. Paris: Editions Sociales.
Orléan, André. 2011. *L'empire de la valeur. Refonder l'Économie*. Paris: Éditions du Seuil.
Schefold, Bertram. 2017. *Great Economic Thinkers from the Classicals to the Moderns*. Routledge Studies in the History of Economics.
Stiglitz Joseph E. 1987. The Causes and Consequences of the Dependence of Quality on Price. *Journal of Economic Literature* XXV (March): 1–48.
Vigo, Iara. 2010. *Foucault's Archaeology of Political Economy*. Palgrave Macmillan.

PART I

An Archeology of Economic Science: From the Physiocrats to the Neoclassics

CHAPTER 2

History of Sciences and Epistemology

This chapter aims to define the different conceptions regarding the nature of epistemology and, ultimately, to determine the relative weight of internal and external history in these different approaches. This leads us to elaborate a reflection on the nature of scientific explanation, the relationships between subject and object, and the Historicity or universality of Science; this also leads us to question the concept of scientific progress, at least with regard to Economics.

After having defined the concept of episteme, as well as the different epistemes that characterize the different epistemological temporalities, in the context of a comparison with Kuhn and Lakatos, I will emphasize the explanatory value of this concept and its limits.

History of Science and Epistemology: Internal History Versus External History?

The Different Conceptions

While economic methodology is conceived as an economic discipline, epistemology is a discipline that belongs to philosophy, more specifically to philosophy of science.

Internal history concerns the methodology employed within a given paradigm; external history is directly related to the evolution of the

A. Herscovici, *Value, Historicity, and Economic Epistemology*, https://doi.org/10.1007/978-3-031-21157-7_2

different paradigms within which different methodologies were developed.

Within the scope of the mainstream approach, and of the hypothesis of the autonomy of the scientific field, internal history is able to explain the evolution of Science and is based on scientific neutrality; economic methodology has to be studied by economists, independently of philosophy.

On the contrary, historicism must be defined from these two dimensions that are inseparable: "Indeed philosophy and methodology could no longer be regarded as distinct, but were rather in an interactive relationship" (Dow 2020, pp. 3, 4). *Such approach emphasizes the explanatory value, the historical limits of the different paradigms* and the need to resort to Epistemology, in its philosophical definition, in order to assess these limits. Contrary to mainstream discourse, methodology is not a neutral tool, but it is historically determined; such approach characterizes most part of heterodox economics (Idem, p. 12).

There are several conceptions regarding the History of Sciences:

(i) A first conception, which I will call idealist, starts from the hypothesis of the autonomy of Science; the more orthodox strand (Popper 1959; Grangier 1993) supports the thesis of full and total autonomy. In this case, it is possible to speak of Science progress; this progress translates into an expansion of the explanatory power of the systems elaborated: this progress is, in a way, cumulative, and it translates into an expansion of the precision of the analysis and the reliability of the predictions elaborated from these models. This analysis implies the universality of scientific laws (Popper, Hayek).

(ii) Other conceptions, on the contrary, will not limit the object of the History of Sciences to its Internal History; External History will be one of the variables that allow me to study these evolutions.

In this regard, Merton's position is particularly interesting: if, on the one hand, there is a determinism exercised by external history (sociological, political, historical, institutional elements), this determinism is only partial (Merton 2013, p. 121): "Philosophy, religion, science are particularly constrained by the preexisting stock of knowledge and belief and are only indirectly and ultimately influenced by economic factors (cf. Engels and

Marx 1935, 1, p. 386)." This implies that "that the ideological spheres exhibit a certain degree of independent development (…)" (Idem, p. 28).

Kuhn's position is complementary in the following sense: as the evolutions of Science are explained, at least in part, from external variables, these evolutions are not cumulative, and it is no longer possible to speak of Science progress; these evolutions are discontinuous, and they are characterized by ruptures.

These approaches will explain the evolution of Science both from the determinism exerted by external variables and by the internal logic of the scientific field. The problem can be summarized as follows: to what extent is the choice of objects of study, the problems to be solved and the methods adopted, the products of the autonomous logic of the field of scientific production and/or external variables?

> "The historian of science must conceive ideas as facts. The epistemologist must conceive facts as ideas based on their insertion in a system of thought." (Bachelard 1989, p. 17)

The historian of Science thus studies the modalities of formation and evolution of ideas, and the epistemologist constructs and interprets these facts based on the coherence of different historically determined scientific systems. The historian of Science analyzes the elements linked to external history, that is, the way in which facts were chosen and designed; the epistemologist studies the coherence of the scientific *démarche* with regard to the choice of facts and the coherence of the mechanisms by which these facts are explained.

Foucault's approach may be defined as a "*meta-epistemology*": an epistemology of the epistemological criteria adopted by scientists at different times. This approach is, by nature, incomplete and partial: it is a Droste effect, as this feedback effect can be repeated infinitely. In this sense, it is possible to state that Foucault advocates a method, a method that is characterized by its historicity, and that, at the same time, he highlights the limits of this method (Vallois 2015, p. 4).

The Autonomy of the Scientific Field and the Progress of Science

The Autonomization Process

It is important to note that Epistemology only appeared once the Sciences were emancipated, at least in part, from external political, religious and social powers; the same kind of observations apply equally to aesthetics or linguistics (Merton 2013, p. 176; Bourdieu 1979).

The approach that guides the present research intends to study these two dimensions to explain the evolution of Economic Science (Scheler speaks of codetermination, *op. cit* Merton). As I have shown in previous works (Herscovici 2019), the domination of Neoclassical Economics is not explained by its epistemological superiority but, essentially, by external variables.

From this conception, the progress of science, as it exists, is limited to a certain paradigm (Kuhn 1991) or a certain episteme (Foucault 1966), but it is not able to explain the passage from a paradigm to other. This is explained by the *incommensurability* of different paradigms. Within the same episteme, or the same paradigm, we find here what Balibar calls *points of heresy* (2020, p. 141):

> "Epistemological conflicts are relativized, that is, represented as surface phenomena, in relation to the general system (or structure) within which it is inscribed."

This interpretation of Foucault's concept of episteme highlights two movements: the internal logic that operates within a given system of thought, and the external logic that determines this system. The controversies that arise within a given system do not modify the logic that characterizes that paradigm: for example, the oppositions between the analyses of Ricardo and Marx are situated within the same system of thought, that of Classical Economics (Foucault 1966; Balibar 2020, p. 145). The same kind of observation can be made about the 1990s debate between new classical and new Keynesians.

Bourdieu reaches similar conclusions: "[…] from internal struggles, only partial revolutions can emerge, capable of destroying the hierarchy, but not the game itself" (Bourdieu 1984, p. 199): beyond these apparent (and superficial) conflicts, the rules of the game that characterize the social field remain. The perennity of the social field is characterized by the existence of a consensus regarding the problems to be solved (Idem, p. 222).

Foucault thus affirms the intrinsic historicity of different fields of knowledge, historicity being defined as the "epistemological disposition" (Foucault 1966, p. 274). On the other hand, the existence of a field of scientific production presupposes a prior emancipation from the activities that will be carried out within this field: emancipation from different forms of external power. This emancipation represents the necessary and sufficient condition for the field to develop its own mechanisms, and thus distance itself from other spheres of power.

In his theory of social fields, Bourdieu defines a field of production as a *relatively* autonomous social space that produces, from endogenous and specific mechanisms, its own instances of legitimation, production and consumption, that is, its operating modalities. Modern Science was born in the Renaissance, from the moment that it was no longer directly subordinated to religious and political power; the greater the distance from powers outside the field, the greater the autonomy of the field and the freedom of the actors who act in this field.

This emancipation, and the resulting autonomization, can only take place in liberal democracies, where there is a developed public space, in the Habermassian sense; perhaps, it is for this reason that part of the Sciences and Arts developed in ancient Greece, in the context of democracy. In authoritarian states, or in societies in which political power is linked to a divine order, such autonomy does not exist: interference in the logic of these fields is incompatible with the autonomy necessary for the development of this field (Merton, 2013, p. 176).

A Relative Autonomy

From this approach, it is necessary to question and redefine the autonomy of the scientific field, the articulations and the respective weight of internal History and external History, in relation to the evolution of Science.

Social and historical determinisms allow explaining the evolution of Science. The evolutions are not explained only by the internal logic of the field of scientific production: "[…] if circumstances produce men, men produce circumstances" (Marx and Engels 1845, p. 39). The Sartrean concept of project at the same time asserts the existence of autonomy and external determinisms; this autonomy is limited by these determinisms. The project expresses its autonomy based on the choices made within a predetermined general framework; the degree of freedom of actors working in this field depends on the choices they can make (Sartre 1986, p. 137).

Nevertheless, this autonomy remains relative: the influence of other social fields is mediated by the specificities of the field in which they operate: conflicts that appear within the field, or between different fields, are a specific manifestation (because they are mediated) of political, religious or ideological conflicts. With regard to the cultural field, for example, conflicts that, within the field, appear as purely aesthetic, are a manifestation of external political conflicts (Bourdieu 1979; Herscovici 1994); the same kind of observations can be applied to the scientific field.

From an epistemological point of view, the study of a specific field of production cannot ignore the set of social, historical and political components that characterize the society in which it operates:

> "The sociology of knowledge emerged with the signaling hypothesis that even truths should be considered socially explainable, should be related to the historical society in which they emerged." (Merton 2013, p. 115)

The study of the evolutions of different social fields cannot ignore the historical situations in which these fields are inserted. On the contrary, "idealistic" analyses ignore, by hypothesis, the elements of this context, and are limited to a purely internal study: the evolution of Science would be the product of its autonomous logic, that is, of its internal History. The implications are as follows:

(i) Within the scope of a Hegelian logic, the manifestation of the Objective Spirit causes a "self-determination of the concept" (Marx and Engels 1845, p. 47). Aesthetics, Science or Language will only be analyzed in terms of this internal logic.

(ii) This refers to the hypothesis of a human nature, that is, to certain universal elements present in all societies and all times; this human nature is invoked by most classical and neoclassical economists. On the other hand, according to Popper (and according to Hayek, too, but for other reasons), scientific laws must, by nature, be universal. The objective of Science is to discover the truth that is embedded in the objects that are analyzed: this refers to different conceptions regarding the very definition of the object and the subject. This scientific progress is closely linked to the discovery of universal laws and the existence of a human nature (Veblen 1899, p. 39).

(iii) From this perspective, it is possible to speak of progress in Science; there would be an autonomous and cumulative development of the "Idea" towards increasingly "explanatory" formalizations. The evolution of Science is conceived as a long journey towards the discovery of the truth contained in the studied objects.

For Popper, the progress of Science is the product "(....) *of the free competition of thought*" supported by institutions that guarantee scientific objectivity (1972, p. 194, emphasis added). This thesis, in addition to demonstrating a naive positivism, implies that scientific institutions are socially neutral instances and are able to guarantee this scientific objectivity: social conflicts are voluntarily ignored, and totally absent from these scientific institutions.

I can simply provide the following counter-arguments: renowned scientific journals represent an important element of appreciation and differentiation within the academic community, within the symbolic "market" inherent to this type of production. The legitimacy, i.e., the symbolic capital, directly depends on this type of publications. Nevertheless, an empirical analysis of these markets allows me to refute, in its entirety, the Popperian thesis:

- The degree of legitimacy of different scientific journals depends on the ranking determined by the "scientific community." In different instances of consecration (Universities, departments and research institutes), the evaluation of different journals is the object of several conflicts between different fractions of the scientific community: this confirms Bourdieu's thesis according to which classification system (*classement* in French) is the product of a political struggle (Bourdieu 1984, p. 83).
- Within these conflicting relationships, "orthodoxy" dominates the field; it takes advantage of this situation to build barriers to entry, in relation to different heterodoxies. In the more specific case of Economics, these barriers to entry are manifested in the following way: for a heterodox economist to be able to publish in one of these most valued journals, he will have to justify his methodological choice and then implement his analysis, while an orthodox economist will not need to justify his choices. There are barriers to entry in order to achieve the same legitimacy. So a heterodox economist will have an additional workload, in relation to an orthodox economist. In this case, the structuring of the scientific

field itself is not explained solely from its internal logic, but from political conflicts that translate into scientific conflicts.

Historicity and Epistemology

The General Problem

The Epistemological Position

The oppositions between the idealist and the materialist position are directly related to the opposition between universalism and historicism, between determinism and methodological indeterminism; this debate refers directly to the nature of scientific laws, and to the definition of subject and object.

Seventeenth-century methodological determinism is found, in its most elaborate form, in the works of Kant, Leibniz and Descartes. What is the nature of "reality," how is it possible, in the case of Science, to define the nature of the object of study and its relations with the subject who implements this study?

Kant's Philosophy is characterized by the hypothesis according to which the world exists outside of us: reality exists as a "real" and immutable fact (Fournier and Rigal 2007, p. 3), and Science is able to objectively analyze this reality to reveal its mechanisms; the ultimate aim of Science is to discover the "truth." The epistemological project of this deterministic view is to produce *universal knowledge* (Ong-Van-Cung 2018, pp. 7 and 11), that is, knowledge that is totally independent of different historical contingencies. Leibniz thus elaborates the *mathesis universalis*, which makes it possible to conceive as a "(…) formal science of order and measure (…)" (Idem, p. 9).

This objective and positivist conception of Science presupposes the neutrality of the subject. If, on the one hand, the object of Science is to discover natural and universal laws, the subject must possess these same qualities. The Cartesian cogito states that "«I *think, therefore I am*"; it is necessarily true, every time *I* utter this statement or conceive it (Descartes 1647, méditation seconde). *I* is a transcendental subject insofar as it is "neutral," devoid of any historical dimension; *I* is a universal subject.

Finally, this type of deterministic approach presupposes that the systems are (a) stable systems, in the sense of being able to predict their trajectories (Vercelli 1991); (b) universal, by nature and (c) that the laws of nature are analyzed from a mathematical determinism.

A system is stable when its evolutions are not hypersensitive to initial conditions (Herscovici, 2019, Vercelli, op. cit.); in this case, it is possible to speak of universality of scientific laws.[1] The Cartesian scientific truth is explained by the fact that it corresponds to the mathesis universalis (Ong-Van-Cung 2018, p. 11): if the laws of the universe can be deciphered from mathematics, the resolution of the problems that Nature presents corresponds to the solving of a mathematical problem. Science uses mathematical determinism to solve these problems (Dahan Dalmenico 1992, p. 400).

In this regard, it is interesting to note that, in Economics, mathematical determinism was widely used: the approaches linked to General Equilibrium, but also those that deal with the problem of transforming values into production prices, are formulated from a system of simultaneous equations: the "explanation" consists of solving this system from a single solution. On the other hand, the system is deterministic: from the moment we know this system of equations, it is possible to predict the evolution of this system.

When the system is unstable, it is hypersensitive to these initial conditions (Israël 1992, p. 258). As measurement instruments have limited accuracy, it is never possible to define exactly these initial conditions; therefore, it is not possible to predict the evolution of the system, which characterizes the *methodological indeterminism* (Vercelli 1991).

It should be noted that methodological determinism is associated with universalism, as the system does not depend on initial conditions; scientific laws are by nature universal in the Popperian sense. In other words, the "world" exists independently of the subject who observes it, as an external and immutable reality: scientific truth consists in deciphering, using a mathematical tool, the laws that govern this reality.

Ultimately, the different conceptions regarding the nature of the subject and the object justify the differences that exist between determinism and methodological indeterminism.

The theses that I called idealistic aim to determine universal scientific laws, that is, laws that depend neither on the context in which they were created nor on the subject who formulated them.

[1] This is Popper's position (1959).

The Subject and Object of Science

The epistemological rupture appears with regard to the object and the subject. Hayek states, in several works, that the aggregated analytical categories are not facts, but intellectual constructions: the object cannot be defined independently from the subject's habitus. Thus, aggregate mechanisms do not constitute objective facts and cannot constitute the object of study of economics. Hayek rejects this approach in order to choose as a concrete object of study the objective facts that, according to him, are limited to the individual behaviors of economic agents. As highlighted by Boianovski (1992, p. 84):

> "(...) Hayek's approach assumes the existence of an objective reality that is independent of the agents' subjective perceptions, which ignores the fact that actions based on subjective expectations of the state of the world will cause external reality to *change*." (Caldwell 1988, p. 529)

In the specific case of Hayek, in addition to the criticisms that can be addressed to positivism, it should be noted that such a methodological choice is incompatible with an analysis in terms of *path dependence*, which implies that time is logical, not historical.[2]

Popper reaches a similar conclusion: he claims that, according to historicist theses, "(...) most objects (...) are theoretical constructions" (1972, p. 170) and deduces that these analyses confuse "(...) theoretical models and concrete things" (Idem.).

Nevertheless, from this refutation of the existence of objective facts, at the macroscopic level, these two authors deduce that scientific laws must be universal. In this regard, it should be noted that the existence of universal laws is directly linked to the philosophy of Kant, Descartes and Leibniz: it is about discovering the truth, that is, the essence, by nature permanent, of the studied reality.[3]

Other approaches refute this conception of reality, that is, of the world. Regarding this conception, or more precisely the conception of Feuerbach, Marx and Engels (1845, p. 24) state that he "(...) does not see that the sensible world that surrounds him is not a given object determined for all eternity and always the same (...), but a historical product (...)".

[2] At this respect, see Davidson (1996) in relation to immutable reality and historicity.

[3] In Economics, this translates into the substantial hypothesis (cf. p. 81).

With regard to language, for example, Bourdieu (and to a certain extent Foucault too) shows that language analysis cannot be reduced to linguistic, semantic or grammatical analysis of what is being said, but that it is necessary to know who speaks and *from what "social and historical place" this person speaks* (Bourdieu, 1982).

Heidegger also claims the historicity of the world: "That historical research, like all sciences, is increasingly and factually 'dependent', as a way of being on Dasein, on the 'dominant conception of the world', it is not necessary to repeat it." Any science is constituted, first, by the choice of a theme (Fournier and Rigal, 2007, p. 295): "Reality can only be discovered from an already revealed world" (Être et temps, § 43 (a), p. 247 [202–203]).

These approaches allow refuting the hypothesis of an immutable and ahistorical reality, an external reality that it is possible to know objectively, regardless of the sensitive world proper to the subject who carries out the observation.

The observation carried out in this way is implemented from a given language, from a given *point de vue* (Bourdieu 1984, p. 16); it is not possible to dissociate observation and reality. Sensitive objects are not dissociated from objects of thought (Marx and Engels 1845, p. 1), which imply that reality cannot be conceived independently of these sensitive objects. This allows me to refute the idealist conception, that is, the definition of a determined and immutable external reality; this implies redefining the objective to be achieved by Science, as well as the very concept of Science progress.

The subject is a historical subject: he is not transcendent but, on the contrary, he speaks from a *certain place*, located historically, sociologically and temporally. With regard to Economics, for example, contrary to what neoclassical economists did, it is neither possible to develop a system based on the hypothesis of a total rationality exercised by a generic and abstract Man,[4] the Homo Economicus, nor to attribute to the human being a natural propensity to exchange (Smith 1776). The same kind of observations can be made regarding the concept of labor used by classical economists: such concept does not constitute an invariant component of humanity, but corresponds to the specific form in the capitalist mode

[4] The abstract and universal character allows the construction of a totally ahistorical archetype which, if it can be applied to any time and to any type of society, is not able to explain any specific situation.

of production (Marx 1859, p. 169). The critique of political economy carried out by Marx is based on this type of distinction and thus allows proposing a historical analysis.

On the other hand, the "world" is not an object that has its own characteristics, but a pure mental and intellectual construction mediated through concepts, through a specific language (Fournier and Rigal, 2007, p. 7). The self of "I think, therefore I am" has to be replaced by "I speak, therefore I am"; the "I" is an intrinsically historical being, which uses the mediation of language in its perception of the world.

Some Examples in Economic Science

The epistemological rupture that prevails in Economic Sciences is defined in terms of these two antagonistic conceptions: Kant's conception and Heidegger's conception, with regard to the nature of reality. Neoclassical analysis is directly linked to this first conception; I will illustrate this from the capital controversy and the implicit assumptions that underpin the entire theoretical framework of the theory of rational expectations.

The Cambridge Controversy

In the famous capital controversy between the two Cambridges, the neoclassical position asserts that it is possible to conceive and measure a certain amount of heterogeneous capital independently of the value of distributive variables and that, consequently, the aggregate capital is represented by physical quantities. This hypothesis allows formulating the following conclusions: (a) the "value" of an aggregate amount of heterogeneous capital is constant, that is, it does not vary over time (b) capital is a component that can be found in any type of society, and at any time (Piketty 2013); capital is universal, and (c) finally, the distribution of income, that is, the relative share of wages and profits in the national product, is determined from the quantities of the factors of production and their scarcity. This implies the universalization of social and economic mechanisms inherent to a historically determined system, the capitalist system.

In this regard, it is possible to speak of "*capital-centrism*": all societies and all economic structures are analyzed using the same conceptual tools. On the other hand, the capitalist system represents the most elaborate form of society, a form towards which any type of society will "naturally" arrive.

The Rational Expectations Theory

The implicit hypotheses from which the Theory of Rational Expectations (TRE) was elaborated (Lucas 1975; Sargent and Wallace 1975), is the pure product linked to the exacerbation of this approach: all agents elaborate their expectations integrating the available information into the relevant theoretical model, that is, into the neoclassical General Equilibrium (GE) model. From an epistemological point of view, it is difficult, if not impossible, to sustain such a hypothesis:

(i) This implies that the only theoretical model that allows an observation of reality to be carried out is the neoclassical one. From an epistemological point of view, it is possible to state that the TRE uses the hypotheses of Descartes, Leibniz and Kant, hypotheses linked to Classical Mechanics: the subject is transcendent, the definition of the object is objectively carried out and the ultimate objective of Science is to reveal the intrinsic truth embedded in reality.

(ii) From the point of view of economic analysis, this thesis is hardly sustainable: as shown by several economists (Keynes 1936; Arrow 1974; Grossman and Stiglitz 1976), the concrete reality of the market, that is, the simultaneous existence of a demand and a supply, in given point in time, implies in the heterogeneity of expectations. Such heterogeneity can only be explained from the moment that expectations are elaborated based on different theoretical models. On the other hand, rational expectations elaborated on the basis of the Keynesian model will produce Keynesian results (Neary and Stiglitz 1983), and not neoclassical ones.

(iii) Finally, the sociology of knowledge allows understanding why the Neoclassical School, founded on subjective hypotheses, like any other school, is able to appear as objective. The orthodox school (the mainstream) that dominates the social field, in this case the university field, manages to "(...) impose its subjective representation (...) as an objective representation" (Bourdieu 1984, p. 93); the different heterodoxies, due to the fact that they are dominated, cannot acquire the legitimacy that would look as objective in the eyes of actors operating in the field.

More generally, Neoclassical Economics, based on a tradition inherited from the Physiocrats, conceives economic mechanisms as natural and ahistorical: (a) natural mechanisms because they do not depend on the will of individuals (Tsoulfidis 2017, p. 4) (b) ahistorical mechanisms due to the fact that they do not include institutions in market analyses (Idem, p. 17).

On the contrary, institutional elements are present in Classical and Keynesian Economics:

- As stated by Ricardo (1821), the wages that correspond to the reproduction of the labor force are determined as a function of social and historical variables that vary depending on the periods studied. On the other hand, in the Sraffaian scheme, distributive variables are determined exogenously: these wage-setting mechanisms can be assimilated to institutional mechanisms (Boyer 1987; Hodgson 1988).
- In Marx's economy, the very concepts of capital and commodity, and the system of property rights that characterize them, are "institutional" mechanisms that are directly related to a historically determined system, the capitalist system (Herscovici 2013).

It is interesting to note in this regard that, in several economics articles, economists invoke "empirical evidence" to validate their analyses. Even if the formula may seem elegant, within the scope of a historicist perspective linked to the dissociation between the subject and the object, this formula is nothing more than an *epistemological incongruity*: *the concrete level* (Marx 1859, pp. 165, 166) *represents the more complex analytical level. It has to be conceived as the result of scientific knowledge, and not as its starting point*: it is necessary "(…) to rise from the abstract towards the concrete (…)" (Idem, p. 165). Empiricism is the opposite of evidence.

Episteme and Economic Science

The Scientific Community: A Heroic Hypothesis

The different epistemological schools, in order to formulate their results, resort to the scientific community as a legitimizing instance. Several questions arise regarding the nature and modalities of action of this scientific community:

(a) First, to what extent is it possible to speak of a scientific community as a homogeneous community? Due to the struggles and conflicts that appear in the field of scientific production, would it not be more appropriate to speak of scientific communities, in the plural[5]?
(b) This fragmentation, not to say the "balkanization" of this community, is explained by the coexistence of various paradigms, or scientific research programs.
(c) This fragmentation allows me to justify and explain what Kuhn calls the incommensurability of paradigms, and thus question the relevance of the concept of scientific progress:

> "Economic theory is, however, a discipline that does not actually progress with the passing of time, or at least not in the way that physics and medicine do, by purging earlier theories of their errors and gradually organizing and monitoring them in the light of significant new results." (Lucarelli and Lunghini 2012)

The epistemologically insurmountable oppositions and conflicts between the different paradigms do not allow the establishment of a single demarcation criterion (in the sense defined by Popper) common to all these scientific communities: *a program that can be described as degenerative, in relation to a given scientific community, will be judged progressive, in relation to the criteria used by other communities.* "Each theoretical orientation or paradigm has its own problems, its own sets of specified questions" (Merton 1973, p. 8).

The "naturalist and universalist" theses ignore this multiplicity of contradictory interests and implicitly affirm the homogeneity and ideological neutrality of the scientific community; this is Popper's and Hayek's position.

It is interesting to highlight the contradictions present in Popper's epistemology: on the one hand, Popper (1959) refutes positivism, stating that any observation of reality is carried out from a certain theoretical framework. On the other hand, the falsifiability criterion consists of comparing the theoretical results of the model with the facts observed in reality. But,

[5] Neophytes, in various speeches, speak of economists as if this community were homogeneous. Given the conflicts and incompatibilities between different schools, such discourse reveals a profound ignorance of Economic Science.

if every observation is, by nature, an interpretation based on a theory, it is not possible to carry out a neutral observation, that is, one devoid of this theoretical and subjective dimension. Thus, it is not possible to reconcile, as Popper does, antipositivism and apply the criterion of falsifiability (Herscovici 2002).

In this respect, Lakatos' position is more comprehensive. On the one hand, this author affirms the primacy of internal History, as an element that explains the evolution of a given Science (1970, p. 92): he intends to carry out a rational reconstruction of the History of Science. On the other hand, a scientific research program is defined by a hardcore and a protective belt: this hardcore is constituted by irrefutable hypotheses accepted by the scientific community (Idem, p. 99).

In these irrefutable hypotheses are embedded historical, institutional and ideological components, and they directly determine the construction of the object of study of Science, the relevant judging problems and the scientific criteria adopted, which limit the explanatory value of the Internal History of Science, in which it concerns their evolutions.

Despite the explicit desire to resort only to internal History, in an implicit way, *Historicity is present in Lakatos' works*, based on the following elements:

(i) The criteria used by the scientific community to legitimize irrefutable hypotheses change over time.
(ii) In opposition to a degenerative PPC, Lakatos defines a progressive PPC because it can predict certain occurrences: consequently, a progressive PPC at one time can become degenerative at another, which highlights the historicity of the analysis.

These irrefutable hypotheses reflect the subjective values espoused by members of the scientific community. This corresponds exactly to Wittgenstein's definition of Philosophy: Philosophy is defined "as all the primitive propositions that are assumed as true without proof by the various sciences" (1922). On the other hand, Schumpeter (1949, apud Lucarreli, 2012) states "That prescientific cognitive act which is the source of our ideologies is also the prerequisite of our scientific work. No new departure in any science is possible without it." Wanting to expel External History through the door, it goes back through the window.

As the different members of this community do not share the same ideological components, it is no longer possible to establish this consensus, which corresponds to the fragmentation of the scientific community.

Based on these observations, it is possible to state that the concept of progress in Science is conceivable only within a certain system of thought (paradigm, Scientific Research Program, or episteme); its cumulative character can only be intra-systemic. If internal history is analyzed based on epistemology, that is, based on the internal coherence of the considered system, external history explains the changes in systems that punctuate the evolution of science. *The epistemological continuities that characterize each system are "disturbed" by the discontinuities that characterize the presence of different systems and the incompatibilities that this produces.*

In the scope of this research, I will use these two dimensions: epistemological analysis, as it relates to the internal coherence of the considered system, and analysis linked to the Sociology of Knowledge, to explain paradigm shifts. The legitimacy of each paradigm, within the scientific community, is the product of these two types of determinism; the relative autonomy of the scientific field makes it possible to carry out an epistemological analysis, without reducing its internal logic to external determinants—nevertheless, sociological determinants make it possible to explain and *clarify what, by definition, epistemological analysis insists on ignoring or hiding*. The position of a given current in the scientific field can be explained from these two dimensions: within the scope of the options chosen in this book, I will show that the dominant position of the mainstream in Economics is not explained, in large part, by its internal Historicity.

Foucault's Contribution

Episteme: A First Approach

The concept of episteme, as it was forged by Foucault, is essential: Foucault's analysis is not limited to an analysis of the object of Science, but it also includes the subject, historical and social conditions from which the subject chooses his object and builds his narrative, and the way in which these evolutions explain the transformations of the subject, the object and their relations. Foucault defines episteme as:

> "The set of relations between sciences, epistemological figures, positivities and discursive practices, that allows understanding the game of restrictions and limitations that, at a given moment, are imposed on the discourse (...) episteme is not what we can know about a period, due to technical insufficiencies, mental customs, or the limits imposed by tradition; it is what, in the positivity of discursive practices, makes the existence of epistemological figures and sciences possible." (Foucault 1969, pp. 250, 251)

While the philosophies deriving from Descartes and Leibniz consider a transcendent and universal subject, beyond historical contingencies, Foucault, on the contrary, includes the analysis of this subject in his study:

> "Finally, the objective of my project is to build an archeology of the subject. Method is an archeology of knowledge, and the precise domain of analysis is what I shall call technologies; I mean the articulation between certain techniques and certain types of discourses about the subject." (Ong-Van-Cung 2018)

The intrinsic historicity of the analysis makes a double archeological and genealogical approach necessary: archeological in that it "digs" into the past to find the archives produced in each epoch—genealogical to study the conditions under which the different scientific schools were born, developed and declined.

Such a choice is incompatible with any form of positivism and/or naturalism, which leads (a) to emphasize the continuities and discontinuities[6] that characterize the evolution of Science; (b) to deny a long trend of progress in Science, that is, a progression towards the truth; (c) to refute the existence of a rationality and a scientific objectivity that would overcome historical contingencies.

The "naturalistic" conception means that all epochs are studied based on the same criteria: for the "universalists," this method is valid, since the criteria used are universal. Thus, the Neoclassical School analyzes the evolution of Economic Science with a cumulative progression whose result necessarily leads to the neoclassical Scientific Research Programm. Consequently, all epochs are studied in light of the same criteria. For example, neoclassical economists see Ricardo's differential rent theory, as the forerunner of marginalist analysis; as I demonstrated in previous works

[6] This term is widely used in Foucault's work, specifically in "L'archéologie du savoir."

(Herscovici 2019), in order to maintain its internal coherence, this type of interpretation has to empty the specific content of this specific analysis in order to integrate it into the neoclassical PPC.

For historicists, on the contrary, it is an *epistemological anachronism*:

> "It is not about knowledge described in its progress towards an objectivity in which current science could be recognized: what we want to reveal is the epistemological field, the episteme where knowledge (…) conceived independently of any criterion it refers to its rational value or to its objective forms (…) and thus manifests a history that is not that of its growing perfection, but that of its conditions of possibility." (Foucault 1966, p. 13)

It is already possible to establish a parallel with Kuhn's approach (1991): within each episteme, there is a certain consensus regarding the problems to be considered and the methods used to "solve" these problems. This corresponds to solving problems using tools provided by normal Science. In addition to the oppositions that manifest themselves within the field of scientific production, there is a tacit agreement on certain "rules of the game." In Lakatos' terminology, it is possible to state that the controversies are related to the auxiliary hypotheses, but they do not represent a threat in relation to the hard core, which allows avoiding the *modus tollens*.

The Different Epistemes

The periodization proposed by Foucault distinguishes three different epistemes (Foucault 1966).

(a) The *preclassic episteme* (until the end of the sixteenth century) presents the following characteristics: the world is characterized by signs deposited by God, signs that are revealed from the similarities between its different components. The interpretation of these signs is carried out from the principle of similarity.

The analogy is widely used (Foucault 1966, pp. 36 and 47), as highlighted by the category of the microcosm (Idem, p. 46); the observations carried out at the micro level will be extended to the macroscopic level (and vice versa), on the basis of equivalences, analogies and similarities: analogies that allow comparing the functioning of the human body and the astrological mechanisms, for example: the game of similarities allows revealing the omnipresence of God.

(b) The *classical episteme* (seventeenth and eighteenth centuries) intends to reveal the Order of the world (ibid., 1966, pp. 73, 86) based on the interpretation of signs: these signs are deciphered, organized and classified based on scientific knowledge. They can only be revealed and acquire a precise and univocal meaning from their representation carried out from a *mathesis* and/or a *taxomania* (Idem, p. 88). The order of the world is represented from the Cartesian interpretation. With regard to economics, Quesnay's general framework is representative of this type of démarche. The object of knowledge is the order that prevails in Nature, and the scientific representations constructed to explain nature use a logical time, which is by nature reversible (Israël 1992; Herscovici 2019).

To this episteme corresponds a *deterministic* conception of Science, represented by Classical Mechanics; Descartes, Laplace and Leibniz are part of this global logic. Scientific laws are of the same nature as natural laws and, consequently, they are *universal*. This episteme represents the first step towards the emancipation and autonomy of the scientific field: the internal logic substitutes progressively and partially the religious power. The natural order will be analyzed from the stable equilibria that Science allows discovering.

Voltaire, one of the most brilliant author of the Enlightenment, ironically highlights the limits of these two epistemes, the preclassical and the classical ones: regarding the first, Zadig makes the following statement: "Nothing more successful (…) than a philosopher who reads in this great book that God has placed before our eyes: the truths he discovers belong to him: he nourishes and uplifts his soul (…)" (Voltaire 1747). With regard to the classical episteme, when Candide asks Pangloss if, after all the misfortunes he has suffered, he always believes that everything is better in the best of all worlds, the latter responds as follows: "(…) I am a philosopher; it is not right to deny, Leibniz cannot be wrong, and the pre-established harmony being the most beautiful thing in the world (…)" (Voltaire 1759).

(c) According to Foucault, historicity appears in the episteme linked to modernity, from the end of the eighteenth century onwards.

> The object of study is Man, the human being defined in his finiteness and in his productive activities. In Economics, this is reflected in the primacy of production over circulation (Foucault 1966, p. 271); production is conceived as the human activity that allows scarcity to be temporarily removed.

Human activities occupy a central role in economics; they make it possible to dominate Nature and thus compensate for the limitations Nature imposes on humanity. The production relations are no longer conceived as the use of the wealth provided by Nature but, on the contrary, by the control that Man exercises over Nature, and by the social relations that allow the implementation of these production activities (Ricardo, Marx). Contrary to what the Physiocrats claimed, nature no longer lavishes its riches; on the contrary, as emphasized in Ricardo's theory of differential income, it is "greedy." Scarcity appears, and the function of labor is to reduce this scarcity: labor becomes a central element in economic analysis.

The emancipation of Economics as a Science appears in the classical episteme and is based on the episteme linked to modernity. In the classical episteme, the divine Order is replaced by the order of nature; in modernity, this natural order is replaced by the appearance of Man and his productive activities (Foucault 1966, p. 16). *Modernity is characterized by the existence of a "purely" economic order.*

This economic order is characterized by *the active role of Man, as an economic subject by definition*: his action determines this order. On the contrary, preclassical and classical epistemes were linked to a holistic conception of society and human activities (Dumont, 1985), because the individual has no active role in determining this order, because the individual is a "passive" subject.

In Classical Economics, this action is manifested mainly through the mediation of labor and institutions; in Neoclassical Economics, by the subjective and exogenous preferences of economic agents, in the absence of institutions (Table 2.1).

The preclassical episteme is characterized by the direct interference of the Christian religion, and more specifically Catholic, in the field of economics: time is infinite, and linked to the belief in an afterlife.

The classical episteme has the following characteristics: scientific laws are conceived as natural laws and, consequently, universal. These laws are deciphered from mathesis, that is, from the mathematical tool; they are universal and deterministic, and can be represented by stable equilibria.

Table 2.1 The different epistemes

	Order	*Tools*	*Method*	*Time*
Pre-classical Until XVI century	Divine	Analogies Similarities	Revelation	Infinite Reversible
Classical¨ XVII/XVIII century	Nature	Representation Mathesis Stable Equilibria	Universalism Methodological determinism	Logic and reversible
Modernity	The Man	Hybrides Equil. versus disequilibrium	Determinism versus indeterminism	Reversible versus irreversible

Time is purely logical and reversible, and comparable to space (Carvalho 1983–1984).

Modernity is defined based on the following elements: the analysis is centered on the individual, and economic activity, that is, the very definition of the object of study is defined on the basis of scarcity.

A non-deterministic reading of these authors corresponds to the instability of equilibria and the irreversibility of time; equilibrium can be unstable. As far as Neoclassical Economics is concerned, as I will show, time and agents' decisions are reversible, whether in the context of pure and perfect Walrasian competition or in the conditions of contestability of markets.

Episteme, Historicity and Economy

Episiteme and Nature of Time

The preclassical episteme is characterized by the primacy of the religious order, and more specifically, of the Catholic order: the philosophy of forgiveness and confession, at the symbolic level, is translated by the reversibility of time and human decisions. For these reasons, time is "infinite" and reversible.

The classical episteme conceives time as intrinsically reversible. Within the scope of the deterministic method that characterizes Classical Mechanics, time is comparable to space, and, consequently, reversible.

In modernity, and especially with regard to Economics, certain schools use reversible time, and others use irreversible time.

Foucault defines modernity based on the finitude of Man, the emergence of scarcity, the central role of labor, which makes it possible to temporarily overcome this scarcity (1966), and by introducing time into economic analysis.

What is the nature of scarcity? For Sraffa and the neo-Ricardians, it is intrinsically historical and social: in the theory of differential rent, better quality land becomes scarce for a certain level of demand, which is the result of a certain degree of development of society (Ricardo 1821). For the neoclassicals, scarcity is natural and is evaluated in quantities.

In modernity, time is the manifestation of man's scarcity and finitude. In Ricardo and Marx's work, time is present: labor time determines the value of commodities, capital rotations determine the rate of profit.

Here, it is necessary to consider three different conceptions of time: the "eternal" time linked to the preclassical episteme, the logical time that corresponds to the classical episteme, this time being, by nature, reversible, and the irreversible time that corresponds to Historicity, this Historicity being compatible only with irreversible time; these different conceptions of time are particularly important, with regard to the internal coherence of the different paradigms of Economic Science, and to define compatibilities and incompatibilities between these different paradigms.

Equilibrium and Normative Versus Unbalanced and Realistic Approaches

Certain authors interpret Classical Economics as an economy of disequilibrium (Duménil and Lévy 1987)[7]: the process of convergence of market prices to values defined by production prices is justified by the agents' reaction to an initial situation of disequilibrium. Equilibrium, as it is carried out, is carried out *ex post.*

Up to a point, we can make the same observations with respect to Keynesian economics: it is an economy of disequilibrium. The fact of relaxing the hypothesis regarding constant long-term expectations allows providing an endogenous explanation of the economic cycle, and to build dynamic models in which the movement is explained by the agents'

[7] It is possible to demonstrate formally, from Ricardian, Marxist and Keynesian approaches, that the system produces endogenous fluctuations and that it does not systematically converge to a long-term equilibrium position (Goodwin 1967; Setterfield 1999; Herscovici 2002).

reaction to an initial disequilibrium (Herscovici 2019); such reactions translate into changes in long-term expectations.

With regard to the first point, it is important to emphasize that long-term expectations partly determine investment, and that, based on the multiplier, changes in investment correspond to more than proportional variations in output and employment. The cause of economic movement cannot be explained solely from an exogenous variable: the animal spirit. For this reason, it is necessary to endogenize, at least partially, long-term expectations (Idem).

Second, the fact of relaxing the hypothesis concerning constant long-term expectations allows the elaboration of dynamic models in which the equilibrium is "undetermined" and in which the agents' reaction allows for an eventual convergence towards this equilibrium (Setterfield 1999).

In Neoclassical Economics, on the contrary, equilibrium is carried out *ex ante* and is stable. Consequently, certain problems arise with regard to the concrete modalities of realizing this equilibrium: the famous Arrow paradox. Contrary to Classical Economics, Neoclassical Economics is an Economics of equilibrium.

Neoclassical Economics is essentially normative: it analyzes economic reality from the deviations presented, in relation to a state of pure and perfect competition. It does not explain the concrete modalities of competition, its dynamics, nor the modalities from which, from an initial disequilibrium, the system returns to the equilibrium position.

In opposition to this normative approach, Classical Economics allows analyzing the concrete modalities of competition (Naveen 2015; Tsoulfidis 2017, p. 108); it is a *"realistic" approach*, in the sense that it is not normative.

While Classical and Keynesian analyses allow the analysis of competitive dynamics, the neoclassical construction assumes that competition has already acted, and that equilibrium is already achieved.

The Walrasian general equilibrium is an ex ante equilibrium, centralized by the auction mechanism: it is determined before the agents act—it is centralized by the fact that the Walrasian auctioneer centralizes the responses provided by the different components of demand—it is "fictitious" in that exchanges are not carried out while prices do not allow for matching supply and demand. In this regard, we can note that neoclassical methodology was the target of several criticisms, both by Classical Economics (notably the neo-Ricardian school) post-Keynesian economics, and by the Austrian school, particularly with Hayek (1950).

Marshall's interpretation of market prices and natural prices radically modifies the content attributed by classical economists to this concept: for the latter, the market price is the product of an initial disequilibrium between demand and supply (Naveen 2015, p. 8). The eventual convergence towards natural prices is the result of the agents' reaction: (a) the eventual "long-term" equilibrium is not carried out ex ante, but ex post (b) the adjustments are made gradually and not instantaneously. On the contrary, Marshall assimilates the market price with the short-term equilibrium price: "The market price of everything, i.e. its price for short periods, is determined by the relations in which the demand for it stands to the available stocks of it (...)" (Marshall 1920, p.333). We can conclude that these two conceptions are antagonic (Schefold 2018, p. 24).

In the same way, the Keynesian macroeconomic equilibrium is not systematically associated with the equalization of demand and supply: under the mechanisms of path dependence, it is the result of the agents' reaction in relation to an initial disequilibrium, *in the form of a change in long-term expectations*, depending on their degree of achievement (Setterfield 1999; Duménil and Lévy 1987).

Due to these methodological observations, it is possible to conclude that all attempts made to integrate Classical and Keynesian analyses in the neoclassical framework fail: to implement this integration, it is necessary to drain their main components. The interpretation of Keynes made by neoclassical authors (Friedman and/or Mankiw, for example) limits Keynes' analysis to the short term, it does not work with uncertainty, nor with the path dependence that, in my view, characterizes Keynesian analysis. I will cite just two examples:

(i) Friedman (1974), for example, considers that the demand for money depends, within a negative correlation, on the interest rate. This is contrary to what Keynes states in Chapter XIII of the General Theory (GT): money fulfilling the function of reserve of value, its demand depends on Liquidity Preference, and not on the interest rate; rather, the interest rate depends on the demand for money, via Liquidity Preference (this theme will be developed in Chapter 7).
(ii) The analyses in terms of menu costs (Mankiw 1985) only study the response of the different components of supply in relation to a shock, by nature exogenous, of demand: what is left of a

Keynesianism that ignores, by hypothesis, the modalities of demand formation?

Kunh and Foucault

Convergences and Divergences

Foucault built the concept of episteme in the book "*Les mots et les choses*" and continued using it in "*L'Archéologie du savoir*." In the continuation of Heidegger's writings, based on the refutation of the existence of a transcendent subject, Foucault elaborates an intrinsically historical analysis. From there, a series of questions arises: how is Foucault going to define the historicity of Sciences? He states that "In a culture and at a given time, there can only be one episteme, which defines the conditions for the possibility of any knowledge" (1966, p. 179).

The very concept of episteme implies that the History of Science is the History of its discontinuities; Foucault thus states that the object of study of the History of Ideas consists in "(...) specifying the different concepts that allow us to think about discontinuity" (1969, p. 12). In this regard, I cannot fail to draw a parallel with Kuhn's (1991) analysis.[8]

For both Kuhn and Foucault, the History of Sciences cannot be conceived as a universal and cumulative History. Kuhn's concept of scientific revolutions corresponds exactly to the ruptures and discontinuities defined by Foucault. *While continuity can only be intra-paradigmatic, or intra-epistemic, discontinuities are related to changes in paradigms or episteme*: Science can be cumulative only within a given paradigm.

The concept of episteme is related to various scientific disciplines; Kuhn's paradigm is more restricted: it applies to a particular discipline, and not to a set of disciplines. However, *the difference is not related to the time horizon*, but to the areas where it can be applied.

Nevertheless, certain authors (Vigo 2010, p. 219) differentiate these two concepts based on the temporal dimension; a given episteme would be composed of several paradigms, since it is part of the same discursive practice. For example, the only element that (neo-)Ricardianism and marginalism have in common is the fact that they developed in a

[8] Foucault recognized the importance of Kuhn's contribution (1991).

phase marked by the relative autonomy of Economic Science. Furthermore, these two systems of thought do not share any epistemological component: (a) The object of study, the nature of the time used, the incorporation of Historicity are different and totally incompatible; (b) the inclusion of these two research programs in the same episteme can only be realized on the basis of emptying the specific content of the hardcore of these two programs.

The progress of Science can only be conceived within the same paradigm, based on commensurability; it is a short-term intra-paradigmatic mechanism. On the contrary, incommensurability is a long-term inter-paradigmatic phenomenon: both Kuhn and Foucault's study is a long-term analysis.

Foucault does not explain the transition between different epistemes; Kuhn explains the transition from one paradigm to another, this from the proliferation of anomalies, that is, facts that the dominant theory is not able to explain. Thus, during this transition period, it is possible to observe the temporary coexistence of two paradigms and explain the paradigm changes.

Kuhn was aware of Foucault's limits when he wrote that Foucault "is scarcely interested in the processes by which [the] system [he describes] is led to transform itself" (Kuhn 1994: 160–161).

Finally, how is it possible to solve the problem of the unicity of the episteme and the paradigm? Foucault states that, at a given moment, there is only one episteme, which defines all possibilities for the production of knowledge (Foucault 1966, p. 179). Kuhn claims that scientific revolutions are characterized by the disappearance of the paradigm that is the object of anomalies, and by the development of the new paradigm. Thus, for these two authors, there cannot be a permanent coexistence of several paradigms, or epistemes.

Scientific production in Economics is a counterexample: how is it possible to explain this coexistence of different epistemes in a given historical period? In the case of Economics, each school of thought is characterized by elements inherited from different epistemes. For example, Classical Economics employs elements linked to the classic episteme (the idea of a natural order) and modernity: man as an economic subject. A given school of thought is not the pure product of a given episteme, but the *hybrid* product of different epistemes.

Another analysis allows understanding the coexistence of paradigms, or scientific research programs (SRP): Lakatos (1970, 1978) shows that, generally, a progressive SRP initially develops from a dominant PPC that becomes degenerative, but this coexistence can remain, depending on the time necessary to be able to compare the results of the new SRP with the facts.

The analyses linked to the Sociology of Science (Bourdieu, Merton) also allow explaining the coexistence of several paradigms, in the same period: from Bourdieu's theory of social fields, the field linked to scientific production is characterized by a struggle between different actors to dominate, symbolically, the field, which presupposes the permanence of incompatible paradigms, and a hierarchy of paradigms, according to the different degrees of legitimacy. The modification of the power relations translates into a historicization of the field and, consequently, of the paradigms and criteria that allow legitimizing the productions. The sociological and economic mechanisms in the field of scientific production are similar to those in the artistic and cultural field (Herscovici 1994).

Such static dimension may be seen as a criticism in relation to Foucault's analysis, and would explain the coexistence of incommensurable paradigms in the same period.

The Dynamics of Change

How to explain the passage from one paradigm to another and from one episteme to another?

(a) For Kuhn, the paradigm enters into crisis when various anomalies arise. This means that the considered paradigm is no longer able to explain facts that characterize the studied period or, more precisely, facts that are recognized as pertinent. Thus, this paradigm progressively disappears. However, Kuhn also points out that the definition of the facts that constitute the object of study itself depends on the paradigm within which they are chosen.

The primacy of a given paradigm is explained by its ability to explain certain facts and, simultaneously, to choose the facts to be studied. The explanation provided by Kuhn consists in combining the elements of internal history and external history to explain the evolution of Sciences. Internal History consists in evaluating the capacity of different paradigms to explain the chosen facts; External History emphasizes that the choice of these facts is explained from sociological and historical variables.

(b) The concept of episteme, as defined by Foucault, is different: it does not conceive Science in terms of the possibilities it offers to explain certain facts, but in terms of the elements that characterize the episteme to which it belongs, that is, due to the historical structures that allowed the construction of these issues.

In Foucault's work, the weight of internal history is less in relation to Kuhn's analysis: it is neither possible to compare different epistemes nor to assess their respective scientificities. *In Foucault, the incommensurability of epistemes is absolute, while, for Kuhn, the incommensurability of paradigms is relative*: the former prohibits any comparison, while the latter allows them. In this sense, in Kuhn's analysis, there is a relationship between the different paradigms,[9] due to the fact that their explanatory powers are compared; for Foucault, the different epistemes are, by nature, incomparable. Such a conception leaves open the question regarding the passage from one episteme to another; Foucault does not explain the social and historical dynamics of this passage.

In Kuhn's view, the incommensurability of paradigms, or epistemes, is not absolute: there is always a moment when there is communication between these different paradigms, whether it is just to highlight existing incompatibilities or explain the dynamics of change. It is the démarche of Kuhn and Lakatos.

In the second part of this work, I will analyze three controversies based on the following issue: What is the nature of the rupture generated by these controversies? Should they be interpreted as an opposition between different epistemes, or as simple oppositions within the same episteme?

References

Arrow, Kenneth J. 1974. Limited Knowledge and Economic Analysis. *American Economic Review*, March.

Bachelard, Gaston. 1989. *La formation de l'esprit scientifique*. Paris: Librairie Philosophique J. Vrin.

Balibar, Étienne. 2020. *Passions du concept. Épistémologie, théologie, politique. Écrits II*. Paris: La Découverte.

[9] A similar démarche is made by Lakatos (1970), when this author defines a progressive scientific research program, which is born from a program that is becoming degenerative (Herscovici 2019).

Blaug, Mark. 1992. *The Methodology of Economics or How Economists Explain*, 2nd ed. Cambridge: Cambridge University Press.
Boianovski, Mauro. 1992. Hicks, Hayek e a dinâmica monetária wickselliana. *Revista Brasileira de Economia*, Rio de Janeiro 46 (1, January/March): 77–95.
Bourdieu, Pierre. 1979. *La distinction*. Critique sociale du jugement. Paris: Les éditions de Minuit.
———. 1982. *Ce que parler veut dire. L'économie des échanges linguistiques*. Paris: Fayard.
———. 1984. *Questions de Sociologie*. Paris: Les Éditions de Minuit.
Boyer, Robert. 1987. *La Théorie de la régulation: une analyse critique*. Paris: La Découverte.
Caldwell, Bruce. 1988. Hayek's Transformation. *History of Political Economy* 20 (4): 513–541.
Carvalho, Fernando Cardim de. 1983–1984. On the Concept of time in Shacklean and Sraffian Economics. *Journal of Post Keynesian Economics* VI (2, Winter): 265–280.
Dahan Dalmedico, Amy. 1992. Le déterminisme de Pierre-Simon Laplace et le déterminisme aujourd'hui. In *Chaos e Déterminisme*. Paris: Editions du Seuil.
Davidson, Paul. 1996. Reality and economic theory. *Journal of Post Keynesian Economics* (Summer): 479–508.
Descartes, René. 1647. Les méditations métaphysiques de René Descartes. http://classiques.uqac.ca/classiques/Descartes/meditations_metaphysiques/meditations_metaphysiques.pdfavailable. Accessed 22 March 2022.
Dow, Sheila. 2020. *Economic Methodology, the Philosophy of Economics and the Economy: Another Turn?* Division of Economics, Stirling Management School, University of Stirling, Stirling FK9 4LA, UK
Duménil, G., and Lévy, D. 1987. The Dynamics of Competition: A Restoration of the Classical Analysis. *Cambridge Journal of Economics* 11: 133–164.
Dumont, Louis. 1985. *Homo aequalis. Genèse et épanouissement de l'idéologie économique*. Paris: NRF, Editions Gallimard.
Feyerabend, Paul. 1975. *Against Method*. London: New Left Books.
Foucault, Michel. 1966. Les mots et les choses. Paris: Tel Galimard.
———. 1969. *L'archéologie du savoir*. Paris: Gallimard.
———. 1971. Foucault responds 2. *Diacritics I* 2: 60.
———. 1978. La société disciplinaire en crise. In *Michel Foucault, Dits et écrits: 1954-1988, tome II, 1976-1988*, ed. Daniel Defert and François Ewald, 532–534. Paris: Gallimard.
Fournier, Françoise, and Élisabeth Rigal. 2007. Gérard Granel et l'analyse heideggérienne du «scandale pour la philosophie». *Cahiers philosophiques* 2007/3 (N° 111).

Friedman, M. 1974. A Theoretical Framework for Monetary Analysis. In *Milton Friedman's Monetary Framework: A Debate with His Critics*, ed. R.J. Gordon, 1–62. Chicago: University of Chicago Press.

Goodwin, Richard M. 1967. A growth cycle. In *Socialism, Capitalism and Economic Growth*. Cambridge: Cambridge University Press.

Grangier, Gilles-Gaston. 1993. *La Science et les Sciences*. Paris: Presses Universitaires de France.

Grossman, S.J., and J.E. Stiglitz. 1976. Information and Competitive Price System. *The American Economic Review* 66 (2, May).

Hayek, Friedrich H. 2009 [1950]. *The Pure Theory of Capital*. Auburn, AL: The Ludwig von Mises Institute.

———. 1952. *Scientism and the Study of Society*. Glencoe, IL: The Free Press.

Heidegger, Martin. Être et temps, Edition numérique hors commerce. http://www.rialland.org/heidegger/.

Herscovici, Alain. 1994. *Économie de la Culture et de la Communication*. Paris: L'Harmattan.

———. 2002. *Dinâmica macroeconômica: uma interpretação a partir de Marx e de Keynes*. São Paulo: EDUFES/EDUC.

———. 2013. As metamorfoses do valor: capital intangível e hipótese substancial. Reflexões a respeito da historicidade do valor. *Liinc em Revista* 10: 560–574.

———. 2019. *Essays on the Historicity of Capital*. Palgrave Macmillan.

Hodgson, Geoffrey M. 1988. The Approach of Institutional Economics. *Journal of Economic Literature* 36 (1, March): 166–192.

Israël, Giorgio. 1992. L'histoire du déterminisme et ses rencontres avec les mathématiques. *Chaos et déterminisme*, op. cit.

Keynes, John Maynard. 2009 [1936]. *The General Theory of Employment, Interest and Money*. New York: Classic Books America.

Kuhn, Thomas S. 1991 [1962]. *A estrutura das revoluções científicas*. São Paulo: Editora Perspectiva.

———. 1994. Paradigms of Scientific Evolution: Thomas S. Kuhn. In *The American Philosopher: Conversations with Quine, Davidson, Putnam, Nozick, Danto, Rorty, Cavell, MacIntyre, and Kuhn*, ed. G. Borradori, 153–167. Chicago, IL: University of Chicago Press.

Lakatos, Imre. 1970. History of Science and Its Rational Reconstructions. In *Proceedings of the Biennial Meeting of the Philosophy of Science Association*, vol. 1970, pp. 91–136.

———. 1978. *The Methodology of Scientific Research Programs*. Philosophical Papers Volume I Edited by John Worral and Gregory Currie. Cambridge: Cambridge University Press.

Lucarelli, Stefano, and Giorgio Lunghini. 2012. *The Resistible Rise of Mainstream Economics the Dominant Theory and the Alternative Economic Theorie*. Bergamo University Press Edizioni Sestant.

Lucas, Robert E. 1975. Equilibrium Model of the Business Cycle. *Journal of Political Economy* 83 (6, December): 1113–1144.

Mankiw, Gregory. 1985. Small Menu Costs and Large Business Cycles: A Macroeconomic Model of Monopoly. *The Quarterly Journal of Economics* 100 (2, May): 529–537.

Marshall, Alfred. 1920. *Principles of Economics*, 8th ed. London: Macmillan and Co., Book II.

Marx, Karl. 1972 [1859]. *Contribution à la critique de l'économie politique*. Paris: Editions Sociales.

Marx, K., and F. Engels. 1972 [1845]. *L'idéologie allemande*. Paris: Editions Sociales.

Merton, Robert K. 1973. *The Sociology of Science*. Chicago: Chicago Press University.

———. 2013. Ensaios de Sociologia da Ciência, Editora 34, São Paulo.

Naveen, Kanalu. 2015. Krishna Bharadwaj's "Return to Classical Theory": An Attempt Towards an Archaeological Reconstruction. *The European Journal of the History of Economic Thought*.

Neary, J.P., and J.F. Stiglitz. 1983. Towards a Reconstruction of Keynesian Economics. *Quarterly Journal of Economics* XCVIII.

Ong-Van-Cung, Kim Sang. 2018. Certitude et inquiétude du sujet. Foucault et Heidegger lecteurs de Descartes. https://journals.openedition.org/methodos/4983. Accessed May 2021.

Piketty, Thomas. 2013. *Le capital au XXIème siècle*. Paris: Editions du Seuil.

Popper, Karl. 1959. *The Logic of Scientific Discovery*. Hutchinson & Co.

———. 1972. *The Poverty of Historicism*, 2nd ed. London: Routledge & Kegan Paul.

Ricardo, David. 1821 [2001]. *On the Principles of Political Economy and Taxation*, 3rd ed. Kitchener, ON: Batoche Book.

Sargent, Thomas J., and Neil Wallace. 1975. "Rational" Expectations, the Optimal Monetary Instrument, and the Optimal Money Supply Rule. *Journal of Political Economy* 83 (2, April 1975): 241–254.

Sartre, Jean-Paul. 1986. *Questions de méthode*. Paris: Editions Gallimard.

Schefold, Bertam, 2018, *Continuity and Change in the Transition from the Classical to the Neoclassical Theory of Normal Prices*, not edited.

Setterfield, Mark. 1999. Expectations, Path Dependence and Effective Demand: A Macroeconomic Model Along Keynesian Lines. *Journal of Post Keynesian Economics* 21 (3): 479–501.

Smith, Adam. 1980. *Inquérito sobre a natureza e as causas da riqueza das nações*, vol. I. Lisboa: Fundação Calouste Gulbenkian [Original: *An Inquiry into the Nature and Causes of the Wealth of Nations*. London: Methuen and Co Ltd., 1776].

Tsoulfidis, Lefteris. 2017. Economic Theory in Historical Perspective. *The Journal of Philosophical Economics: Reflections on Economic and Social Issues* X (2, Spring).

Vallois, Nicola. 2015. Michel Foucault and the History of Economic Thought (Michel Foucault et l'histoire de la pensée économique). *Oeconomia* (5–4): 461–490.

Veblen, Thorstein. 1899. The Preconceptions of Economic Science. *The Quarterly Journal of Economics* 13.

Vercelli, Alessandro. 1991. *Methodological Foundations of Macroeconomics: Keynes After Lucas*. Cambridge: Cambridge University Press.

Vigo de Lima, Iara. 2010. *Foucault's Archaeology of Political Economy*, Iara, Copyright 2010 Publisher, Palgrave Macmillan UK.

Voltaire, François-Marie. 1747. *Zadig ou la destinée*. Lyon.

———. 1759. *Candide ou l'optimiste*, Édition *princeps, Genève.*

Wittgenstein, Ludwig. 1922. *Tractatus Logico-Philosophicus*. Kegan Paul, Trench Trubner & Co.

CHAPTER 3

From Physiocratic School to Neoclassical Economics

Mercantilism has as object, the study of money and its intrinsic value, and it does not get to study economics as a relatively autonomous system, which encompasses production, consumption and exchange. Economic Science, i.e., the study of the economic system as a whole, was born with the Physiocracy, developed with Smith, Ricardo and Marx, and later with Marginalism. I will study the different episteme that characterizes the Classical and the Neoclassical Schools, as well as the internal ambiguities of each one.

The Physiocratic School and Adam Smith

Physiocracy

From Physiocratic approach, the object of study of Economics is constituted from the determination of value and commercial exchange: money no longer has intrinsic value, it becomes a sign of value and thus makes possible the development of commercial exchanges (Foucault 1966, p. 187): "It is because gold is money that it is precious. Not the other way around."

Value is linked to labor applied to Nature, only this kind of labor being productive: the value thus produced (i.e., the exchange value called *valeur vénale* by Quesnay [1759]) is greater than the costs necessary to implement this production; while the other branches of production only transform the value created in the productive sector, labor

A. Herscovici, *Value, Historicity, and Economic Epistemology*, https://doi.org/10.1007/978-3-031-21157-7_3

applied to nature produces a net surplus. This concept of surplus is present throughout classical economics, from Smith to Ricardo and Marx (Dumont 1985, p. 107). Economic laws are part of a natural order, as private property, for example (Cartelier 2008, p. 17).

The concept of Natural Law, as defined by Quesnay (1759, pp. 69 and 74) highlights the fact that wealth is defined in terms of utility: this natural right is defined as "(…) the right that man has to enjoy things" (Idem). *Utility determines simultaneously use value and exchange value; on the other hand, the surplus, produced with human labor, is the source of such utility. We can observe this ambivalence in regard to the value theory, and an equivalency between wealth and value.*

Nevertheless, this utility can be expanded through exchange, and this through the following mechanism (Foucault 1966, p. 211): as the labor applied to Nature produces a surplus, the production carried out by A surpasses its needs: A will want to exchange this surplus on the market, which has no use for him, and this to acquire B's production, which will provide him with greater utility. A will want to exchange his commodity, buying the commodity from B as long as the utility of his surplus is less than the utility provided by the commodity produced by B (and vice versa). The exchange will be carried out until the utility provided to A by B's commodities equals the utility provided to A by its own commodities, which Turgot (apud. Foucault 1966, p. 211) calls estimated value *(valeur estimative)*. Thus, value already has a double dimension: that linked to needs, and that linked to exchange, that is, the exchange value.

Here, we can observe the foundations of traditional microeconomic analyzes that will be developed in the context of Neoclassical Economics: the theory of value linked to subjective utility, the concept of substitution rate, decreasing marginal utility and utility maximization by each agent that participates in the exchange.

The labor value theory, as an explanatory element of exchange value, appears secondary in this mechanism (Dumont 1985, p. 109), while utility and exchange play a fundamental role. On the one hand, the generalization of exchange presupposes the prior determination of values, that is, the prices of commodities linked to the utility value; but, on the other hand, exchange determines the value attributed to the commodity by different agents, that is, its exchange value (Foucault 1966, p. 209).

This analysis allows resolving the paradox of water and diamond, initially enunciated by Galiani and Turgot (and later by Adam Smith):

the theory of subjective utility allows justifying the fact that, for a given individual, the utility of diamond may be superior to that of water.

Finally, the universalist dimension permeates the Physiocratic school: economic laws are conceived as being natural laws, that is, disconnected from their historical and social determinants.

Adam Smith: Labor Value Versus Utility Value?

The Labor Value Theory

Adam Smith was undoubtedly influenced by Physiocratic thought: nevertheless, he will add fundamental elements in relation to the construction elaborated by the Physiocrats:

a. The concept of productive labor is no longer limited to labor applied to nature. The value, that is, the natural price, is determined from the productive labor, whether applied to Nature or Industry.
b. Smith designs the mechanisms that will allow, as Ricardo and Marx later did, justifying the primacy of the sphere of production over the sphere of realization. This primacy of production is expressed by the fundamental and regulatory role played by ***natural prices*** (or production prices in Marx's analysis).

The natural price of a commodity is determined based on the quantity of labor necessary to produce it (Smith 1776, p. 159): this price allows the remuneration of labor, capital and land rent, at their respective natural rates. If the market price (the effective price at which the good is sold) is different from the natural price, one of the components of the natural price (wages, profit or land rent) is remunerated at a rate different from its natural rate (Idem, p. 163).

As the situation becomes competitive, the deviations between market prices and natural prices will systematically disappear: if, for example, the market price is higher than the natural price, this means that one of the components of natural prices is remunerated at a rate higher than its natural rate. There will be a transfer of capital, or labor, towards this sector (ibid., p. 165): the increase in the supply of capital or labor translates into a decrease in their respective real remuneration rates, until these rates equal the value corresponding to the natural rates.

The natural price, defined in the sphere of production, constitutes the regulatory element. Market prices fluctuate from the value of these natural prices: "The natural price is therefore, as it were, the central price, towards which the prices of all goods continually tend" (ibid., p. 163).

Nevertheless, ambiguities arise with regard to the relationships between the respective roles of production and circulation spheres:

i. "The division of labor (…) is limited by the size of the market" (ibid., p. 99). In other words, the productive capacity of labor, and consequently the value of commodities, is determined by the extent of the market, that is, by the sphere of circulation.
ii. Smith's theory of labor was elaborated from this same ambiguity. The theory of commanded labor is stated as follows: "The value of any commodity, therefore, to the person who possesses it, and who means not to use or consume it himself, but to exchange it for other commodities, is equal to the quantity of labor which it enables him to purchase or command. Labour, therefore, is the real measure of the exchangeable value of all commodities" (ibid., p. 121).

Smith's theory of value is defined in terms of two dimensions, one linked to production and the other to circulation. In fact, we can consider the exchange between A and B, and the respective commodities mA and mB. The mA value is determined by the amount of labor incorporated in mB; likewise, the value of mB is determined from the amount of labor incorporated in mA. Thus, value is defined simultaneously, in production and in exchange spheres (Dumont 1985, p. 225).

Utility

Beyond this theory of labor value, other concepts elaborated by Smith are directly related to utility value and announce the further developments made by the Neoclassical School, starting from marginalism.

i. The thesis according to which the competitive market constitutes a superior and socially efficient order is present in the baker's parable: "It is not from the kindness (…) of the butcher, the brewer or the baker that we can expect our dinner, but from the consideration in which they have their own interest" (ibid., p. 95)

   This statement implies two things:

(a) exchange is an essential element that allows the realization of the exchange value of commodities. This exchange is justified, as the Physiocratic school already explained, by the subjective theory of value and it verifies the decreasing marginal utility hypothesis (ibid., p. 89).
(b) In the line of thought of Mandeville (1732), this statement implies that there is a convergence between individual interests and the collective interest. This mechanism was formalized by Pareto and, in the context of the first welfare theorem, associated with general equilibrium, in a situation of pure and perfect competition.

In the Theory of Moral Sentiments, Smith tries to reconcile Christian morality with ostentatious consumption, i.e., private vices with public virtues, in the same way that Mandeville does (Alcouffe, Massot-Bordenave 2018, p. 334): in regard to the Fable of the Bees, he claims that "If the love of magnificence, a taste for elegant arts and improvement of human life (…) is to be regarded as luxury, sensuality, and ostentation, (…) it is certain that luxury, sensuality, and ostentation are public benefits (…)" (1759, p . 285).

In this way, prefiguring Pareto, he denies the antogonic interesses of the different social classes. Pareto's formalization presupposes, among other things, that there is no conflict of interest between the different agents participating in the exchange because the increase in one agent's utility does not conflict with the other agent's utility.

ii. Despite adopting the labor value theory, Smith develops the modern concept of marginal disutility, to explain the value of goods and the supply of labor:

> "What one thing is really worth to the man who acquired it and who wants to get rid of it or exchange it for something else is the effort and fatigue it can save him by imposing it on other people. What we buy, with money or in exchange for other goods, is acquired through labour, just like what we get at the cost of the effort of our own body." (Smith 1776, p. 120)

- This mechanism was developed by Neoclassical Economics, regarding the determination of the labor supply: to maximize his utility function, the homo economicus increases its labor supply until the marginal utility of income corresponding to the last hour of labor sold equals disutility which corresponds to the last working hour.

On the other hand, Smith thus tries to reconcile the two dimensions present in the theory of commanded labor: labor as the only component of the cost of production and as disutility that a commodity saves for those who buy it. *Two dimensions are present in Smith's theory of value: one linked to production and the other to circulation.* These ambiguities highlight the fact that, in the sphere of production, in order to be exchanged commodities previously possess a value, which is related to the substantial hypothesis (cf. p. 52).

- Smith thus tries to escape the contradiction that characterizes the labor theory of value: if labor is the measure of value of the set of goods produced, this unit of measurement must be constant. But if the value of labor is determined by the value of the goods that make up the basic basket of workers, this value cannot be constant (Schumpterer 1954, p. 276).
- As noted by Dumont (1985, p. 228), the solution that consists in determining the value of labor from its disutility can only be valid if this disutility is always the same: "A day of slavery or plowing is so hard for a man today as it was for a man a thousand years ago" (Canant, apud. Dumont 1985). Labor would be an invariable measure of value:

> "Equal quantities of labour, at all times and places, may be said to be of equal value to the labourer. In his ordinary state of health, strength and spirits, in the ordinary degree of his skill and dexterity, he must always lay down the same portion of his ease, his liberty, and his happiness. The price which he pays must always be the same, whatever may be the quantity of goods which he receives in return for it." (Smith 1776, p. 120)

This hypothesis presupposes the existence of invariants.

The Ambivalence

Several concepts elaborated by Smith in Wealth of Nations are ambivalent: (a) they relate to the theories of labor value and utility value (b) These concepts present elements that were developed later by the Neoclassical

School, but, at the same time, others that are incompatible with the mechanisms through which the Neoclassical School used them. (c) Smith uses two concepts of utility: the first conception is defined as an intrinsic quality of the good; the paradox of water and diamond emphasizes an *objective conception of utility*, similar to that of Ricardo and Marx. Nevertheless, regarding the division of labor, Smith justifies the exchange from the subjective theory of value, from the same mechanism highlighted by the analysis of the Physiocrats (Quesnay 1759, p. 89) and, later, by the marginalists.

For example, the baker's parable can be interpreted in two ways:

(a) The Neoclassical School developed this mechanism based on Pareto's optimal and the two welfare theorems. Nevertheless, within this epistemological framework, these mechanisms act from the moment that economic agents are able to exercise a substantive rationality, in the sense defined by Simon.

(b) On the other hand, Mandeville's Fable of the Bees, or the baker's parable, clearly show that the rationality of agents is, by nature, bounded, and this for the following reasons: the performance of individuals is driven by their self-interests, and they are not aware of the implications linked to their individual performances.

Thus, the rationality they exercise is, by nature, limited, as they cannot assess, ex ante, the implications linked to their decisions. The *tour de force* operated by the market consists in transmuting private vices into public virtues: in this respect, Smith invokes the invisible hand and Hayek the spontaneous order of the market, *without specifying the modus operandi from which the market manages to operate this transmutation.*

We can observe that Hayek refutes the mechanisms highlighted by the Neoclassical School based on this type of argument, that is, because it refutes the fact that agents are able to exercise a substantive rationality.

Substantive rationality is defined as follows: in an initial unbalanced situation, individuals know the process that allows them to return to a balanced position, and use it. Individuals know and use, consciously and rationally, the mechanism that makes it possible to return to the equilibrium position (Arrow 1986, p. 236). The actions of agents are totally conscious and voluntary.

This is not the case with regard to Smith's or Hayek's views, for example: the return to equilibrium, for Smith, or the implementation of efficient regulation, for Hayek, is not due to the conscience or rationality of the agents, but by the invisible hand or the spontaneous order. *This perspective refers to a higher order, a natural order, as individuals are not able to interfere in this "celestial" and/or natural mechanism* (Tsoulfidis 2017, p. 4).

This approach is incompatible with the existence of path dependence, because the actions of individuals do not modify the equilibrium position (or the modalities of regulation) that prevails in the long run; such equilibrium is predetermined and, consequently, does not depend on the agents' performance. It is the position adopted by Neoclassical Economics.

(c) Finally, we must study the relationship that exists between bounded rationality and the coordination effected by the market game. For Smith and Hayek, for example, this bounded rationality corresponds to a social efficiency implemented by the market: the competitive game makes it possible to reconcile a multitude of individual interests and, based on endogenous mechanisms, the competitive market is self-regulated.

For other authors, on the contrary, the limited rationality of agents endogenously generates instability, which means that the market is no longer self-regulated. For Keynes, strong uncertainty implies that the rationality of agents is, by nature, limited; the system produces endogenous fluctuations (Herscovici 2019): at the point of effective demand, Keynes states that, in most cases, due to insufficient labor demand, workers cannot equate the disutility of labor with the utility of the income that comes from the sale of this labor (GT, pp. 41 and 42).

In the same line of thought, Goodwin (1967, 1992) shows, in models that it is possible to describe as Ricardian, that the system never reaches the equilibrium position and that the market system is, intrinsically, unstable. Grossman and Stiglitrz (1980) even formulate similar results.

In summary, it is possible to say that Smith's work allows us to understand the nature of the transition from Physiocracy to the further developments of economic theory. Some elements were used by Classical Economics, mainly by Ricardo and Marx: the concept of natural price represents a fundamental element of classical economics, either in its Ricardian or Marxist strand. Using quantities of labor as a unit of measurement of the value of commodities, Smith points to the need to build a commodity whose value is constant: Ricardo also tried to solve this logical problem.

On the other hand, other elements were developed by the Neoclassical School: (a) part of the value formation is determined in the sphere of circulation (b) the concept of the invisible hand was formalized from the Pareto optimum, and applied to the aggregate level with the first welfare theorem (c) prior saving allows investment to be financed, and thus constitutes an intertemporal consumption choice; this conception was widely developed by Neoclassical Economics, notably in growth models.

As stated by Vigo (2010, p. 193), the elements present in Smith's work correspond to a transition period: nevertheless (a) Smith incorporated part of the legacy of the Physiocratic school, with regard to utility and (b) his discoveries were incorporated into different epistemes: that developed by the classical school and its modern developments, and the one which corresponds to Neoclassical Economics. I will demonstrate later why these two schools do not belong to the same episteme.

The hybrid character of Smith's thought is explained by the fact that he uses concepts that come from three types of epistemes: the preclassical, due to its animistic character, the classical, due to the concept of natural order and the modern, with respect to the hedonistic dimension. For this reason, his work has been subject to different and incompatible interpretations and developments: the neoclassical ones and the Ricardian and Marxist ones. At this respect, Veblen (1899, p. 24) highlights the relation between Smith's approach and the neoclassical one, and claims that "There is no wide breach between Adam Smith and the utilitarians, either in details of doctrine or in the concrete conclusions arrived at as regards questions of policy."

In a different manner, in terms of long-term evolutions of Economic Thought, I claim that *Smith's work can be conceived as a "bifurcation point,"* a point from which the classical school (Ricardo, Marx and the neo-Ricardian) and the Neoclassical School chose different directions: "So it appeared that a choice had to be made between a return to the classical Ricardian approach or to modern intertemporal equilibrium (...)" (Schefold 2016).

The Labor Value Theory: Ricardo and Marx

The Ricardian Theory of Value

The Incorporated Labor Theory

Ricardian theory, and the neo-Ricardian developments partially resolve the ambiguities present in the previous analyses: it definitively excludes any reference to utility, it eliminates the utility of its investigations and thus affirms the primacy of production over circulation:

i. The Ricardian theory of value excludes from its field of investigation goods that are not reproducible from an industrial process, and whose value is only determined by their intrinsic scarcity. The value of these goods depends only on their scarcity:

   > "Some goods have their value determined only by their scarcity. No labor can increase the quantity of such goods (...). Their value is totally independent of the amount of labor originally required to produce them, and fluctuates with changing wealth and preferences of those who wish to own them." (Ricardo 1821, pp. 43 and 44)

   Thus, the Ricardian theory of value excludes from its field of investigation the goods whose value can only be explained from the subjective theory of value: Ricardo cites the example of statues, paintings, rare books and wines of specific quality, and observes that the value of these goods fluctuates with the modification of tastes and preferences (Idem). As these preferences change over time, the value of those goods changes accordingly.

ii. Ricardo defines the object of Economic Science as the study "(...) of the laws that regulate the distribution (...)" of the national product (1821, p. 19). The mechanisms that make it possible to explain the modalities of product distribution among capitalists, workers and landowners come from his theory of labor value. I will now explain this relationship:

   - (a) In Ricardo's works, natural prices represent the center from which market prices will oscillate, based on intersectoral capital transfers. In this regard, Ricardo refers directly to Chapter VII of the Wealth of Nations, adopting Smith's position (Ricardo 1821, p. 79); he qualifies the deviations between market prices and natural prices as temporary and accidental (Idem). In the tradition of classical economics, natural prices (or production prices for Marx) constitute the regulators, that is, the equilibrium value towards which market prices converge.

- (b) The question is now: what determines these natural prices? The amounts of direct and indirect labor needed to produce these goods, says Ricardo. Although Ricardo enunciates all the causes that can invalidate his theory of labor value, he considers that "(...) all the great variations that occur in the relative value of goods are produced by a greater or lesser amount of labor that, at different times, is necessary to produce them" (**h1**) (Idem, p. 56).

  As hypothesis h1 is relaxed, Ricardian labor theory of value presents logical inconsistencies, as Ricardo himself recognizes. The works of Sraffa and the neo-Ricardian school solved this logical problem, starting from the famous Cambridge controversy, whose results can be summarized as follows: when capital is heterogeneous, the value of an aggregate amount of capital depends on the value of distributive variables.
- (c) Despite these problems, Ricardo admits, as a proxy, that labor determines the value of commodities: it is from the value thus defined that Ricardo will deduce his theory of distribution, and oppose Adam Smith.

  The value of the commodity is determined by the amounts of direct and indirect labor necessary for its production: this value will be distributed among capitalists, wage earners and landowners. Consequently, a variation in value can only be explained by a variation in the amount of labor incorporated, and not from a variation in remuneration for labor, capital or land rent: "No change in wages could produce any change in the relative value of such goods" (ibid., p. 52).

Thus, income distribution is explained as follows: first, it depends on the value created by labor. Second, *the remuneration of the three factors of production (capital, labor and land) is indeterminate*: contrary to the Walrasian theory of *service producteur*, or to Clark's theory (1891), the different factors of production do not receive as remuneration their respective contributions to the product. If the totality of the value to be distributed is determined from the theory of value, *the relative parts of each factor are indeterminate. This corresponds, in the neo-Ricardian construction, to the exogenous determination of distributive variables.*

> "(...) a characteristic of Ricardo's theory—indeed, of the classical theory in general—is that of being made of blocks which are logically separate (...)" (De Vivo 1988, p. 183). (...) "This conception was particularly useful, in that it separated value and distribution, making the former independent of the latter." (Idem, p. 184)

On the one hand, this allows us to understand why certain components of Classical Economics were developed by the neoclassical economists and other elements by the different heterodoxies. On the other hand, the blocks constituted by the theory of value and distribution provided fundamental elements to refute the neoclassical theory, whether from Marxism or from the Neo-Ricardian School.

Ricardo refutes the Smithian theory of value, and this in two points:

- Ricardo's theory of value is not compatible with Smith's claim that the value of wheat increases when the value of land rent increases. The only reason that can explain the increase in the value of wheat is the increase in the amount of labor needed for its production; there is an inversion of causality in Adam Smith's reasoning (Ricardo 1821, op. cit., p. 70).
- There is no convergence between individual interests and the general interest: as demonstrated in the theory of differential income, there is an antagonism between income and wages on the one hand, and the profits of capitalists, on the other.

We can interpret Ricardo's theory as a desire to move away from utility and its subjective dimension, putting in its place an "objective" measure of value: the quantity of labor. The primacy of production, and the conditions that prevail in this sphere, represent an important moment in the creation of a science that aims at "objectivity," and this for the following reasons: it provides an objective measure of exchange value, and this analysis is totally disconnected from any moral a priori or any subjective element.

It is possible to state that with Ricardo, Economic Science becomes relatively autonomous in relation to other disciplines and emancipates itself in relation to moral or religious values.

The Ricardian Concept of Capital

Contrary to what we can read in several books of economic theory (Blaug 1992, p. 98; Schumpeter, II 1954, p. 134), the structure of the model elaborated by Ricardo and by the neo-Ricardian school is neither hypothetical-deductive, nor lacking a historical dimension.

The value of a given amount of aggregated and heterogeneous capital intrinsically depends on the value of distributive variables. Due to the historically determined value of these variables, *the closure of the system is essentially historical, and not hypothetical-deductive* (Chick and Dow 2001).

This procedure is incompatible with neoclassical methodology: admitting, by hypothesis, that this value is constant, at various points in time, implies that the value of these distributive variables is equally constant. It is a denial of the historical movement itself.

On the other hand, the theoretical closure of the Ricardian system implies that the determination of wages (and, consequently, of profits) is exogenous. This means that wages are not determined from the demand and supply of labor (indeed, there is no labor market); in the absence of a labor market, this determination can be institutional.

For these reasons, I have to disagree with Blaug (1992, p. 53) when he writes that, regarding Ricardo, that "(…) the historical, the institutional, and the factual, which had figured, the prominently in the writings of Adam Smith, faded into the background (…)".

Marx

This movement will develop with Marx; at the same time, Marx historicizes the analysis, and resolves, at least partially, some formalizations relating to the labor theory of value.

In his book "Contribution to the Critique of Political Economy," Marx reconstructs the different moments of the creation and autonomy of Economic Science, from mercantilism to Ricardo, based on the different historical forms assumed by labor. Following Ricardo, Marx will exclude use value from his research to study mainly exchange value: "Although it is related to social needs, consequently to the social set, use value does not express any social relation of production" (Marx 1859, p. 8). In this regard, he shows that the process of formation of exchange value is implemented from the alienation of use value (Idem, p. 25).

Nevertheless, if Marx recognizes that Ricardo was the economist who managed to elevate Classical Political Economy into its most elaborate form (ibid., p. 37), in the name of historicism, he will criticize Ricardo's analysis: according to Marx, "(…) Ricardo considers the bourgeois form of labor as the natural, eternal form of social labor" (ibid.) and thus speaks in an anachronism.

Marx will substitute the concept of labor *en général* used by classical economists by the concept of abstract labor, this being the characteristic assumed by labor in the capitalist system. He theoretically refutes the view of Smith and Ricardo according to which, in "primitive" societies, the concrete modalities of material life would be based on the same mechanisms as those that prevail in capitalist societies. Nevertheless, as I will show, Marx's historicization of analytic categories is limited.

Regarding the problem of transforming values into production prices, Marx goes beyond Ricardo: he demonstrates that, apart from the specific case in which the organic composition of capital in different sectors is the same, (a) there is, at the sectoral level, a systematic deviation between values and prices and that (b) at an aggregated level, the value/price deviation is obligatorily equal to zero[1] (Le capital, Livre III).

Finally, Marx explains, from his theory of value and exploitation, the antagonism between wages and profits. Thus, Marx's economics is largely based on the Ricardian theory of value, even if he modifies it: these changes are expressed through the historicization of analysis, the substitution of the generic concept of labor by the concept of abstract labor, the concept of antagonism between classes by the concept of exploitation, and by the resolution, at least partially, of the transformation problem.

Even if these theories are inscribed in different political projects, this cannot hide the epistemological continuity that exists between these two authors. Marxism is fully situated in the "*epistemic disposition*" of the nineteenth century (Foucault 1966, p. 274; Dumont 1985, p. 177): in the terminology used by Bourdieu (1979), I could say that, beyond the oppositions, these different schools agree on the problem to be studied.

[1] For a detailed presentation of such mechanism, see Herscovici (2002).

In terms of Internal History, in the sense defined by Lakatos, or of archeology and the structuring of knowledge, in Foucault's view, Classical Political Economy is established with these two authors, based on the following elements: the primacy of production, the construction of a theory of value that rests essentially on labor, a theory from which it is possible to deduce the distribution modalities, and the attempt to build a science based on objective criteria: the labor as source and determinant of this exchange value.

Neoclassical Economics: The "Triumph" of Utility Value

The Theory of Subjective Utility Value

The theory of value based on subjective utility constitutes an alternative explanation in relation to the theory of labor value: based on the writings of utilitarian philosophers (Mill, Jevons, Menger), a theory of utility value based on subjectivity is developed: individuals' preferences are fixed and exogenous, and, by nature, subjective. Such a conception makes it possible to elucidate the paradox of water and diamond: the subjective utility of diamonds may be superior to that of water, due to this subjective dimension.

The "Homo Economicus" is rational insofar as he maximizes his total utility, minimizing pain and maximizing pleasure: the consumer maximizes the utility that results from his consumption, the capitalist maximizes his profit.

On an aggregated level, when the conditions of pure and perfect competition are verified, the system naturally reaches an optimum situation, the so-called Pareto optimum.[2] This system of pure and perfect competition works as soon as the following conditions are met:

[2] The first welfare theorem demonstrates that, in a state of pure and perfect competition, the general equilibrium (GE) corresponds to a Pareto optimal situation. What I call Neoclassical Economics is composed of a structure that systematically associates GE and social efficiency, this efficiency being evaluated based on Pareto's criterion. In this regard, see Herscovici (2019).

(a) Preferences express the subjective choices of individuals, and these choices are determined individually, without relationships with other agents (Orléan 2011, p. 58).

This characteristic is incompatible with strategic behaviors, that is, with the generalization of the agents' interdependence. Prices thus reflect the intensity of the need: if, for a high price, the consumer decides to buy the good, this means that the utility provided by his purchase will be at least as intense as the effort needed to acquire this good; as seen, this perspective was initially developed by the Physiocrats and by Smith.

(b) The homogeneity postulate is verified: the price summarizes all the information necessary for agents to be able to assess, ex ante, the utility. Quality determines price (Herscovici 2019): a high price systematically corresponds to a high quality. There is no uncertainty with regard to quality or with regard to the possibility of evaluating, ex ante, such quality. As the marginal utility decreases, with respect to a homogeneous good, consumers will necessarily diversify their consumption basket to maximize their total utility.

Neoclassical approach is based on the following hypotheses:

i. There is complete autonomy of the economic agent: their decisions do not depend on the decisions of others or on their preferences. Preferences are exogenous and constant (**h1**). This corresponds to the concept of consumer sovereignty: their preferences are completely autonomous, and there will be no interference from any external agent with regard to the determination of those preferences. This is why Neoclassical Economics rejects psychology outside its field of investigation (Popper 1959).[3]

ii. The price system provides all the information necessary for agents to maximize their objective functions, based on the *homogeneity postulate* (**h2**). In Lancaster's (1966) analysis, exchanged goods are conceived as utility providers to consumers, as the price system freely discloses the characteristics of these goods; this process is characterized by its objectivity. Goods have an *intrinsic quality*, and

[3] Certain analyses linked to behavioral economics, those that introduce psychology into the field of study, even formulate results that are incompatible with the hard-core components of Neoclassical Economics.

prices provide the proper signal to spread information regarding this quality. The subjective dimension appears in the choices that each consumer will make, depending on their individual preferences, with regard to the characteristics of these goods.

iii. Equilibrium is carried out from the centralizing mechanism represented by the Walrasian auctioneer (the *crieur de prix*, in the terminology used by Walras), in the context of a *tâtonnement* process, during which the auctioneer proposes a price, the consumers answering with the quantities desired (**h3**). Exchanges are effectively carried out only when, for the advertised price, supply is equal to demand; equilibrium is determined ex ante, before agents act in the market (Duménil and Lévy 1987).[4]

iv. The adjustment towards the equilibrium position, that is, to a unique equilibrium that corresponds to the Pareto optimum, depends on other conditions:

(**h4a**) Individual rationality has to be parametric (Orléan 2011, p. 89); the agents' choices are based solely on prices, without any relationship with other agents.

(**h4b**) While the choice process is being carried out, preferences have to be constant, as well as prices.

(**h4c**) Finally, agents are price takers: no agent can modify the prices determined in the market by the game of supply and demand.

The Aggregate Quantity of Capital

The orthodox conception of capital (and the famous controversy of capital initiated at Cambridge in 1960 by Piero Sraffa) perfectly illustrates the universalist thesis, and its limits with regard to Economics. In fact, the theoretical construction proposed by Neoclassical Economics assimilates capital to the material means of production, and wealth to capital, which allows reasoning in real terms, that is, in quantities (Schumpeter, II 1954, p. 288).

It is possible to reason in this way when the economy produces a unique good (the "economy" of corn in Ricardo's parable). In this case,

[4] Several authors have already observed that this mechanism does not allow explaining how, from an initial position of imbalance, the system returns to equilibrium (Arrow 1986; Vercelli 1991).

the overall profit rate is determined from the following relationship:

$$Profit\ rate = \frac{Product - (capital\ costs + wages)}{capital\ costs + wages} \tag{3.1}$$

All components of the profit rate are measured in corn quantity, a homogeneous good: total production, costs linked to the initial investment in terms of quantity of corn to be sown, wages paid that correspond to the reproduction of the labor force (Garegnani 1980).

Logical problems arise when the goods, and more specifically, the capital, are heterogeneous: it is necessary to measure production, capital cost and labor remuneration in a common unit, that is, in economic value. We are faced with a logical impossibility: the profit rate is determined from three components determined in value, but the rate of profit is already embedded into these values. To know the rate of profit, it is necessary to know this same rate of profit in advance[5]; in this regard, Schefold (2017, p. 14) speaks of circularity.

For this reason, Neoclassical Economics, without further justification, considers that, at an aggregate level, it is possible to conceive a magnitude that represents a heterogeneous amount of capital. Capital is thus conceived in physical quantities, that is, in real terms. I can illustrate this mechanism from the following parable: a table, in its purely material dimension, will always be a table, in any historical period and in any society. This procedure assimilating capital to a quantity, this quantity being timeless and ahistorical.

The refutation of this hypothesis was elaborated by Sraffa (1960), and the proposed mathematical solution shows that the distributive variables (wage rate and profit rate) determine the value of an aggregated amount of capital. Thus, the value of an amount of capital varies as a function of changes in the value of distributive variables, which represents a clear manifestation of the historicization of the concept of capital, and a refutation of the universalist hypothesis.

Capital is a category that applies only in a capitalist society, and does not have this universal dimension. If we conceive capital as a social relationship, we can deduce that this analytical category is not universal; consequently, the hypothesis according to which a quantity of capital can

[5] The profit rate of the capitalist is a component of the capital value and of the wage goods.

be represented by a constant magnitude implies a permanence of social relations, which is a denial of the historical movement itself.

In universalist approaches, capital is conceived as an ahistorical, or suprahistorical, analytical category. I can summarize this debate as follows: according to this "universalist" conception, capital is evaluated in physical quantities, its magnitude is constant and determined independently of historical and social specificities (wages, profit, interest rate, etc.).[6] Capital has an intrinsic value, which represents an obvious manifestation of the substantial hypothesis. We can thus speak of the "cosification" of capital and economic relations, as opposed to its historicization: capital is conceived "(...) as a mass of material objects serviceable for human use" (Veblen 1998, p. 8).

This approach leads to asserting that the propensity to exchange is a characteristic of human nature, which prevails in all societies. Due to this implicit hypothesis, when Adam Smith cites the example of hunters and fishermen, in a hypothetical primitive society (1776), he affirms that the product of hunting and fishing is entirely destined for exchange. All the modern works of economic anthropology and economic history show, on the contrary, that in non-capitalist societies, production is not carried out with a view to exchange in the market, but in function of other social, political or symbolic purposes: self-consumption, symbolic exchanges linked to a gift economy, religious purposes, etc. Material production is based on a logic linked to use value, social use value, and not exchange value (Braudel 1985).

Based on these hypotheses, the "universalist" authors claim that economic laws are, by nature, universal. In this regard, I will cite three authors who, in my view, in addition to their differences, belong to this universalist school:

(a) For Hayek, any theory has to be universal, because it chooses the performance of individual agents and their relationships as an object of study. In this regard, Hayek claims that a monopoly price in Egypt, four hundred years before Christ, or a monopoly price practiced today, will be explained from the same law (Hayek 1952, p. 118).

[6] See Herscovici (2019).

(b) Popper intends to make an epistemological critique of historicism, and more particularly of Marxism, based on the following argument: if scientific laws were historical, there would be no way to explain the mechanisms that allow understanding the passage from one period to another (Popper 1972, p. 131). On the other hand, a historical law, by its nature, cannot be falsified (1959): it is always possible to invoke the fact that certain initial conditions were not verified to justify the non-verification of the results foreseen by this law (Herscovici 2002).

(c) Piketty, in fact, uses the same hypothesis: he analyzes the rate of return on capital from year 0 of the Christian era to 2200 (2013, p. 566). In addition to the problems relating to the measurement of capital, this study assumes that capital constitutes a universal analytical category, intrinsically associated with any form of material production, at any time and in any type of society. As the different anthropological, historical and economic studies emphasize, *capital is a social relationship*: assimilating capital and material production specific to each type of society necessarily leads to universalizing this concept, denying the specificities of the different societies studied and, ultimately, to consider that the mechanisms inherent to capitalism are inscribed in human nature: such analysis is based on the hunters and fishermen's parable, whose production, according to Adam Smith, is destined to be exchanged.

History of Economic Thought, Episteme and Historicity

Episteme and Nature of Ruptures

Foucault's analysis allows us to study the nature of the ruptures that characterize long-term evolutions, and notably the controversial ones inherent to Economics: *these controversial ones have to be interpreted as incremental ruptures, which occur within the same episteme, or as fundamental ruptures that relate to the emergence of a new episteme?* The three controversial ones that I will study in the second part of this work will be analyzed from this perspective.

(a) Does the neo-Ricardian school's radical refutation of Neoclassical Economics take place within the same episteme or, on the contrary, from two different epistemes? Foucault does not provide elements of an answer, as he does not analyze the marginalist school, which, in my view, represents one of the limitations of Foucault's analysis.

If the marginalist school fits the episteme of modernity (Vigo 2010, p. 191), the neo-Ricardian critique is an internal critique. If, on the contrary, the marginalist school corresponds to another episteme, this critique becomes an external critique, and the limits of this critique come from the incommensurability between two epistemes. Nevertheless, it seems to me that this criticism is, simultaneously, internal and external: internal because the Cambridge controversy refutes the neoclassical foundations: the law of decreasing marginal productivity, the hypothesis of constant scale returns and the construction of functions of aggregated production—external, due to the fact that this criticism starts from the labor value theory instead of the subjective value theory.

(b) The second controversial concerns Hayek's criticisms of standard Neoclassical Economics: in this regard, I will demonstrate that these two schools share several common elements in their respective hard cores.

(c) The third controversy highlights the refutation of the neoclassical model aggregated from the post-Keynesian critique, and more specifically, in relation to the nature of money and finance. Post-Keynesian economics uses a time that is by nature irreversible, which, in the presence of strong uncertainty, characterizes a historicist approach (Davidson 1996). The neoclassical universe defines itself, on the contrary, by a reversible time, and verifies the ergodicity postulate. These two schools come from different epistemes.

This type of analysis is different from the one carried out by Foucault, as it can imply the comparison between two epistemes. On the other hand, *the incommensurability of paradigms, or epistemes, is not absolute*: there is always a moment when there is communication between these different paradigms, if only to highlight existing incompatibilities. It is the *démarche* of Kuhn and Lakatos.

A Taxonomy of Different Schools of Thought

Physiocracy

Physiocracy is the hybrid product of preclassical and classical episteme: the abundance provided by nature is a divine gift, economic laws are of the same nature as natural laws, they are universal, Quesnay's Tableau Économique corresponds to a logic of representation, the object of study of Economics is mainly defined by the use value, and wealth and value are equivalent concepts. Labor only contributes to transforming the elements existing in Nature, and to materializing the surplus provided by Mother Nature (Foucault 1966, p. 268).

Scarcity is explained from the need (the "besoin" in French), that is, from the utility (Idem); this utility varies according to the individuals, and it decreases according to the quantity consumed. Nature, she, meets the needs.

Smith

Smith's work, due to the ambiguities presented, uses elements that belong to the three epistemes defined by Foucault:

i. Labor is conceived as a negative utility, that is, a disutility: this conception comes directly from the divine order, that is, from the preclassic episteme. After having committed the original sin, Adam and Eve were expelled from paradise and had to work to survive. From there, labor became the punishment inflicted by God.

   On the other hand, labor is the true measure against which all goods are to be evaluated: as a unit of measure, its value must be constant. The answer given by Smith consists in stating that the disutility of labor is constant, which presupposes the existence of invariant elements inherent to human nature:

   This element is characteristic of the classical episteme, in function of this universal dimension of modernity: Ricardo tried, in vain, to find a standard commodity whose value is constant, that is, whose value does not depend on distributive variables.

ii. The baker's parable shows that there is a convergence between individual interests and the general interest. This parable allows reconciling Christian morality with self-love, the love of the other with the love of oneself; this analysis has not been able to completely break its ties in relation to the preclassical episteme and the divine order that characterizes it.

iii. Nevertheless, the paradox of water and diamond (Smith 1776, p. 117) prefigures Classical Economics and, more generally, what Foucault calls modernity:

- use value is conceived as an objective quality that is part of the commodity body: it is considered as natural, that is, it is rejected outside the field of study (Smith, Ricardo and Marx). This approach reveals the substantial hypothesis adopted in Economics (cf. p. 70 and 71), and corresponds to the primacy of the sphere of production over the sphere of circulation.
- Nevertheless, in the physiocratic tradition, Smith resorts to subjective utility to explain and justify the development of exchanges and the division of labor, which contribute to the social welfare:

  > "Each worker has a much larger amount of their own labor than they can use; it is possible for him to exchange a large quantity of his own products for a large quantity (…) of theirs (of other workers)." (op. cit., p. 89)

  We can observe the similarity with the arguments developed by the Physiocratic school, and with the elements that herald the marginalist economy: individual utility is subjective, marginal utility is decreasing and the exchange corresponds to the maximization of individual utility functions as, via the calculating substitution rate, the individual maximizes his total utility.
- Finally, Smith interprets the generalization of exchange as the action of an invisible hand, as these exchanges spread "abundance across different social strata" (Idem.). The invisible hand mechanism reappears here.

In several passages in The Wealth of Nations, Smith asserts that money is neutral. This neutrality is a means that makes possible the generalization of exchange and its beneficial effects for society. However, money cannot determine exchange relations, for the following reasons: being a commodity, its value is determined by labor. As the quantities of labor, it can command vary, its value varies as well, and it cannot constitute a unit of measure. For Smith, labor determines the value of goods, because the value of labor itself is, by hypothesis, constant: "(…) only labor, whose value never varies, is the genuine and true standard in terms from which the value of all other goods can, at any time and place, be estimated and compared" (ibid., p. 124).

As I will demonstrate later, the primacy of the sphere of production has two implications: first, it discards the explanatory power of the sphere of circulation (exchange, the game of supply and demand), second, it means that money is neutral.

It is interesting to note that Marx adopted the first interpretation, while the marginalist school the second; Ricardo adopted both hypotheses.

Based on these hypotheses, saving is conceived as a purely real mechanism, in the sense that it is not monetary: investment depends on previous savings, and this savings promotes economic growth. This is the reason why Smith states that "(…) thrift, by increasing the fund for the maintenance of productive workers, tends (…) consequently, to increase the exchange value of the annual product of the land and of the country work" (ibid., p. 592). Savings is conceived as an intertemporal choice of consumption; the same results were later formulated by Say:

(a) Profits are "(…) solely determined by the value of the capital employed, and are greater or lesser depending on the volume of that capital" (ibid., p. 149). It is a "supply economy" in the sense that profits determine economic growth.
(b) Here, we observe the frontal opposition with the vision of Keynes and Kalecki, with regard to the role of expenditure in the dynamics of economic growth: in Smith's view, this growth is determined by previous savings, that is, by the renunciation of immediate expenditures, while for Keynes (1936) and Kalecki (1939), growth depends on these present expenditures.
(c) Finally, this nature of saving and money causes Global Demand to remain the same as Global Supply, for any product level: What is annually saved is so regularly consumed (…) (Smith, 1776, p. 593). This corresponds exactly to the theory of loan funds in Walrasian macroeconomics: this theory implies that there is equality between global supply and demand, for any level of output: "(…) he anticipates the classical theory

of money neutrality and Say's law" (Alcouffe and Massot-Bordenave 2018, p. 259).

In order to refute this economy, in Chapter XIV of the General Theory, Keynes will initially refute this theory. Thus, citing Hobson, Keynes opposes Smith's theory, based on the following argument: an excess of savings translates into an insufficiency of consumption. In this case, there will be an excess of supply, that is, an insufficiency of global demand (GT, p. 281): "(…) it is consumption that limits production and not production that limits consumption" (Hobson 1889; apud Keynes 1936).

(d) Nevertheless, in this discussion, Smith introduces an element that is totally incompatible with the neoclassical approach, and that was developed extensively by Marx: the dichotomy between productive and unproductive labor, which represents a legacy of the Physiocratic system, and allows developing, from the classic matrix, analyzes based on the concept of surplus. Marx thus deduced his theory of exploitation, and Sraffa the whole of his theory (Garegnani 1980).

(e) Money is neutral, as it does not fulfill the function of store of value: "The only use of money is to allow the circulation of consumable goods" (Smith 1776, p. 595).

iv. Finally, Smith assimilates value and wealth, which is also a legacy of the Physiocratic system: this can be explained by the duality present throughout Smith's work, that is, by the ambivalence between a theory of value linked to utility and another to labor (Dumont 1985): "The increase in income and capital corresponds to the increase in wealth" (Smith 1776, p. 181).

Regarding the periodization established by Foucault, it is possible to say that Smith uses components that come from the three epistemes: some elements linked to the preclassical episteme, due to references to a divine order—other elements linked to the classical episteme, due to the "naturalist" components—components that announce modernity, components that were widely used by Ricardo and Marx—and, finally, elements that were developed by the Neoclassical School. With regard to this last point, Smith's theory of value "hesitates" between an analysis in terms of labor costs and in terms of subjective utility: "(…) sometimes he is as a cost of production theorist, while others see him as a forerunner of general equilibrium analysis" (Vaggi and Groenerwegen 2003).

For this reason, part of his work has been developed in the context of Classical Economics, and another part from a marginalist perspective. If each of these interpretations has an internal consistency, the choice made necessarily implies that, in order to take away the present ambiguities, certain hypotheses are adopted and others must be rejected.

Ricardo and Marx

Ricardo and Marx exclude use value from their investigation in order to focus their analysis on exchange value. This hypothesis was already, in part, present in Smith's theory, when this author elaborates an "objective" conception of use value; it was taken up by Marx, when he states that use value is natural, while exchange value is, by nature, social: on the other hand, exchange value determined from abstract labor constitutes the substance of commodities: "Commodities are exchanged because they have value, and they have not value because they are exchanged" (1867, Livre I, p. 69).

These statements are particularly significant: they make it possible to assert the primacy of the sphere of production in relation to circulation and correspond to the substantial hypothesis: goods have a substance that determines their value. What is the nature of this substance? Historical or universal? (cf. p. 83).

It should be noted that, for the Classics, this primacy of the sphere of production is synonymous with the primacy of production in relation to circulation, that is, the effects of the game of demand and supply are only temporary. *With regard to the neoclassicals, this primacy of the sphere of production is interpreted as the primacy of the real sphere in relation to the monetary and financial sphere*. There are two different interpretations: if Ricardo adopted Say's law, for Marx, money is not neutral (Herscovici 2002).

Finally, the time used can be reversible, or irreversible: several authors conceive production prices as the long-term position that the system achieves, they use a reversible time and ignore the phenomena of path dependence. It is possible to provide another interpretation of production prices from a time that is by nature irreversible, from a neo-Ricardian and Marxian perspective (Idem).

The Neoclassical School

The Neoclassical School is likewise heterogeneous: it contains elements that belong to the three epistemes defined by Foucault:

(a) Methodological individualism, as used by the Neoclassical Research Program, uses the analogies and similarities proper to the preclassical episteme *to reduce macroeconomic mechanisms to their microeconomic foundations.*

(b) It borrows characteristic elements of the classical episteme: the universality of scientific laws (cf Popper), the representation of the order of the world from a mathesis (the particularly complex formalization prevails) and the existence of a cumulative progress of Science.

- Time, by nature, as well as the decisions of economic agents, is reversible, which is one of the characteristics of the classical episteme. The iteration mechanism (the Walrasian auctioneer) that makes possible to instantly achieve general equilibrium, in the set of markets, translates into "false exchanges": exchanges are effectively carried out only when the advertised price is the one that allows for equalization of demand and supply. The relaxation of this hypothesis causes the markets to close out of balance, as a result of rationing (Bénassy 1984 and Stiglitz 1987).
- One of the characteristics of pure and perfect competition resides in the hypothesis of free entry and free exit in the industry, in Marshall's own terms. This hypothesis is adopted both in the founding models of neoclassical theory (Marshall and Walras) and in modern competition theories (Baumol's theory of contestable markets).

(c) Finally, neoclassical theory maintains an ambiguous relationship with the episteme linked to modernity: the concept of scarcity, a central concept that defines the object of study, is devoid of any social, institutional and historical dimension, and is related to physical quantities.

Generally speaking, neoclassical economists study the contributions inherited from the past in light of the criteria in force today, criteria adopted in their Scientific Research Program. The epistemological strategy developed by the Neoclassical School consists of integrating all schools into its theoretical framework: in this perspective, bastard Keynesianism, in Joan Robinson's own words, in the scope of the interpretation made from the IS/LM graphics, is reduced to a neoclassical General Equilibrium model with short-term prices rigidity.

- The construction of Homo Economicus, rational being par excellence, is an attempt made to build an ahistorical and transcendent subject, provided with a universal and instrumental rationality applicable at any time and to any social activity. This methodology is applied to various social fields, such as sociology, psychology, legal sciences and political sciences: in the 60 s, based on the works of Gary Becker, Neoclassical Economics decided to study the economics of family and marriage, politics, corruption, etc.

References

Alcouffe, Alain, Massot-Bordenave, Philippe. 2018. *Adam Smith en Occitanie*. Toulouse: Privat Histoire.

Arrow, Kenneth J. 1986. Rationality of Self and Others in an Economic System. *The Journal of Business* 59 (4): 385–390.

Bénassy, Jean-Pascal. 1984. *Macroéconomie et théorie du déséquilibre*. Paris: Dunod.

Blaug, Mark. 1992. *The Methodology of Economics or How Economists Explain*, 2nd ed. Cambridge: Cambridge University Press.

Bourdieu, Pierre. 1979. *La distinction*. Critique sociale du jugement. Paris: Les éditions de Minuit.

Fernand, Braudel. 1985. *La dynamique du capitalisme*. Paris: Champs Flammarion.

Carvalho, Fernando Cardim de. 1983–1984. On the concept of time in Shacklean and Sraffian economics. *Journal of Post Keynesian Economics* VI (2)(Winter): 265–280.

Cartelier, Jean. 2008. *Introduction*, *Quesnay. Physiocratie*. Paris: GF Flammarion.

Clark, J.B. 1891. Distribution as determined by a law of rent. *Quarterly E Journal of Economics*, 5 (April): 289–318.

Davidson, Paul. 1996. Reality and economic theory. *Journal of Post Keynesian Economics/Summer* 1996: 479–508.

Chick, V., and S. Dow. 2001. Formalism, logic and reality: A Keynesian analysis. *Cambridge Journal of Economics* 25: 705–721.

De Vivo, Giancarlo. 1988. Ricardo and his disciples: Otthodoxy and Socialism. *History of European Ideas* 9 (2): 183–189.

Duménil, G., and D. Lévy. 1987. The dynamics of competition: A restoration of the classical analysis. *Cambridge Journal of Economics* 11: 133–164.

Dumont, Louis. 1985. *Homo aequalis. Genèse et épanouissement de l'idéologie économique*. Paris : NRF, Editions Gallimard.

Foucault, Michel. 1966. *Les mots et les choses*. Paris: Tel Galimard.

Garegnani, Pierangelo. 1980. Sobre a teoria da distribuição e do valor em Marx e nos economistas clássicos. *Progresso técnico e teoria econômica*. São Paulo: Hucitec-Unicamp.

Goodwin, Richard. 1967. A growth cycle. In *Socialism, capitalism and economic growth*. Cambridge: Cambridge University Press.

———. 1992. *Chaotic Economic Dynamics*. Oxford: Clarendon Press.

Grossman, S.J. and J.E. Stiglitz. 1980. On the Impossibility of Informationally Efficient Markets. *The American Economic Review* 70 (3) (June 1980): 393–408.

Hayek, Friedrich von. 2009 [1950]. *The pure theory of capital*. Auburn, Alabama: The Ludwig von Mises Institute.

———. 1952. *Scientism and the study of Society*. Glencoe, IL: The Free Press.

Herscovici, Alain. 2002. *Dinâmica Macroeconômica: uma interpretação a partir de Marx e de Keynes*. São Paulo: EDUC/EDUFES.

Herscovici, Alain. 2019. *Essays on the Historicity of Capital*. Palgrave Macmillan.

Kalecki, Michal. 1990 (1939). Crescimento e ciclo das economias capitalistas. São Paulo: Hucitec.

Keynes. 2009 [1936]. John Maynard Keynes, Keynes, John Maynard. *The General Theory of Employment, Interest and Money*. New York: Classic Books America.

Lancaster, Kelvin. 1966. A New Approach to Consummer Theory. *Journal of Political Economy* 74 (2): 132–157.

Mandeville, Bernard. [1732] 1988. *The Fable of the Bees or Private Vices, Publick Benefits, Vol. 1*. Indianapolis: Liberty Fund.

Marx, Karl. 1972 [1859]. *Contribution à la critique de l'économie politique*. Paris: Editions Sociales.

Orléan, André. 2011. *L'empire de la valeur. Refonder l'Économie*. Paris: Éditions du Seuil.

Piketty, Thomas. 2013. *Le capital au XXIème siècle*. Paris: Editions du Seuil.

Popper, Karl. 1959. *The Logic of Scientific Discovery*. London: Hutchinson.

———. 1972. *The Poverty of Historicism*, 2nd ed. London: Routledge & Kegan Paul.

Quesnay. 2008 [1759]. *Physiocratie*. Paris: GF Flammarion.

Ricardo, David. 1821. *On the Principles of Political Economy and Taxation*, 3rd ed. Kitchener, ON: Batoche Book 2001.

Schefold, Bertram. 2017. *Great Economic Thinkers from the Classicals to the Moderns*. Routledge.

———. 2016. Continuity and change in the transition from the classical to the neoclassical theory of normal prices, paper presented to the congress *The dissemination, and practice of market economic thought in China and the Commemoration of the 240th anniversary of the publication of An inquiry into the nature and causes of the wealth of nations*. Shangai.

Schumpeter, Joseph A. 1954. *History of Economic Analisis*, vol. II. Oxford: Oxford University Press.

Smith, Adam. 1776. *Inquérito sobre a natureza e as causas da riqueza das nações*, Vol I, 1980. Lisboa: Fundação Calouste Gulbenkian [Original: *An Inquiry into the Nature and causes of the wealth of Nations*. London: William Strahan e Thomas Caldell Editor, 1776).

———. 2005 [1759]. *The Theory of Moral Sentiments*. São Paulo: Metalibri.

Sraffa, Pierro. (1960). *Production of Commodities by Means of Commodities: Prelude to a Critique of Economic Theory*. Cambridge: Cambridge University Press.

Stiglitz Joseph E. 1987. The Causes and Consequences of the Dependence of Quality on Price. *Journal of Economic Literature* XXV (March): 1–48.

Tsoulfidis, Lefteris. 2017. Economic Theory in Historical Perspective. *The Journal of Philosophical Economics: Reflections on Economic and Social Issues* X (2) (Spring).

Gianni, Vaggi, and Groenewegen Peter. 2003. *A Concise History of Economic Thought*. Palgrave Macmillan.

Veblen, Thorstein. 1899. The Preconceptions of Economic Science. *The Quarterly Journal of Economics* 13 (4): 396–426.

———. 1998. Why Is Economics Not an Evolutionary Science. *The Quarterly Journal of Economics* 12 (4): 373–397.

Vercelli, Alessandro. 1991. *Methodological Foundations of Macroeconomics: Keynes and Lucas*. Cambridge: Cambridge University Press.

Vigo, Iara, 2010, *Foucault's Archaeology of Political Economy*, Palgrave Macmillan.

CHAPTER 4

The Different Epistemological Trajectories: From Archeology to Genealogy

Despite the construction of a theory of labor value, the Physiocratic school and Smith's analysis incorporate elements directly related to utility value and announce the further developments elaborated by the Neoclassical School, starting from marginalism. For example, the fact that Smith conceives labor as disutility is justified by the utility value theory, and not the labor value theory.

Then, from different hypothesis, Ricardo and Marx move away from the subjective theory of value and the subjective elements linked to morality or religion; in other words, they allow emancipating Economics from religion, moral, politics and ideology. The classical approach, from labor value theory, substitutes the subjectivity that characterizes morality criteria by objectivity relative to economic relations: relations between men are substituted by relations between commodities, which Marx calls fetishism.

From a different paradigm, based on the subjective value theory, the Neoclassical School intends to carry out an objective analysis and provides the necessary tools to measure economic quantities: for this reason, within the scope of methodological individualism, it considers that the agents' preferences are exogenous and constant.

A. Herscovici, *Value, Historicity, and Economic Epistemology*,
https://doi.org/10.1007/978-3-031-21157-7_4

Autonomization of Economic Science and Substantial Hypothesis

Autonomization of Economic Science

A Progressive Emancipation

There is a progressive emancipation in relation to morals and politics[1]: Adam Smith conceives labor as a disutility: this thesis is still linked to Christian morality and original sin. Ricardo and Marx move away from this conception to reach "objectivity," that is, to build a science totally disconnected from morals, politics and, more generally, from ideology (Dumont 1985, p. 102):

> The mercantile value, as the economic tradition conceives it, is radically distinguished from other social, moral, aesthetic or religious values, in that they present themselves as an objective and calculable magnitude, independent of the actors and their relationships. (Orléan 2011, p. 52)

The moral that prevails in the social sphere is ignored in the economic sphere, as highlighted in the parable of the invisible hand or in the fable of the bees: while social morality is characterized by altruism, economic interests are governed by self-love, that is, by hedonism.

The subjectivity that characterizes morality is progressively replaced by objectivity relative to economic relations: the relations between men are being replaced by the relations between men and goods (Idem, p. 128). This is what Marx calls commodity fetishism. This tradition characterizes all schools of thought, and Neoclassical Economics based on the subjective theory of value does not escape this trend: individual utility, by its subjective nature, is conceived as an exogenous variable (Lancaster 1966).

Classical economics will focus its analysis on the sphere of production. This position is ambiguous, in Smith's work. However, it is established in the work of Ricardo and Marx: the natural price (or production price) constitutes the position from which market prices oscillate. In this regard, Marx states that, due to a double determination, demand and supply mechanism do not explain prices: "If the market price is determined by supply and demand, supply and demand are determined by the market price (...)" (Le Capital, Livre III, p. 205). *The primacy of production can*

[1] In this regard, it is interesting to note that economics was a discipline originated from moral sciences, philosophy or laws.

also be interpreted as the manifestation of money neutrality; it is the reason why classical economists, apart from Marx, implicitly consider money to be neutral (Orléan 2011, p. 28).

Neoclassical Economics introduces an epistemological break, or more precisely, it represents a return to classical episteme: production comes down to a "black box" in which homo economicus maximizes a profit function, and the economic order is assimilated to a natural order. However, it also intends to elaborate an objective analysis and provide the necessary tools to measure economic quantities: "The market appears in the form of an automatic mechanism, absolutely *neutral*, whose function is to register exogenous individual desires, without transforming them" (Idem, p. 67, emphasis added).

The Substantial Hypothesis: A First Approach

The substantial hypothesis would be the common component that, beyond the theoretical and epistemological oppositions and incompatibilities, would result from the (relative) autonomy of Economics and the constitution of a specific field of investigation. This thesis is defended, implicitly or explicitly, by Foucault, Dumont and Orléan.

Regarding Classical Economics, Foucault states that, based on the theory of value, these economists intend to break with mercantilism because "(…) they differentiate the theory of price and that of *intrinsic value* (…)" (1969, p. 178, emphasis added).

Dumont (1985, p. 119) writes that Classical Economics, "(…) tends to conceive the economic process as being rooted much more in a substance (production, labor) than in relationships."

Finally, Orléan assimilates the construction of a theory of value to the substantial hypothesis: "The economic tradition calls 'value theory' the approaches that try to discover the secret of commercial exchange in the hypothesis of a 'substance' or quality that gives goods an intrinsic value" (2011, p. 24).

This approach leads me to ask the following questions:

- (a) To what extent does this substance make it possible to determine the intrinsic value of goods? Can this substance be defined independently of historical and social variables or, on the contrary, does it depend directly on these variables? We find again the oppositions between the historicist and universalist theses. The very concept of intrinsic value implies that economic laws are linked to a natural order, ahistorical by nature.

- (b) What is in common between the theoretical matrices linked to the labor value and those linked to the utility value? Could it be possible, beyond the incompatibilities, to define a common element between these two matrices?
- (c) Finally, how may we consider economic analysis that are not supported by any theory of value, whether labor or utility (I think more specifically about Hayek and Schumpeter)?

In this case, the problem is to define the nature of this substance: *is it universal or does it depend on the historical periods considered*?

- For Classical economics, Neoclassical Economics and the Austrian school, mainly with Hayek, such substance is universal. I will call this position universalist, in the Popperian sense. In it is present a naturalism that works from the invariants proper to human nature; economic laws are of the same nature as natural laws.

Two types of arguments justify this thesis: first, the belief in a human nature that acts as an invariant element across space and time, beyond cultural and historical specificities. Second, if economic concepts are the result of certain social relations, the universalization of these concepts is equivalent to the universalization of social relations that characterize capitalism, that is, the negation of the historical movement, in its social, political and cultural dimensions.

This hypothesis allows analyzing different societies and their material production systems as different phases of the same capitalist-type development process. Based on these hypotheses, it is possible to study "primitive" societies in terms of their backwardness, in relation to a more advanced stage of capitalism development: this is the position of Adam Smith and, to a certain extent, of Ricardo.

This represents the different possible manifestations of the substantial hypothesis, *based on the permanence of social relations;* for this reason, the naturalization of economic concepts makes it possible to resemble these economic concepts with "things" or with quantities, with regard to capital, things that are immutable and defined independently of any social and historical component.

Historicism, on the contrary, is characterized by the fact that it recognizes that the substance that the theory of value reveals is, intrinsically, historical: in other words, *if the goods exchanged have a certain substance, such substance changes quantitatively and qualitatively*. The quantitative dimension is related to the value conceived as a unit of measure, for the same quality; the qualitative one, with the very choice of the substance that served as the unit of measure.

Several Marxist authors consider that, in today's capitalism, value continues to be determined by the quantity of abstract labor incorporated in goods. This is based on the assumption that capitalism is defined by the generalization of the commodity. If, on the contrary, we refute this assumption, abstract labor no longer constitutes the substance that determines value, that is, quantitatively, prices and exchange relations. Due to these qualitative changes, the substance of the value itself has changed, and is no longer constituted by abstract labor (Herscovici 2014); *the logic of the economy of relation has replaced the economy of quantities, and this economy of relation is, by nature, historical* (Herscovici 2019).

Marx, like Ricardo, recognized that, in certain cases, value is no longer determined by the amount of abstract labor: all forms of fictitious capital express this disconnection; on the other hand, in the *Grundrisse* (1857–1861), Marx speaks of the self-destruction of the law of value in advanced capitalism.

Effectively, the substantial hypothesis implies an objective definition of the object of study, and the possibility of reaching, from scientific investigation, this intrinsic value; such a démarche presupposes an impartial observer, that is, a neutral subject.

The Substantial Hypothesis in Different Paradigms

Wealth, Value and Historicity: The Rupture Introduced by Ricardo

Ricardo and the neo-Ricardian developments constitute a double rupture, in terms of the History of Economic Thought: the first rupture is defined in relation to the Physiocratic school and Smith's theory:

- The analysis of Physiocrats is centered on social utility; wealth is provided by production linked to nature. Exchange is only possible as nature produces a surplus, which will be exchanged for other commodities.

Ricardo, on the contrary, differentiates wealth and value:

> "Most errors in Political Economy are due to errors in this matter, in regarding an increase in wealth and an increase in value as having the same meaning, and by unfounded notions of what constitutes a standard measure of value." (1821, p. 190)

The reasoning is as follows (Idem, p. 191): if country A produces goods with a certain quantity of labor, and if country B produces twice as much goods with an equivalent quantity of labor, the value produced by A will be equivalent to the value produced by B, but the wealth of B will be twice as much as the wealth of A, because B produces twice as much commodity as A, with the same amount of labor. In B, the increase in labor productivity translates into an abundance of useful goods, while the total value remains constant. Ricardo deduces that wealth depends directly on the abundance of useful goods, while value is determined by labor and labor productivity. *It is necessary to differentiate wealth and value. Wealth linked to utility increases as a result of the abundance of goods, while value, determined from the quantity of labor, remains constant.*

Ricardo (op. cit., p. 191) highlights the contradictions in the Smithian definition of value: on the one hand, Smith states that a man is rich or poor "(…) depending on the amount of labor (…) that he can buy" (Smith 1776, p. 119). In the example cited, wealth increases while the quantities of labor from which exchange remains constant. Thus, contrary to Smith's analysis, it is not possible to assimilate wealth and value: wealth is related to the abundance of utility goods, according to the terminology used by Ricardo, while value refers to the quantities of labor necessary to produce these goods.

The theoretical implications are as follows:

(a) The fact that Smith assimilates Wealth and Value highlights the influence of the Physiocratic school, and has to be interpreted as a characteristic of the representation proper to the classical episteme (Vigo 2010, p. 179).

(b) The differentiation made by Ricardo between wealth and value constitutes a fundamental epistemological rupture: it rejects outside the field of investigation utility to focus the analysis on production and labor.

(c) Contrary to the hypotheses adopted by Neoclassical Economics, scarcity is not the only foundation of economic value; this highlights the fundamental incompatibility that exists between these two schools, and the fact that *they do not share the components of the same episteme*; it must also be added that the very nature of scarcity is different for these two schools.

There are two ways to increase a country's wealth: in the absence of technical progress, the increase in the production of goods implies a drop in consumption due to the increase in necessary savings: such increase translates into a decrease in global consumption of this country, that is, by "(...) deprivation or the reduction of satisfactions (...)" (ibid., p. 192). When, on the contrary, the productive force of labor increases, the increase in wealth does not translate into a decrease in consumption. Consequently, technical progress translates into an increase in wealth and makes it possible to avoid intertemporal distributional conflicts between social classes.

These analyses allow me to formulate the following conclusions: the object of study of economics moves away from utility, or needs, to focus on exchange value, this value being defined based on the quantities of labor: labor determines wealth.

Based on his theory of differential rent, Ricardo shows that value no longer comes from land, as a divine gift, but from human labor: Economy emancipates itself from the power of the church, which explains its autonomy as a science and, at the same time, affirms its historicity (Foucault 1966, p. 269).

Marx, in the tradition of classical economics, obviously refutes the thesis of mercantilism. What is hidden behind the fetish character of money is the exchange value (Le Capital, Livre I, p. 87), it is the substance that is embedded in commodities and that allows them to be expressed in a common unit of measure: abstract labor. Value has to be created beforehand in production, to enter the sphere of circulation and for goods to be exchanged. In this regard, Marx states that "(...) it is not exchange that regulates the quantity of value of a commodity but, on the contrary, the quantity of value of the commodity that regulates its exchange relations" (Idem, p. 69).

Marx resolves the duality between use value and exchange value based on the concept of alienation of use value: "To be realized as use-values, goods must be realized as exchange-values" (1859, p. 21). This analysis is reminiscent of that of the Physiocrats.

Marx, like Ricardo, will privilege the quantitative relationship to explain the exchange between commodities. The very transformation of concrete labor into abstract labor, which corresponds to the alienation of use value, allows expressing the value of goods in a common unit: abstract labor. Thus, the fetishism of the commodity expresses the fact that relations between men are replaced by exchange relations between commodities, that is, by "(...) relations of things among themselves" (1867, Le Capital, Livre I, p. 77).

This issue is questioned by certain authors: Kurz and Salvadori (2010), for example, support the following thesis, regarding Marx, Ricardo and Sraffa: it is necessary to differentiate the fact that labor is the source of value and the fact that labor is the adequate measure to quantify this value, that is, the exchange ratios. The logical errors found in the theoretical constructions developed by Ricardo and Marx are explained by the fact that these authors chose labor as a unit of measurement of value, and not only as a source of value. For other authors (Meacci 2017), Smith's theory of commanded labor allows solving this problem.

The Classical Economy

A priori, Ricardo adopts a view similar to that of Smith regarding primitive societies: "In the primitive stages of society, the exchange value of such commodities (...) depends almost exclusively on the comparative amount of labor employed in each" (1821, p. 44): the substance of exchange value is labor *en général*. This statement would be valid for any type of society, and for any age. In this example, Ricardo uses Smithian universalism, based on the following assumption: in any society, material production is elaborated as a function of its exchange in the market, which presupposes that the mercantile logic regulates any type of society.

We can affirm that the implicit anthropological hypotheses on which these conclusions rest, for both Smith and Ricardo, reveal a *European centrism*: the entire history of humanity is conceived based on the sociological norms proper to capitalism. Nevertheless, despite these assumptions, Ricardo's analysis intrinsically has a historicist dimension, for the following reasons:

i. On one hand, Ricardian analysis also uses intrinsically historical tools (cf. p. 105): scarcity is not the attribute of certain goods, but depends solely on specific historical conditions. In the example of the Ricardian differential rent theory, land becomes scarce under certain historical conditions, that is, when economic development is such that better quality land is no longer able to meet the growing demand for corn; best quality land would not be scarce for any level of development of society, that is, for any level of demand for wheat.

ii. On the other hand, Ricardo was aware of the fact that the natural wage, which corresponds to the reproduction of the labor force, is determined by historical, cultural and social variables:

> "It should not be understood that the natural price of labor, although determined in food and basic necessities, is absolutely fixed and constant. It varies in the same country, at different times and differs substantially essentially in different countries, depending on the habits and customs of the peoples." (1821, p. 83)

This observation highlights a historical relativism that, in my view, is present in the framework elaborated by Ricardo.

Marx

Marx, on the contrary, historicizes the analysis, showing that abstract labor, that is, socially necessary labor, is the substance of value in the capitalist system. From a historicist perspective, Marx will refute the universalism of classical economists, especially in Adam Smith's approach. He ironically states that the dogma (this is the term used by Marx) of these economists consists in stating that "(...) things, instruments of labor, for example, are, by nature, capital (...)" (1867, Livre I, p. 87).

The law of value implements a triple transformation: concrete labor is transformed into abstract labor, complex labor into simple labor and individual labor into social labor (Rubin 1980, p. 155). I will focus the analysis on the first and third level of this transformation. Certain ambiguities appear in the argument developed by Marx:

i. Marx recognizes that use value is "natural," that is, universal: utility is determined "(...) by the properties of the commodity body (...)" (1867, Livre I, p. 44) and "(...) does not express a social relation of production" (1859, p. 8). I refute this hypothesis: the utility of material and immaterial goods is not natural, but essentially social and historical. Bourdieu's (1979) analysis, for example, clearly shows that this utility (the "tastes") is socially determined, by the very logic of the social fields of production, and by specific distinction mechanisms (Orléan 2011, p. 26).

ii. On the other hand, Marx starts from the hypothesis according to which the exchange value is determined from social labor. The problem is to study the modalities of transformation of individual labor into social labor: when there is generalization of commodities, the socialization of individual labor expressed mainly through abstract labor (Marx 1894, p. 75). This mode of socialization of individual labor "(...) acquires for this reason a *historical character*, that of a specific mode of social production" (Idem, emphasis added).

However, the historical dimension of the analysis is limited, as it assimilates capitalism to the generalization of the commodity: the main vector for the socialization of individual labor is necessarily the abstract labor incorporated in commodities. This analysis refers to the definition of the capitalist mode of production; for Marx, it is defined from the generalization of the commodity and, consequently, of abstract labor as a modality of socialization of individual labor. Marx assimilates capitalism to an essentially industrial mode of production.

For Braudel (1985), on the contrary, capitalism is not defined in terms of the generalization of industrial production, but in terms of the existence of a specific superstructure. In this case, *the mercantile logic can develop outside the commodity form,* by extending the market logic to various areas of social production. *The socialization of individual labor is implemented based on their validation in the market, based on the price form, independently of any transformation into abstract labor.*

There are other forms of labor socialization that are not linked to the commodity form: (a) the different forms of fictitious capital show that certain goods have a price, that is, they are exchanged in the market, but their valorization is not explained by the amount of social labor required for its production: land, financial titles and works of art, for example (b) this highlights *the autonomy of the price form from value* as the price form may cease to express any relation to the amount of abstract labor.

Thus, the historicity of Marx's analysis is limited by the fact that he implicitly defines capitalism by the generalization of the commodity; even in capitalism, if all abstract labor is social labor, not all social labor is abstract labor. In the same way as cultural products, different types of intangible capital are valued based on specific labor; socialization is implemented due to these specificities. The development of different intellectual property regimes expresses these modifications: they aim to remunerate the product of these highly specific labors, based on the monopoly rent that these rights allow them to earn. This type of remuneration for labor corresponds to the development of all forms of intangible capital, and is different from wages.

iii. In fact, *Marx adopts, at least with regard to his analysis of the capitalist mode of production, the substantial hypothesis*. He recognizes the fact that the substance of goods exchanged on the market is defined by a quantity of abstract labor (1867, Livre I, p. 69).

It should be noted that value is realized in the sphere of circulation and not in the sphere of production, in the monetary form (that is, in the form of price), and not directly from the quantities of labor: if a capitalist spends, for example, 10 hours of labor to produce a good and that the market validates only 7 hours, 3 hours of labor do not constitute social labor; *labor effectively becomes social in the sphere of circulation, and not in the sphere of production* (Herscovici 1994), it is in the sphere of circulation, in the monetary form, that this social character is asserted.

In summary, it is possible to affirm that the works of Ricardo and Marx complete the process of autonomy of Economic Science: the analysis is focalized on the exchange value, and these authors exclude moral or religious considerations from their concerns to elaborate an "objective" analysis of exchange relations.

On the other hand, Ricardo and Marx, breaking away from Physiocracy and Adam Smith, incorporate a historical dimension in their theoretical constructions. However, *this historicity is limited to the study of a capitalist society*: a universalist view of exchange sustains the Ricardian edifice. Marx defines capitalism by the generalization of the commodity, and the law of value that is its own: he does not develop other approaches that correspond to contemporary forms linked to different forms of intangible capital.

The works of Economic History (Polanyi 1992) and Economic Anthropology (Godelier 1969; Mauss 1923–1924) allow refuting the hypotheses adopted by Ricardo; Braudel's (1979) thesis is incompatible with the conception of capitalism adopted by Marx.

Neoclassical Economics: Mercantile Objectivity

Some Preliminary Remarks

The set of elements, hypotheses and axioms on which Neoclassical Economics was and is being built is imbued with universalism; more precisely, social relations, in their historical and political dimensions, are explicitly excluded from the field of investigation, in order to assert this universalism.

I defined the conception of capital used by Neoclassical Economics, and showed how such a conception leads to refuting the historical and social dimensions of economic relations. I would just like to emphasize the following contradiction that characterizes this entire theoretical construction: on the one hand, neoclassical analysis privileges the sphere of circulation, that is, the market, the supply and demand mechanisms. Production activities constitute a "black box": returns to scale are constant, and the firm's activity consists solely of maximizing a profit function, based on certain budgetary constraints. But on the other hand, the Cambridge controversy shows that the neoclassical case is limited to an economy that produces a single good: the corn economy.[2] Obviously, there can be no exchange in an economy that produces a unique good.

The Mercantile Objectivity

This mercantile objectivity, presupposition that supports the entire neoclassical edifice, can be defined based on the verification of the following hypotheses (Orléan 2011, p. 106): the hypothesis of nomenclature of goods, the hypothesis of nomenclature of the states of the world, the auctioneer hypothesis and the convexity hypothesis of preferences. I will successively analyze each of these hypotheses:

The nomenclature of goods

Lancaster (1966) considers that the competitive price system constitutes an adequate signal to disclose the objective characteristics of the goods: it is the objective component with regard to utility. Subjectivity manifests itself at the level of individual preferences: the same characteristic corresponds to different levels of utility, depending on the diversity of individual preferences: goods are only the supports of the utilities that appear on the market.

[2] See Chapter 5.

In this approach, social, historical and relational dimensions are considered exogenous; nevertheless, any market presupposes the existence of certain conventions, that is, of implicit or explicit rules, in order to be able to operate concretely. A market cannot exist without prior socialization, language being the most obvious example, as well as common knowledge (Arrow 1986).

Quality, in its objective dimension (characteristics, in Lancaster's definition), does not constitute an intrinsic property of goods: in the presence of information asymmetries, prices fail to disclose information related to quality (Akerlof 1970). The same type of observation can be made with regard to quality, in its subjective dimension: in the presence of information asymmetries, the same price variation will be interpreted differently by different groups of agents (Grossman and Stiglitz 1976). *The fact that these authors refute the postulate of homogeneity means that quality is no longer an intrinsic characteristic of goods (that is, an exogenous variable) but, on the contrary, an endogenous variable. The example of the efficiency wage clearly shows that the quality of labor is an endogenous variable that directly depends on wages.*

In the neoclassical model, information is one-dimensional Orléan qualifies this mechanism as a nomenclature hypothesis (2011, p. 87): *a social convention previously determines, before agents act in the market, the quality of goods, in their quantitative and qualitative dimensions.* Thus, the homogeneity postulate is verified: quality does not depend on interindividual relations or on prices, and competitive prices are a sign that allows assessing this quality.

The mercantile objectivity defined by Neoclassical Economics only makes sense when the universe in which it operates is devoid of any historical social dimension.

The Hypothesis of the States of the World

The homo economicus maximizes a utility function under certain budget constraints: this maximization can only be implemented from the moment ergodicity hypothesis is verified. There are several limitations in regard to substantive rationality, the main ones being the following:

- Rationality must be substantive: it must allow (a) assessing ex ante the utility, in its objective and subjective dimensions (b) assessing all the implications that result from its choices. In case rationality is limited, in the sense defined by Simon, this maximization will never be effective. Finally, the universe in which it operates has to verify the ergodicity hypothesis, that is, it has to be probabilizable. In the presence of strong uncertainty, in the sense defined by Knight or by Keynes, the conditions that make it possible to maximize an objective function are no more verified, and markets work in disequilibrium (Arrow 1974).

When rationality is limited, concrete possibilities for maximization disappear; when the new institutional economics, in the works of Coase or Williamson, for example, introduces uncertainty into the analysis, contracts become incomplete, agents are no longer able to maximize their objective functions, and Pareto's optimal is no longer achieved (Herscovici 2019).

- Utility would be the successful result of desire (Girard 1972, p. 205). Nevertheless, we can also question the implicit positive correlation that exists between desire and utility: when the price system does not convey all the information regarding the quality of goods, a gap appears between desire and real utility.

The Walrasian auctioneer

The parable of the Walrasian auctioneer fulfills several functions:

i. Exchanges are carried out only when the price announced by the auctioneer equals demand and supply, and are not carried out otherwise: we are in the presence of "false exchanges," which means that, *in the neoclassical universe, time and decisions of the agents are reversible*.
ii. The Walrasian auctioneer centralizes the responses that come from the crowd of consumers, and sends back a signal in the form of price. It is a centralized system in which the auctioneer fulfills a centralizing function. The debate that took place in the 70s highlighted the fact that, theoretically, this centralizing function could either be assumed by the competitive market or by a bureaucratic planning instance (Lange 1942).

iii. The agents act individually, without relationships with each other: coordination is implemented from the auctioneer.
iv. The auctioneer is a parable which means that prices adjust in such a way that equilibrium is automatically and *instantly* reached.

The convexity of preferences

This hypothesis corresponds to the law of decreasing marginal utility. It compulsorily leads consumers to diversify their consumption, to maximize their utility; this mechanism was already analyzed by the Physiocrats to justify the development of the exchange.

This hypothesis presupposes that the choice made by the rational agent is related to homogeneous (identical) goods, and is solely quantitative: the exchange of x units of A against y units of B corresponds to the same level of utility. When goods are highly differentiated, marginal utility is not decreasing, but cumulative: for example, consumption of cultural goods (Herscovici 1994).

In short, mercantile objectivity represents the purest, not to say exacerbated, manifestation of the substantial hypothesis:

i. goods have intrinsic qualities, which imply that historicity and social relations are totally ignored; from there, the analytical categories used to build the theoretical model become universal.
ii. The rational economic agent maximizes its utility by combining prices and quantities (Stiglitz 1987): *it is an economy of magnitudes, an economy from which relations are totally absent* (Orléan 2011, p. 54).

On the other hand, the substantial hypothesis is the necessary and sufficient condition for this economy to function and be socially efficient, and for the price system to be fully transparent.

A Premonitory Intuition from Cultural Economics

The works related to Cultural Economics, although they are little known, were pioneers with regard to the issues that guide this work.

The Exclusion of Cultural Goods from the Field of Economic Theory: The Van Gogh Paradox

The classical theory excluded from its analysis the immaterial goods, and more specifically the symbolic goods:

i. Adam Smith already stated that, by nature, service activities are unproductive: in addition to the work of the sovereign and public servants, the work of "(...) lawyers, doctors, men of letters (...), actors, fools, musicians, opera singers, dancers, etc." (1776, p. 583) is not productive because it does not add value, but essentially constitutes a cost (Idem, p. 581). These activities do not create but destroy value.

Adam Smith limits productive labor to labor applied to the production of material goods, in such a way that labor adds "(...) to the value of the raw materials to which it applies, the value of its own maintenance and the profit of the boss" (ibid.). Labor applied to services is inherently unproductive; only labor applied in agriculture and in the production of material goods would be productive.

ii. Ricardo excludes from his theory of the value goods that cannot be reproduced from labor (1821, p. 44): "Some famous statues and paintings, books and rare coins (...)." Its value is not determined by the amount of labor incorporated, but "(...) it fluctuates with the modification of wealth and preferences of those who wish to own them."
iii. Marx's analysis reaches similar results with regard to symbolic goods: (a) the use value is an intrinsic property of the commodity and is determined from the concrete labor applied in its production (b) the law of value transforms use value into exchange value, and concrete labor into abstract labor (or socially necessary labor).

Marxist economics is unable to determine the value of cultural goods: this value is not determined from the quantities of abstract labor applied in their production, but from concrete, specific labor. The Marxist law of value is not applicable because the transformation of concrete labor into abstract labor does not occur, with regard to cultural goods. Even industrially reproduced, the valorization of the cultural good intrinsically depends on the concrete labor applied in its production.

Neoclassical theory does not provide an alternative explanation: as interindividual relationships are hypothetically ignored, and individual preferences are exogenous and constant, price is just an index of scarcity, and demand components depend on exogenous variables.

What are the determinants of cultural goods value? Neoclassical theory does not allow answering this question either: by definition, based on the hypothesis of methodological individualism, it excludes from its field of investigation the modalities of formation of this scarcity; thus, it considers, implicitly or explicitly, that each cultural good has an intrinsic aesthetic value (Grampp 1987).

From a sociological point of view, this aesthetic value is the product of a process of symbolic accumulation by the artist who produced the cultural good (Herscovici 1994; Bourdieu 1977). This process of symbolic accumulation is explained through a mechanism of social distinction and differentiation; the accumulation thus achieved, that is, the artist's artistic value, is the product of the artist's position within the field of production, in the sense used by Bourdieu (1977).

As economic value intrinsically depends on this symbolic value, that is, on the use value of this good, and as this use value is determined from the relationships that characterize the field of production, neoclassical theory is unable to explain the Van Gogh's paradox.

Thus, both Classical and Neoclassical Schools are faced with the "*Van Gogh's paradox*." What is the economic value of a Van Gogh painting? We do not find an answer in classical theory, because this value is not determined by the amount of labor needed to produce it. On the other hand, in this case, it is not just any human labor, social labor in Marx's terminology, but a specific one. Classical theory cannot explain this paradox. It can only assert, as Ricardo did, that its value depends only on its scarcity (Idem).

Use Value: The Relational, Social and Historical Dimension

It is possible to observe that, for different reasons, the classical matrix and the neoclassical matrix exclude use value from their analysis: this exclusion corresponds to what Orléan calls mercantile objectivity. It is only at this price that it is possible to conceive Economy as an Economy of quantities, as opposed to an Economy of relations (Orléan 2011, p. 54).

This exclusion implies refuting the historical dimension of the analysis and adopting the substantial hypothesis: artistic goods would have an intrinsic value that is reflected in their economic value. It is the implicit thesis that sustains the entire Frankfurt school, which allows affirming, among other things, that jazz and cinema, as well as the whole of the cultural industry, represent "degenerated" forms of Culture. In the name of this intrinsic value, all cultural productions are evaluated in terms of historically determined criteria, which presuppose the existence of universal criteria, that is, a transhistorical one.

The sociological analysis of social fields, as elaborated by Bourdieu (1977, 1979), shows, on the contrary, that the formation of the use value of these cultural goods is the product of the relationships of the different actors that act in this social field, and that the processes of legitimation and delegitimation that act in these social fields change over time: consequently, this analysis highlights a historical relativism, incompatible with any manifestation of the substantial hypothesis.

Economic value depends on use value, and this use value is the product of social relations that prevail in the field of production; relational economy is substituting the economy of magnitudes, historicity is reintroduced in the analysis. The mechanisms that act in this economy are profoundly different from those described by classical and Neoclassical Economics and, to a certain extent, much closer to the Information economy, in the sense defined by Akerlof, Grossman and Stiglitz.

In this economy, there are no regulatory prices from which real prices fluctuate: in the case of classical economics, there is no natural price (determined from the amount of labor) towards which market prices will converge. As far as Neoclassical Economics is concerned, the valuation of these goods is inherently random: the price system is unable to provide information regarding the characteristics of the goods. Consequently, the consumer cannot equate the marginal utility with the price, because he is not able to know, ex ante, this marginal utility. Likewise, in view of this random valuation, the producer cannot evaluate the marginal product ex ante. Thus, economic agents are unable to optimize their microeconomic functions of utility and profit.

Due to the absence of regulatory prices (natural prices or matching of marginal costs and revenues), this economy is particularly unstable and intrinsically speculative: there are no limits within which real prices will fluctuate. In other words, the value of a Van Gogh frame can range between 0 and $+\infty$.

Under these traditional approaches linked to a mainly industrial economy, the production of this type of goods was limited and related to a negligible part of the total production: "These goods, however, are a very small part of the mass of articles exchanged daily in the Marketplace. Without a doubt, most of the goods that are demanded are produced by labour" (Ricardo 1821, p. 44).

This weak economic weight made it possible to overlook these "theoretical anomalies." However, today, the development of all forms of intangible capital is such that these issues resurface with much more acuteness: how to quantify the value of patents, property rights and copyrights held by companies? How to assess the value of companies operating on the internet, especially the economic value of social networks and search engines like Google?

The same kind of observations is valid with regard to the financialization of economies and the parallel development of speculative finance: as a growing share of financial securities became speculative, their value is subject to wide fluctuations. How to quantify the value of these bonds?

Neoclassical Economics disregards this problem as follows:

a. It denies the existence of information asymmetries and price opacity (cf. Chapter 8).
b. It considers that the value of financial securities is tendentially determined by the *fundamental value* of the security. This fundamental value is calculated from the expected earnings in terms of dividend, updated by the current interest rate. These dividends depend on the profits realized by the company in the real sphere (Tirole 2016). Analyses of speculative bubbles, in terms of rational expectations, try to show that, beyond a certain critical value, the speculative bubble must burst, and effective values return to their fundamental values (Fama 1988).

We can draw the following conclusions: the study of the mechanisms that govern the economy of cultural goods was premonitory, in the following sense: *those mechanisms that were considered marginal, and limited to a specific sector, extended to most of the economy, and this since 20 or 30 years.*

This intangible economy is characterized by its speculative dimension and, consequently, by its chronic instability, by the absence of any value that could act as a regulatory mechanism, as highlighted by Van Gogh's paradox. Historicity is at the heart of this economy, and translates into a growing instability of these systems. Value is not an intrinsic characteristic of goods and services launched on the markets, but it is produced endogenously, as highlighted by Keynes and Stiglitz, in regard to the relations between economic agents, and by Bourdieu, in relation to the symbolic dimension. *Economic goods can no longer be conceived as the supports of a universal and perennial substance, but, on the contrary, as the reflection of unstable and versatile social relations.*

The Different Epistemological Trajectories

A Winding Path

A Reconstruction of Internal History
From this reconstruction of the different moments during which Economic Science is created and transformed, we can observe that there is no direction, trend or, more precisely, progression. Thus, together with Kuhn and Feyerabend, and contrary to Popper, it is not possible to speak of progress in Science: certain questions have not been clarified: for example, is value created in the sphere of production, or of circulation? If value is created in the sphere of circulation, how can value be justified from the quantities of labor applied in production? However, in order to be an object of exchange, goods must have, beforehand, an established value in the sphere of production. On the other hand, if value previously exists in the sphere of production, as an intrinsic characteristic of the commodity, how, and to what extent, is it transformed into circulation?

Perhaps, this is why both the Physiocrats and Adam Smith resorted to both utility and labor to explain the modalities of formation of exchange value: for Physiocrats, exchange is explained from the subjective marginal utility. Smith, on the contrary, regarding the paradox of water and diamond, refutes utility as a source of value in the name of objective utility: water and diamond have an intrinsic utility, the same for all individuals; nevertheless, he uses a theory of subjective value as well. Ricardo and Marx somehow manage to dispel these ambiguities; they focus analysis on exchange value, attach little importance to use value and do not resort to utility to explain this exchange value.

We can observe a return to the subjective theory of value with the Neoclassical School: given certain logical insufficiencies linked to the theory of labor value[3] the General Equilibrium (GE) model, to which Pareto's optimal is associated, with the first theorem of welfare, constitutes an elegant solution that can be manipulated with the mathematical tool.

These epistemological trajectories become even more complex: certain authors, such as Schumpeter or Hayek, for example, did not adopt any theory of value, nevertheless, their works were important stages in the construction, and deconstruction, of Economic Science. Joan Robinson states, regarding Ricardo, Marx and Sraffa, that, in these models, "(...) there is no advantage in introducing value as a unit of measure" (1980, p. 89). Finally, Keynes does not adopt an explicit theory of the value of work, although he claims that everything is produced from labor.[4]

Thus, it seems to me more realistic to indicate the main controversies that punctuated the different stages related to the construction of this Science.

Some Controversies About the Theory of Value

The Labor Value

Marxism, as well as the entire economy linked to the labor value theory, was the target of violent criticism, based on the controversy regarding the problem of transforming values into prices. If the labor value does not allow deducing prices, the theory of value becomes totally "metaphysical" and does not provide an adequate, or at least coherent, framework for studying economics.

Ricardo had already faced this problem, as well as Marx. From the 1950s onwards, mathematical economists (for example, Bortkiewicz 1959) tried to demonstrate that there is no solution in accordance with the results set out by Marx, this representing a disconnection between labor value systems and price systems. This would invalidate the labor theory of value.

From the 1960s onwards, responses emerged, both from Marxist and neo-Ricardian authors. It is possible to formally resolve the problem of transformation within a Marxist (Shaik 1984; Duménil 1980; Lipietz 1983) or a Ricardian (Sraffa 1960) perspective. This answer unfolds in

[3] The search for an invariable measure of value, for Ricardo, and Marx's logical errors regarding the transformation of values into prices.

[4] See Herscovici (2019).

radical criticisms addressed to Neoclassical Economics, starting from the controversial Cambridge.

Utility Value, Neoclassical Theory of Capital and General Equilibrium

Finally, from the 1960s onwards, the neoclassical construction, dominant at that time, faced various types of criticisms to which, in my opinion, it was unable to respond; these criticisms are even more relevant, as they are internal criticisms:

i. The Cambridge controversy, which began with Sraffa (1960), allows us to question the entire internal logic of the neoclassical aggregate model: in his 1926 work, Sraffa refutes the Marshallian foundations on which standard neoclassical microeconomics was built. As macroeconomic analyses mainly use microeconomic fundamentals, the refutation of Marshallian analysis leads to the refutation of the dominant macroeconomics. Already, in 1930, regarding a controversy with Robertson, Sraffa declared that: "(…) Perhaps I ought to have explained that, in the circumstances, I think it is Marshall's theory that should be discarded" (1930, p. 9).

This attack is reinforced in the 1960 book, in which Sraffa questions the possibility of conceiving the value of an aggregate amount of heterogeneous capital as being a magnitude that does not depend on the value of distributive variables. Samuelson himself failed, in his own words, to solve this problem (the famous neoclassical parable).

ii. Arrow (1974), who was one of the authors who contributed to introducing time into GE models, highlights the limits linked to the hypotheses on which this model was built: the existence of uncertainty, in the sense defined by Knight, is incompatible with the adjustment towards equilibrium. On the other hand, the *tâtonnement* mechanism does not allow explaining how the system reacts, in a situation of disequilibrium, to return to equilibrium (Arrow 1986).
iii. From the 70s onwards, the Information Economy led by Akerlof (1970), Stiglitz and Grossman (1976, 1980), highlights the explanatory limits of the standard neoclassical model, since it refutes

> the homogeneity postulate. The endogenization of qualities and the introduction of information asymmetries in the neoclassical model lead to conclusions incompatible with the hardcore of the neoclassical research program: markets are no longer Pareto efficient, markets are rationed and demand and supply curves are atypical. For this reason, Stiglitz proposes an alternative paradigm linked to the Information Economy (2000).

If, as stated by Foucault, from the eighteenth century onwards, "(...) political economy began to exist with its own object and its internal coherence" (1966, p. 179), we can observe that the path taken to build this science takes many back and forth, that the internal coherence is only partial, that is, it is not free from contradictions and controversies, and that, from the different schools that have emerged, it is not possible to discern a trend.

Keynes Versus Neoclassical Economics: Blaug's Interpretation

Certain analyses try to establish a link between the birth and development of Keynesian thought and certain conditions linked to external history: Blaug, for example, states that (a) the research program initially elaborated in the General Theory is characterized by an "(...) excess of empirical content" (Blaug 1975, p. 416) (b) and that if, in the 1930s, it could be considered as a progressive program due to the fact that the macroeconomic equilibrium was characterized by the permanence of involuntary unemployment, it later became degenerative as it was no longer able to explain, nor predict, the main economic developments (Idem, p. 414). In other words, the Keynesian research program would be the product of a historical period characterized by the existence of structural unemployment.

I do not agree with such issues and this for the following reasons: the post-Keynesian research program is not limited to the elaboration of short-term policies with the sole objective of reducing unemployment. It constructs an alternative theoretical universe, in relation to the neoclassical universe, a universe from which money and finance are of a different nature, as are the modalities of macroeconomic adjustment. It also provides an endogenous interpretation of economic movements, allows building dynamic growth models that integrate path dependence processes; finally, it allows making explicit the current dynamics proper to the current financial speculation (Herscovici 2019).

The Incommensurability of Different Paradigms

An Episteme Proper to Economic Science?

What episteme defines Economic Science, or more precisely, is it possible to distinguish, through these evolutions, an episteme to define modern economic science, from Adam Smith to Neoclassical Economics?

Kuhn's epistemology (1991) allows stating that two competing paradigms cannot coexist for a long time: the paradigm that fails to resolve certain anomalies is substituted by another that is able to resolve them.

The very concept of Science progress is meaningless: the evolution of Science is not oriented in a determined direction (Idem, p. 213), but it changes due to the diversity of problems that are considered relevant for the scientific community. Sciences do not evolve from a cumulative process (ibid., p. 225), but from ruptures; scientific revolutions are not guided by a logic of cumulative progress, but determined by interests that change over time, that is, by historical and sociological variables: "(...) the judgment that leads scientists to reject a previously accepted theory is always based on something more than this comparison of theory with the world" (ibid., p.108). External history, in its temporal dimension, is one of the elements that determine these various scientific revolutions, that is, it determines the change in paradigms.

In relation to Economic Science, Kuhnian epistemology is partially explanatory: it emphasizes that its evolutions are neither cumulative nor linear, that its developments do not follow a determined trend, that it is not reducible to an autonomous logic, that is, to its internal history, in the sense defined by Lakatos (1978). But, contrary to what Kuhn claims, it is characterized by the coexistence of several paradigms: at a given historical moment, the existence of a dominant paradigm does not translate into the disappearance of the other paradigms.

Thus, it is not possible to speak of an episteme proper to Economic Science, neither to Modern Economics: the matrix linked to the labor value theory and the neoclassical matrix, abstracting from the divergences within each of them, do not have a minimum of common elements that allow me to state that they they belong to the same episteme: the very definition of the universe, the methods used, and the type of economic and monetary policy advocated have nothing in common. These two paradigms are totally incommensurable, in that there is no point of communication possible.

Nevertheless, certain authors state that "Foucault considered the 'Marginalist Revolution' as inserted in the same epistemic context of Ricardo" (Vigo 2010, p. 219).

This thesis is justified as follows: (a) The role of Man, in both cases, is fundamental: he becomes the object of study of Economics (Idem, p. 215) (b) Scarcity appears and highlights the finitude of human being (c) In both cases, the mechanisms can be represented using mathematical language (ibid., p. 219): the "Ricardian vice" and the formalizations proper to the maximization of microeconomic functions or general equilibrium.

In relation to (a), I showed why the Ricardian conception incorporates Historicity, notably with regard to the determination of wages, and why the neoclassical conception is totally abstract, in the sense that it is devoid of social and historical components. In relation to (b), I will emphasize, notably from Sraffa's conception, why the Ricardian concept of scarcity is intrinsically different from the neoclassical concept. Finally, if these two schools use a mathematical tool (mathesis universalis), the modalities of resolution of the systems thus elaborated are totally different: while the neoclassical model uses a "purely" mathematical determinism, *the closure of the Ricardian system (the same observation being valid for the Marxist system and the Keynesian system) is based on the historical determination of exogenous variables: the value of distributive variables, in the case of the neo-Ricardian model, the long-run expectations, in Keynes's analysis.*

So, I cannot agree with this these: the very definition of the object of study, the method used, the conception of time and history make the two systems of thought totally incompatible.

I will echo the words of Bharadwaj when she writes that "My attempt, in this paper, will be to argue that the analytical inadequacies, as well as the a-historicity that appears to plague the mainstream theory, arise from the specific structure of the theory of value and distribution based on demand and supply" (Bharadwaj and Schefold 2017, p. 54).

These observations highlight the difficulties inherent to studies in terms of the History of Economic Thought and Economic Epistemology[5]: despite being desirable, it is particularly complex, not to say impossible, avoid to assess the past based on today's criteria.

Historians are confronted with the same type of problems: on the one hand, History is interpreted based on criteria proper to the current period. It is particularly difficult not to rewrite the past in light of the present; it is the option, implicit or explicit, of several historians and several economists who work with the History of Economic Thought. Blaug (1992), for example, proceeds in this way: "This resolutely sought to appraise past ideas from the perspective provided by contemporary economics" (Backhouse 2002, p. 648). In this sense, the method advocated by Foucault is much more related to the History of mentalities: it tries to reconstruct the mentalities that prevailed in the different periods studied.

The Definition of the Object of Study

The very definition of the object of study shows that there is no consensus regarding the own definition of the field of investigation of this Science. Robbins (1945, p. 83) defines the object of Economic Science as the efficient allocation of scarce resources with alternative uses: "Economics is the science which studies human behavior as a relationship between ends and scarce means which have alternative uses." This object is constituted by scarce means that must be rationally allocated, that is, from the maximization of certain objective functions.

I will focus my analysis on the nature of the scarcity invoked here: for Neoclassical Economics, this scarcity is natural, that is, devoid of any historical component. This feature is justified from the substantial hypothesis. In the construction of aggregate production functions, of the Cobb–Douglas type, the scarcity of production factors is evaluated based on the ratios between the amount of capital and the amount of labor; this assessment in terms of quantity presents itself as the most obvious expression of the universalization of analysis, its "objectivity" and its scientific status.

[5] In the conception I adopted, it is not possible to differentiate these two approaches: History of Economic Thought is conceived as the study of long-term evolutions of Economic Science and, consequently, as the relations of continuity and discontinuity between different paradigms (Dow 1985, p. 4).

The law of decreasing marginal productivity is stated from the relative quantities of production factors; when one of the factors is abundant, in relation to the other factor, its marginal productivity is decreasing. Solow's (1956) growth model and the trend towards the steady state are explained by the decreasing marginal productivity of capital.

In Ricardo's analysis of differential income, on the contrary, the scarcity of the best quality land causes the appearance and increase of the relative share of land rent, and the fall of the relative share of profit. The cause of this mechanism lies in the "Development of society and wealth" (Ricardo 1821, p. 97), a development that directly translates into an increase in the demand for wheat. As Sraffa wrote (1925, p. 37): "The characterization of the Ricardian theory, acknowledged by us as fundamental, i.e., assigns an economic cause rather than a physical cause to the diminishing productivity (…)." Ricardo's analysis incorporates this historical dimension: scarcity is, by nature, social and historical, while it is conceived as a natural fact, in neoclassical analysis.[6]

These two antagonistic conceptions correspond to theories of distribution that are also antagonistic: in Ricardian analysis, the divergence of interests between, on the one hand, landowners and workers, and capitalists, on the other, is totally explicit. In the neoclassical aggregate model, distribution is explained from the Walrasian concept of *service producteur*, or the contribution of production factors to the product (Clark 1891): these analyses emphasize the convergence of interest and deny, by definition, any distributive conflict.

Ricardo introduces a definitive rupture, in relation to Physiocracy and the nascent utilitarism: in his analysis, contrary to Physiocracy, nature is no longer the source of wealth and becomes "avaricious" (Foucault 1966, p. 268). On the other hand, this analysis is centered on production and no longer on the satisfaction of human needs. In this sense, marginalism represents a reconnection with the Physiocratic school.

Finally, it is interesting to analyze, from an epistemological point of view, the interpretation that neoclassical economists give of the Ricardian theory of land rent: from Marshall (1920) to Clark (1931) and Blaug (1992), these economists interpret the theory of Ricardo as the premises of marginalism: in this regard, Clark states that: "The Ricardian law of rent (…) is the first great example of the marginal method,

[6] For similar reasons, it is possible to state that both Marx and Keynes conceive scarcity as a social fact, not a natural one.

later to become the key-stone of the entire system of economic theory" (1931, Vol. 4, p. 6). To arrive at such results, it is necessary to ignore one of the main Ricardian hypotheses (the increasing heterogeneity of cultivated land as a cause of decreasing marginal productivity), in order to find an equivalence between quantities and values. This is equivalent to denying all of Ricardo's original contribution: according to Schumpeter, these economists "(…) do not generalize Ricardo's scheme but instead destroy it" (Schumpeter 1954, p. 739).

The thesis I defend is as follows: given this incommensurability of different paradigms, or Scientific Research Programs, *we have a frontal opposition between schools that incorporate this historical dimension and those that refute it in the name of universalism* (Bharadwa and Schefold 2017, p. 24). The analysis in terms of episteme aims to highlight the historicity of different systems of thought and, consequently, their relativity.

References

Akerlof, G. 1970. The Market for "Lemons": Qualitative Uncertainty and the Market Mechanism. *Quarterly Journal of Economics*, 84 (3): 488–500.

Arrow, Kenneth J. 1986. Rationality of Self and Others in an Economic System. *The Journal of Business* 59 (4): 385–390.

———. 1974. Limited Knowledge and Economic Analysis. *American Economic Review* 64 (March): 1–10.

Backhouse, Roger E. 2002. *The Penguin History of Economics*. London: Penguin Books.

Bharadwaj, Krisnha, and Bertan Schefold. 2017. *Essays on Piero Sraffa, Critical Perspectives on the Revival of Classical Theory*. London: Routledge.

Blaug, Mark. 1992. *The Methodology of Economics or How Economists Explain*, 2nd ed. Cambridge: Cambridge University Press.

———. 1975. Kuhn versus Lakatos, or Paradigms Versus Research Programmes in the History of Economics. *Hope* 7 (41): 399–433.

Bortkiewicz, Ladislauss. 1959. *von, "Essai de rectification de la construction théorique fondamentale de Marx dans le troisième livre du Capital."* Paris: Cahiers de l ISEA.

Bourdieu, Pierre. 1979. *La distinction*. Critique sociale du jugement. Paris: Les éditions de Minuit.

———. 1977. L'économie de la production des biens culturels, theâtre, peinture, littérature. *Actes de la Recherche en Sciences Sociales n.13*. Paris: les Éditions de Minuit.

Braudel Fernand. 1979. *Civilisation matérielle, économie et capitalisme* XVème–XVIIIème siècle. Amand Coli Paris.

———.1985. *La dynamique du capitalisme*. Paris: Champs Flammarion.

Clark, J.B. 1891. Distribution as Determined by a Law of Rent. *Quarterly Journal of Economics* 5 (April): 289–318.

Clark, J.M. 1931. Distribution. In *Encyclopcedia of the Social Sciences*. Macmillan.

Dow, Sheila. 1985. *Macroeconomic Thought. A Methodological Approach*. Oxford: Basil Blackwell.

Duménil, Gérard. 1980. *De la valeur aux prix de production*. Paris: Economica.

Dumont, Louis. 1985. *Homo aequalis. Genèse et épanouissement de l'idéologie économique*. NRF, Paris: Editions Gallimard.

Duménil, G., and D. Lévy. 1987. The Dynamics of Competition: A Restoration of the Classical Analysis. *Cambridge Journal of Economics* 11: 133–164.

Fama, E. 1988. Market Efficiency, Long Term Returns and Behavioral Finance. *Journal of Financial Economics* 49 (3) (September): 283–306.

Foucault, Michel. 1966. *Les mots et les choses*. Paris: Tel Galimard.

———. 1969. *L'archéologie du savoir*. Paris: Gallimard.

Girard, René. 1972. *La Violence et le sacré*. Paris: Grasset.

Godelier, Maurice. 1969. *Rationalité et irrationalité en économie*. Paris: Librairie François Maspéro.

Grampp. 1987. William D. The Rent in the Fabric. *American Association Annual Meeting*. Chicago.

Grossman, S.J., and J.E. Stiglitz. 1976. Information and Competitive Price System. *The American Economic Review* 66 (2) (May 76).

———.1980. On the Impossibility of Informationally Efficient Markets. *The American Economic Review* 70 (3) (June): 393–408.

Herscovici, Alain. 1994. *Économie de la Culture et de la Communication*. Paris: L'Harmattan.

———. 2014. As metamorfoses do valor: capital intangível e hipótese substancial. Reflexões a respeito da historicidade do valor. *Liinc Em Revista* 10: 560–574.

———. 2019. *Essays on the Historicity of Capital*. Palgrave Macmillan.

Kurz, Heinz D., and Neri Salvadori. 2010. *Sraffa and the Labour Theory of Value. A Observations*, 187–213. London: Routledge.

Kuhn, Thomas S. 1991 [1962]. *A estrutura das revoluções científicas*. São Paulo: Editora Perspectiva.

Lakatos, Imre. 1978. *The Methodology of Scientific Research Programs*, Philosophical Papers Volume I, ed. John Worral and Gregory Currie. Cambridge: Cambridge University Press.

Lancaster, Kelvin. 1966. A New Approach to Consummer Theory. *Journal of Political Economy* 74 (2): 132–157.

Lange, Oscar. 1942. The Foundations of Welfare Economics. *Econometrica* 10 (3/4) (July–October): 215–228.

Lipietz, Alain. 1983. *Le Monde enchanté. De la valeur à l'envol inflationniste*. Paris: La Découverte/Maspéro.
Marshall, Alfred. 1920. *Principles of Economics Macmillan and Co*, 8th ed. London: Book II.
Mauss, Marcel. 1923–1924. *Essai sur le don*. in l'année sociologique, tome I, Paris.
Marx, Karl. 1972 [1859]. *Contribution à la critique de l'économie politique*. Paris: Éditions Sociales.
———. 1973 [1857–1861]. *Grundrisse, Foundations of the Critique of Political Economy* (Rough Draft). Penguin Books in association with New Left Review.
———. 1976 [1867, 1894]. *Le Capital, Critique de l'économie politique*. Paris, Livre I e III: Editions Sociales.
Marx K., and F. Engels. 1976 [1845]. *L'idéologie allemande*. Paris: Editions Sociales.
Meacci, Fernando. 2017. On Adam Smith's "Original Error Respecting Value. *Adam Smith Review* 10: 286–301.
Orléan, André. 2011. *L'empire de la valeur. Refonder l'Économie*. Paris: Éditions du Seuil.
Polanyi, Karl. 1992 (1944). *The Great Transformation. The Politic and Economic Origins of our Time*. Boston: Beacon Press.
Ricardo, David. 1821. *On the Principles of Political Economy and Taxation*, 3rd ed. Kitchener, ON: Batoche Book 2001.
Robbins, Lionel. 1945. *Nature and Significance of Economic Science*, 2nd ed. revised and extended. London: Macmillan and Co.
Robinson, Joan. 1980. *Further Contributions to Modern Economics*. Oxford: Basil Blackwell Publisher.
Rubin, Isaak I. 1980. *A teoria marxista do valor*. São Paulo: Brasiliense.
Schumpeter, Joseph A. 1954. *History of Economic Analysis*, vol. II. Oxford: Oxford University Press.
Schefold, Bertram. 2017. *Great Economic Thinkers from the Classicals to the Moderns*. Routledge.
Shaikh, Anwar. 1984. La transformation des prix directs en prix de production. In *L'Economie Classique. Nouvelles perspectives*, ed. Gilbert Abraham-Frois. Paris: Economica.
Smith, Adam. 1980. *Inquérito sobre a natureza e as causas da riqueza das nações*. Fundação Calouste Gulbenkian, Lisboa, Vol. I, 1980 [Original: *An Inquiry into the Nature and Causes of the Wealth of Nations*. London: Methuen and Co Ltd., 1776).
Solow, R.M. 1956. A Contribution to the Theory of Economic Growth. *Quartely Journal of Economics* 70: 65–94.
Sraffa, Piero. 1925. Sulle relazioni fracosto e quantitá prodotta. *Annali di Ecónomia* II (1): 277–328.

———. 1926. The Laws of Returns under Competitive Conditions. *The Economic Journal* 36 (144) (December): 535–550.

———. 1930. '"A critique" and "A rejoinder" in "Increasing Returns and the Representative Firm": A symposium'. *Economic Journal* 40 (1): 89–92, 93.

———. 1972 (1960). *Produção de Mercadorias por Meio de Mercadorias. Prelúdio para uma Crítica da Teoria Econômica.* Rio de Janeiro: Zahar Editores.

Stiglitz, Joseph E. 1987. The Causes and Consequences of the Dependence of Quality on Price. *Journal of Economic Literature* XXV (March): 1–48.

———. 2000. The Contribution to the Economics of Information to Twentieth Century Economics. *The Quarterly Journal of Economics* 115 (November): 1441–1478.

Tirole, Jean. 2016. *Economie du bien commun.* Paris: PUF.

Vigo, Iara. 2010. *Foucault's Archaeology of Political Economy.* London: Palgrave Macmillan.

PART II

Epistemological Ruptures: Three Contemporary Examples

CHAPTER 5

The Reswitching of Techniques and Its Epistemological Implications: A Deepening of Criticism

This chapter aims (a) to explain the mechanisms from which the problem of reswitching of techniques is formulated and (b) to analyze the implications with regard to the general architecture of neoclassical macroeconomics. One can see how these elements allow refuting the neoclassical theory of income distribution, and why they translate into structural instability. In the first part, I will explain the mechanisms that correspond to the problem of reswitching of techniques; in the second part, I will study the implications linked to the reswitching, with regard to the determinants of income distribution and the equilibrium stability.

> The first question is whether there exists an aggregate production function in which quantities of labour and 'capital' explain both the level of the national product and, by means of the 'marginal products' of the two factors, its distribution. A second question is whether a similar production function can be conceived for any single commodity. The third and most important question concerns the basic premise of the traditional theory of distribution in all its formulations: the notion that a fall of *r* will cheapen the more capital intensive processes of production.
> (Garegnani 1970)

This chapter aims to (a) explain the mechanisms from which the problem of reswitching of techniques is formulated; (b) to analyze the implications with regard to the general architecture of neoclassical macroeconomics and; (c) to show how Sraffa and the neo-Ricardian school propose an

A. Herscovici, *Value, Historicity, and Economic Epistemology*,
https://doi.org/10.1007/978-3-031-21157-7_5

alternative solution. Contrary to the traditional neo-Ricardian view that conceives production prices as the long-term position that the system achieves, regardless of short-term fluctuations (Carvalho 1983–1984), I will show why the system is intrinsically unstable, and to what extent this instability constitutes a deepening of the neo-Ricardian criticism, in relation to the neoclassical economy.

In the first part, I will explain the mechanisms that constitute the microeconomic foundations of neoclassical macroeconomics, the hypotheses on which these mechanisms are based, and their implications with regard to the nature of macroeconomic equilibrium and to the adjustment processes towards equilibrium. In the second part, I will present the different modalities related to the reswitching of techniques. In this regard, I will highlight some logical flaws and thus deepen the criticisms that the neo-Ricardian framework allows formulating in relation to the neoclassical construction.

I will implement my analysis from two levels: the first one relates to a macroeconomic approach in which the economy is divided into two sectors, the one that produces capital goods and the one that produces consumer goods. The second level studies the reswitching of techniques; it is a microeconomic analysis, as it is about maximizing the firm's individual profit from the choice of techniques. In the neoclassical tradition, macroeconomics essentially has microeconomic foundations; thus, the refutation of these Marshallian fundamentals translates into the refutation of the aggregated macroeconomic models.[1] The deepening of the criticism elaborated lies in the fact that, due to the capital controversy, this transition from the micro to the macroeconomic level cannot be carried *out on the basis of the same mechanisms.*

The Architecture of Neoclassical Macroeconomics

The Main Causal Relations of Neoclassical Macroeconomics

The foundations of neoclassical macroeconomics can be expressed by the following propositions:

[1] The systematization of the criticism elaborated by Sraffa (1960) is based on a previous criticism of the Marshallian microeconomic fundamentals (Sraffa 1925, 1926).

Income distribution is determined by the following equation (Denis 1974; Deleplace 2007):

$$Y = r.C + w.L \tag{5.1}$$

(r as the profit rate, w as the wage rate, Y as the product, C and L as capital and labor quantities).

Equation (5.1), in per capita values, is equivalent to:

$$y = k.r + w \tag{5.2}$$

$y = Y/L$ and $k = C/L$.

that is:

$$k = \frac{y - w}{r} \tag{5.3}$$

Equivalent to:

$$k = f(r) \tag{5.3´}$$

with $f' < 0$

(5.3) and (5.3′) define *the substitution principle*, valid for all values of r. The rate of profit is equal to the marginal productivity of global capital:

$$r = pmk = {}^{dy}/_{dk} \tag{5.4}$$

From (5.2), it is possible to write:

$$dy = r.dk + k.dr + dw \tag{5.5}$$

Combining (5.4) and (5.5), we deduce that:

$$-{}^{dw}/_{dr} = k \tag{5.6}$$

Proposition 1 Relations (5.1) and (5.2) show that the distribution of income is determined by the quantity of factors used multiplied by their respective prices, the interest rate and the wage rate. How are these quantities and prices determined?

Proposition 2 The prices of factors of production are determined by matching marginal cost with marginal product, with marginal cost increasing and marginal productivity decreasing.

(5.6) highlights the fact that the abundance, or scarcity, of the production factor determines its price, which is explained by the law of decreasing marginal productivity and the equalization of the price of the production factor with its marginal productivity.

I can define an equilibrium value represented by k^*. When $k > k^*$, there is an abundance of capital. Due to the law of decreasing marginal productivity, the interest rate will decrease; from (5.6), we can deduce that dw/dr increases and, consequently –(dw/dr) decreases, which translates into a decrease of k towards its equilibrium value. When $k < k^*$, the same mechanisms work in the opposite direction: the scarcity of capital causes dr to increase and k to increase.

The convergence towards the equilibrium position is the result of the law of decreasing marginal productivity, which allows me to affirm that, starting from (5.6), the price of the factors of production is determined from its relative scarcity (or abundance). The relative quantities of the factors of production determine their prices. As Harris (1978, p. 219) writes, "The distribution of income is therefore completely determined by technology and 'factors endowments' and (…) relative factor prices reflect scarcity of the factors (…)".

Convergence towards the equilibrium position thus depends on the verification of the law of decreasing marginal productivity: the price of capital will decrease (increase) when it is abundant (scarce). Thus, *the action of the law of decreasing marginal productivity explains the process of convergence towards the equilibrium position.*

However, *when capital is not homogeneous, it is impossible to elaborate the very concept of marginal productivity* and thus deduct the rate of profit. The rate of profit is equal to the marginal productivity of capital, which is equal to the ratio between the change in product and the change in capital. However, in order to know the product in value, it is necessary to know the profit rate in advance; consequently, in order to know the profit rate, it is necessary to know the same profit rate in advance (Garegnani 1980, p. 11).[2]

[2] In regard to another criticism of the marginalist approach, and more specifically the marginal productivity concept, see Marcuzzo and Rosselli (2011).

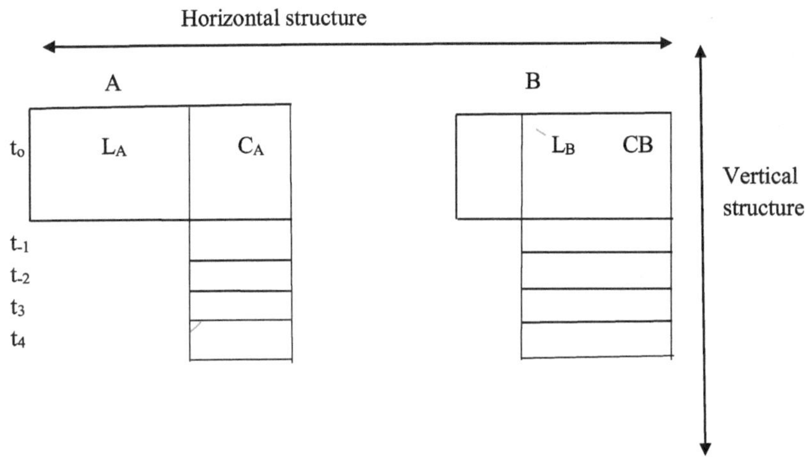

Fig. 5.1 The Ricardian value theory

The Starting Point of Neo-Ricardian Criticism

The main theoretical results of neo-Ricardian theory may be synthesized from the following example[3]: we consider two commodities A and B, each produced by capital C_A and C_B, and some quantity of labor, L_A and L_B. Obviously, C is expressed in labor quantity, in terms of indirect labor:

$$L_A + C_A = L_B + C_B \tag{5.7}$$

In regard to the Ricardian labor theory, relation (5.7) implies that A value is equal to B value:

$$A = B \tag{5.8}$$

Capital is conceived as labor "spent" in the past, as a "*roundabout method of production*" (Hayek 2009); it must get an economic return every period. *The dated labor is evaluated, in each period, based on the current profit rate* (Fig. 5.1).

Relation (5.8) is verified only when the horizontal and the vertical structures are the same for A and B. It will be also verified when the profit

[3] In respect to a complete presentation, see Cohen and Harcourt (2003).

rate is nil (Schefold 2018); notwithstanding, such solution is a no-sense, from an economic perspective. As there are no reasons for the horizontal and vertical structure being the same for the two commodities, A value is different from B value.

If we consider a high profit rate, B value will be greater than A value. As the wages rate increases (which means that profit rate decreases), B value will decrease in relation to A value: dated labor is updated from a smaller rate and current labor from a higher rate.

We can write:

$$V_B = \gamma.V_A \tag{5.9}$$

equivalent to:

$$\gamma = \frac{VB}{VA} \tag{5.10}$$

$$\gamma = \varphi(w). \tag{5.11}$$

$$\gamma' < 0.$$

Proposition 3 *The value of a given quantity of aggregate capital depends directly on the value of the distributive variables*. This applies equally to any type of commodity. In this regard, Robinson (1953–1954, p. 86) states that "Thus the same stock of physical goods represents a larger amount of real capital when the rate of interest is higher (…)."

Stability, Equilibrium Instability and Substitution Principle

The main results of the neo-Ricardian analysis show, without any ambiguity, that there cannot be a stable long-term equilibrium position that the system automatically reaches.[4] In her seminal work of 1953–1954, Robinson comes to this conclusion: "Now, the conditions of equilibrium require that the rate of interest which enters into the cost of equipment

[4] This approach is intrinsically different from the "traditional" neo-Ricardian analyses that conceive Keynesian analysis as a short-term analysis, whereas long-term positions are defined by neo-Ricardian production prices, in the absence of path dependence. In this regard, see Amadeo and Dutt (1987) and Cardim por Carvalho (1983–1984).

be equal to the rate of profit actually ruling (…)" (p. 94). Consequently, the stability of the equilibrium depends on the stability of the distributive variables: "An unforeseen fall in the rate of profit ruptures the conditions of equilibrium" (ibid., p. 100).

This principle can be applied to any type of market, and it necessarily translates into the instability of the meso and macroeconomic equilibrium. I will illustrate this thesis based on the loanable funds' theory and the balanced growth models derived from Solow's model (1956).

The Loanable Funds Theory

Macroeconomic equilibrium depends directly on the existence of the monotonic relationship between interest rate and capital: in the absence of such a relationship, the equalization between investment and savings is not systematically realized (Petri 1998), and macroeconomic equilibrium is, by nature, unstable. This equilibrium is characterized by the fact that global demand is equal to global supply: global supply Og is equal to C + S (consumption and savings), and global demand Dg to C + I (consumption and investment). The macroeconomic equilibrium corresponds to the following relationship:

$$\mathrm{Og} = \mathrm{C} + \mathrm{S} = \mathrm{Dg} = \mathrm{C} + \mathrm{I} \tag{5.12}$$

From (5.12), I deduce that Og > Dg when S > I, and that Dg > Og when I > S:

$$\mathrm{Og} - \mathrm{Dg} = \mathrm{S} - \mathrm{I} \tag{5.13}$$

We can consider that the economy is divided into two sectors, sector 1 which produces the production goods and sector 2, the consumer goods. If $\mathrm{Dg} = \mathrm{D}_1 + \mathrm{D}_2$ and $\mathrm{Og} = \mathrm{O}_1 + \mathrm{O}_2$, starting from (5.13), I can write:

$$\mathrm{O}_1 + \mathrm{O}_2 - (\mathrm{D}_1 + D_2) = \mathrm{S} - \mathrm{I} \tag{5.14}$$

That is:

$$(\mathrm{O}_1 - \mathrm{D}_1) - (\mathrm{D}_2 - \mathrm{O}_2) = (\mathrm{S} - \mathrm{I}) \tag{5.15}$$

(O_i and D_i represent sector *i* supply and demand respectively).

Equation (5.15) highlights the conditions of stability of the macroeconomic equilibrium: when I = S, the global demand remains equal to the global supply. Sectoral disequilibrium is offset and does not affect the global equilibrium: the macroeconomic equilibrium is stable. In contrast, when S is different from I, sectoral disequilibrium translates into a global disequilibrium, which means that the macroeconomic equilibrium becomes unstable.

Within the scope of the neoclassical matrix, the equilibrium is systematically realized from the loanable fund market, based on a variation in the interest rate. When, for example, there is an excess supply of funds in relation to demand, savings is higher than investment: the interest rate decreases, and the substitution principle acts in such a way that investment increases until it equals savings. Consequently, *in the neo-Ricardian perspective, the refutation of the substitution principle results in the systematic non-equalization of savings and investment, which implies the instability of the macroeconomic equilibrium and, ultimately, the refutation of Say's law* (Herscovici 2002).

Convergence to the Steady State

The same type of observations can be made regarding neoclassical growth models. Automatic adjustments towards the steady state position, in Solow's model (1956), are carried out based on these mechanisms:

$$\dot{k} = s.y - nk \tag{5.16}$$

$\dot{k}$ represents the variation of k; s, the propensity to save; y, the product per capita; and n, the growth rate of the active population.

The steady state (k^*) represents the macroeconomic equilibrium: GDP per capita is constant, and the rate of growth of capital and labor, per capita, is equal to the rate of growth of the population, which corresponds to the full use of the factors of production. At this point, "(...) the real return to factors will adjust to bring about full employment of labor and capital (...)" (Solow 1956, p. 164). Using a Cobb-Douglas production function, *the quantities of factors employed are determined from the equalization between their marginal cost and their marginal productivity, the returns to scale are constant and the law of decreasing marginal productivity is verified* (Fig. 5.2).

From (5.16), we can deduce that if k value is different from equilibrium value, k value will change to reach automatically the equilibrium position. Such equilibration mechanism may be explained in the following manner: in k_1, savings by worker is higher than the investment that corresponds to the steady state (Denis 1974, p. 689): the interest rate

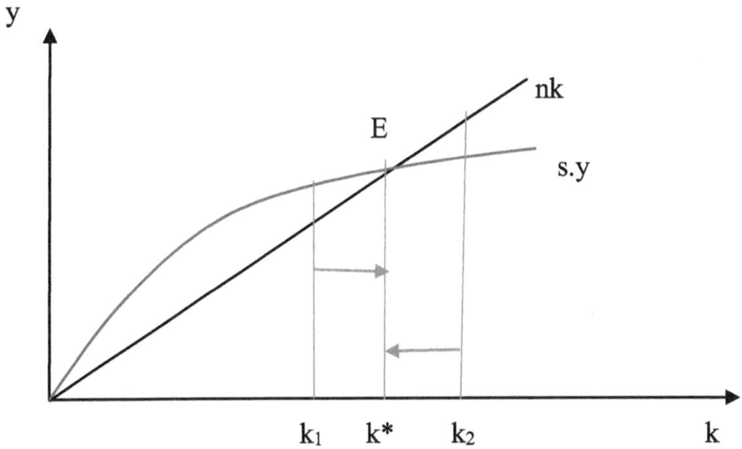

Fig. 5.2 The adjustment in the Solow's model

decreases, investment increases: from the theory of loanable funds, investment and savings become equal, the capital stock increases until it reaches E. From the same mechanism, in k_2, k will decrease until reaching the equilibrium position. It is thus possible to state that the *theory of loanable funds fulfills the role of a stabilizer and allows for the realization of equilibrium.*

On the other hand, the law of decreasing marginal productivity allows explaining the slope of the *s.y* curve and thus justifying *the stability* of the equilibrium position (Solow 1956, p. 167).[5]

In the equilibrium position, global demand is equal to global supply, global savings to global investment, and variations in interest rates allow reaching the global equilibrium.[6] In the neoclassical macroeconomics, the loanable funds theory constitutes the mechanism that ensures the maintenance of equilibrium (Herscovici 2013).

[5] On the contrary, in the models of endogenous growth, the marginal productivity of capital is constant or increasing, which justifies the existence of endogenous technical progress and prevents the system from achieving a steady equilibrium.

[6] I do not consider endogenous growth models as belonging to the Neoclassical Research Program: for example, the law of decreasing marginal factor productivity is not verified.

In Solow's model, equilibrium can also be represented by the following relationship:

$$G.C = s = n \tag{5.17}$$

G is the growth rate of the product; C, the capital coefficient; *s*, the propensity to save; and *n*, the growth rate of the active population.

Relation (5.17) represents stable long-term growth conditions with full employment; in the Solow's model, this relation is always verified, based on the variations of C, variations that are realized from the substitution principle (cf. Eq. 5.3′).

On the other hand, Harrod's instability is explained by the fact that C is constant, as well as the interest rate: as there is no monotonic relationship between the interest rate and the amount of capital, the fact that C (the capital/product ratio) is considered constant allows neutralizing the effects related to the reswitching of techniques (Herscovici 2006), and thus ignoring the substitution principle.

The Reswitching of Techniques: A Deepening of Neo-Ricardian Criticism

The Traditional Presentation

The Fundamental Mechanisms

Initially, let's assume that the economy is divided into two sectors: sector 1 that produces consumer goods, and sector 2 that produces capital goods. We will choose the wage rate as unit of measure. We can write the following system in the following manner:

$$1 = l_a.w + c_a.p_c(1 + r) \tag{5.18}$$

$$p_c = l_c.w + c_c.p_c(1 + r) \tag{5.19}$$

(5.18) and (5.19) $\Rightarrow$

$$w = \frac{1 - c_c(1 + r)}{l_a + (l_c.c_a - l_a c_c)(1 + r)} \tag{5.20}$$

l and c represent the quantities of labor and capital used, the indices a and c relate respectively to sectors 1 and 2, p_c is the price of a unit of capital, w the price of a unit of labor and r the rate of profit.

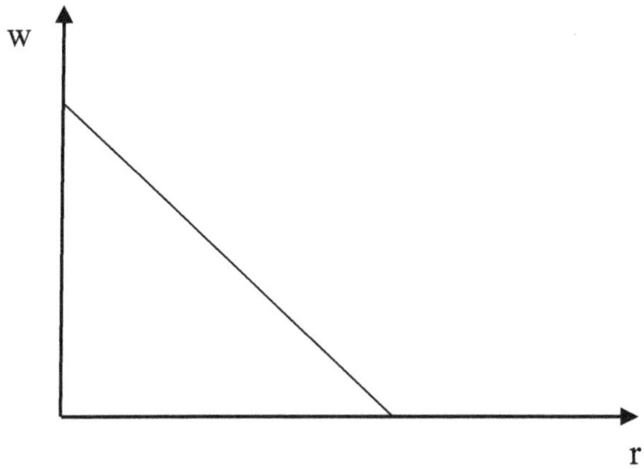

Fig. 5.3 The profit/wages frontier: a linear relation $c_c/l_c = c_a/l_a$

Equation (5.20) shows that there is an inverse relationship between the profit rate r and the wage rate, w.

This relationship is linear if $(l_c.c_a - l_a c_c)(1 + r) = 0$, that is, if:

$$\frac{c_c}{l_c} = \frac{c_a}{l_a} \tag{5.21}$$

Proposition 4 If (5.21) is verified, the relationship between r and w is linear (monotonic) (Fig. 5.3).

Proposition 5 If (5.21) is not verified, the relationship between r and w is not linear anymore (Figs. 5.4 and 5.5).

The Implicit Hypothesis

It is possible to conceive an amount of aggregated capital (Garegnani 1970, p. 154; Harris 1978, p. 231) regardless of the value of the distributive variables, only when Ca/la = Cc/lc.

The nature of the relationship between the wage rate and the profit rate depends on the capital/labor ratio in the two sectors, *capital being valued in quantity* (Ca/la and Cc/lc). Nevertheless, the necessary and sufficient condition to evaluate capital in quantity is that all capitals are homogeneous; in this case, the amounts of capital Cc and Ca are valued independently from the variation in the profit rate and the wage rate.

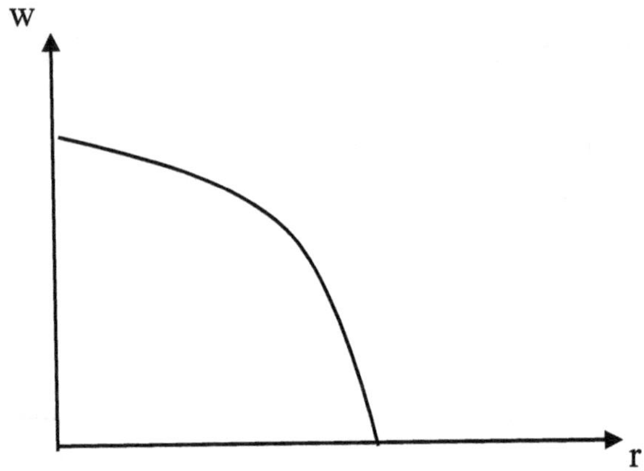

Fig. 5.4 The profit/wages frontier: a non-linear relation (1) $c_c/l_c > c_a/l_a$

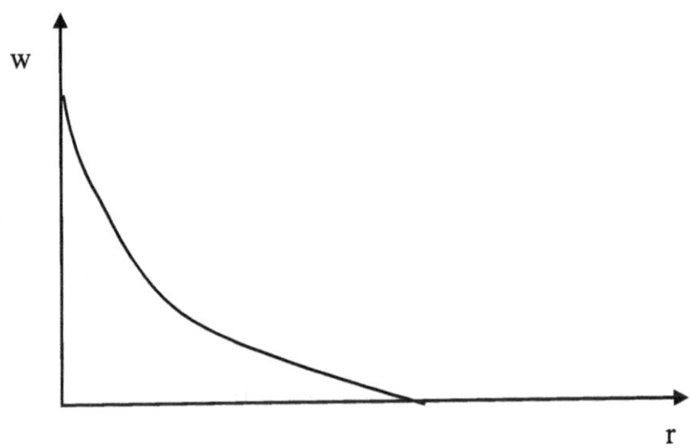

Fig. 5.5 The profit/wages frontier: a non-linear relation (2) $c_c/l_c < c_a/l_a$

The C/l ratio in the two sectors determines the nature of the relationship between *w* and *r*.[7] We are in the presence of an economy that produces a unique good, from this same good and labor: the corn economy evoked by Ricardo.

[7] That is why Samuelson builds a pseudo production function in which "(…) the value of capital for each method was independent from the rate of profit" (Robinson 1980, p. 161).

With regard to the neoclassical case, at the aggregate level, Ca/la = Cc/lc. As capital is valued in quantities of corn, these quantities do not depend on the variation of w and r, and Ca/la = Cc/lc for any value of r and w. In other words, there is an equivalence between quantities and values (Herscovici 2019).

The implications are as follows: when capital is heterogeneous, it is no longer possible to reason in terms of the quantities of capital. It is necessary to express this amount of capital in a common unit, that is, in value. In this case, the value of a given quantity of capital varies depending on the variation of w and r; now, the variations of r and w determine the C/l ratios. The Ricardian differential rent theory highlights the need to reevaluate capital in each period, when it is heterogeneous (Idem).

When capital is heterogeneous, it is not possible anymore to verify Ca/La = Cc/Lc, for all values of r greater than 0. In other words, the Ca/La = Cc/Lc ratio will only be verified, for all positive values of r, if the economy produces a single good. This mechanism highlights the explanatory limits of the theories based on this hypothesis.[8]

The Different Cases

What are the implications regarding the choice of techniques? In the neoclassical case, that is, when Ca/La = Cc/Lc, the relationship between r and w is linear. The neoclassical case is a particular case, while the other cases are general.

The Neoclassical Case

When Ca/la = Cc/lc is checked, there is a linear (monotonic) relationship between w and r. This linearity is verified for the set of techniques, and there is only one point of return for the techniques. The capital/labor ratio (k) depends directly on the relative price of the factors: when the price of capital (the rate of profit) increases in relation to the rate of wages, the more capitalistic techniques are substituted by less capitalistic techniques. *There is thus a perfect substitution of the factors of production, for all values of r, and, consequently, of w* (Fig. 5.6).

Without any ambiguity, technique I is the most capitalistic: it is for this reason that, when the profit rate increases, and exceeds r_1, this

[8] For this reason, Solow (1956), in his growth model, considers an economy that produces a unique good.

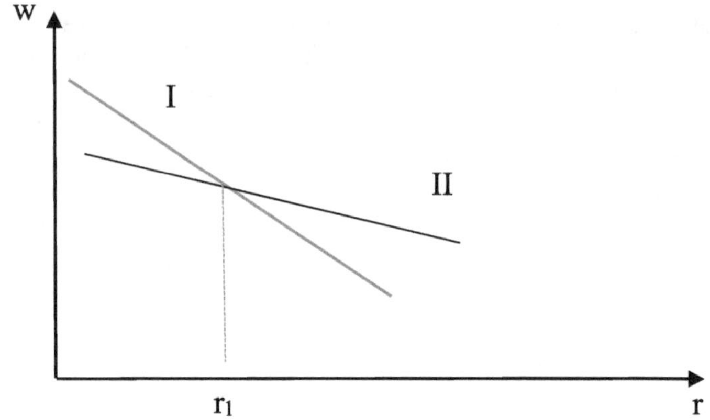

Fig. 5.6 The neoclassical case: the verification of substitution principle

technique will be substituted by technique II, which is more labor intensive. The case that corresponds to the neoclassical hypotheses is a specific case, verified only when Ca/la = Cc/lc, that is, when it comes to an economy with a unique good (Deleplace 2007, p. 472; Solow 1956).

Since goods and capital are heterogeneous, the equality between Cc/lc and Ca/la is no longer systematically verified, which implies that the substitution principle is not verified for all positive *r* values.

The Other Cases: The "Traditional" Presentation

In other cases, when Cc/lc ≠ Ca/la, the relationship between *w* and *r* is not linear (monotonic). Such situations correspond to the following graphs (Hunt 1981, p. 467):

In all of these cases, there is more than one turning point for each technique. This means that, for some values of *r*, a given technique can be considered as the most capitalistic; and that, for other values of *r*, the same technique can be considered as the less capitalistic.

The capitalistic intensity is evaluated from the capital/labor ratio, represented by *k*. Neoclassical economists, starting with Marshall, consider that it is possible to measure a certain amount of heterogeneous capital, and that the value of this amount of capital is constant (Harris 1978). On the other hand, the neo-Ricardian analysis showed that the value of this quantity of capital is not constant, but that it depends on the distributive variables, *w* and *r*. It is the reason why the same technique, depending on the values of *r*, can be considered as the most or least capitalistic: as the value of *k* changes when *w* and *r* changes, logically, ***it is not possible to determine the capitalistic intensity regardless of the level of r and w***. In this regard, Sraffa (1960, p. 100) speaks of a different economic system, due to the fact that "(…) there is no common basis on which a comparison can be made between both methods (…)".

Thus, the cases represented in Figs. 5.7, 5.8 and 5.9, from the moment that capital is heterogeneous, contradict the relationship on which the

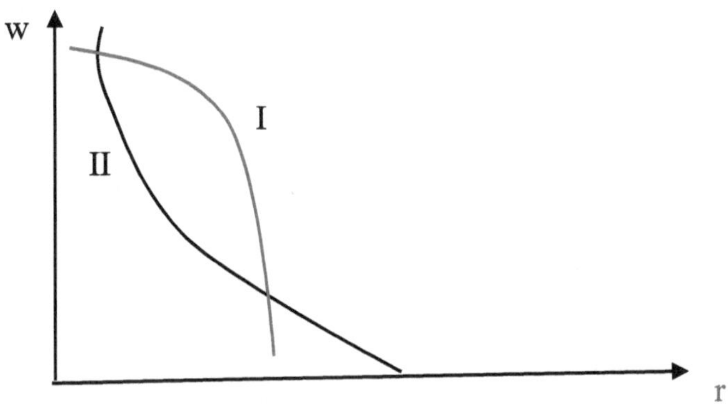

Fig. 5.7 Reswitching (1) (the non-verification of substitution principle)

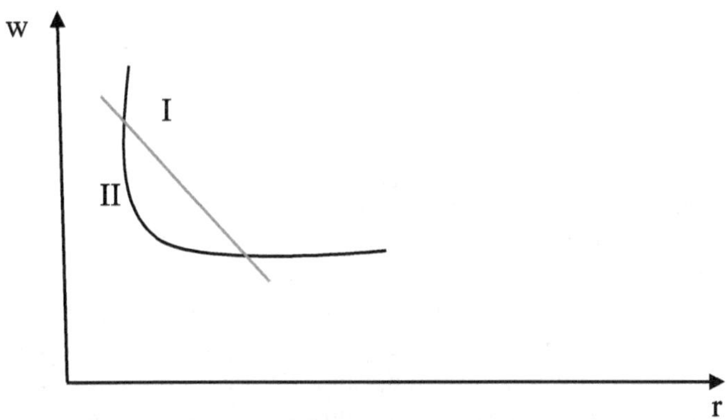

Fig. 5.8 Reswitching (2) (the non-verification of substitution principle)

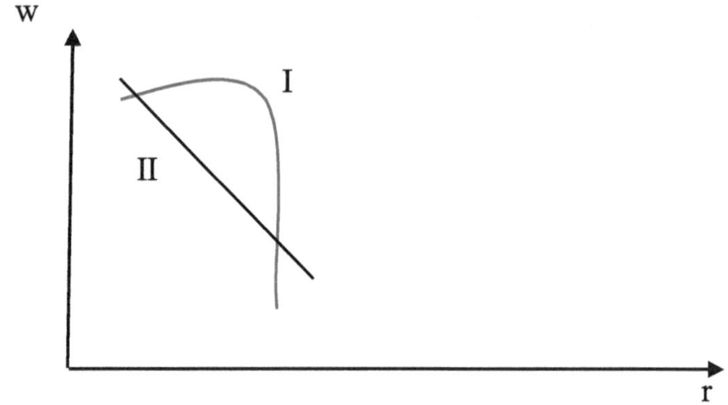

Fig. 5.9 Reswitching (3) (the non-verification of substitution principle)

neoclassical macroeconomics is *based; the relationship between w and r is not monotonic.*

A Deepening of Criticism

Some Logical Fallacies

I will highlight some logical inconsistencies present in this traditional presentation; the resolution of these contradictions allows deepening the criticism that the neo-Ricardian economy formulates in relation to the neoclassical economy.

The substitution principle cannot be verified simultaneously, with regard to the aggregate level and the choice of techniques: when Hunt (1981, p. 463) considers the aggregate level, he considers the quantities of labor and capital used in production in terms of value (and not quantity). *The logical error is as follows: at the aggregate level, the values of the capital employed in the two sectors cannot be constant when the distributive variables change, as specified in the choice of techniques.*

If, at the aggregate level, Cc/lc and Ca/la are equal, at the microeconomic level, each technique translates into a linear relationship between *r* and *w*; but as *r* and *w* vary, according to the logic of the choice of techniques, Cc/Lc and Ca/la, in value, cannot remain the same. *In this case, each technique can no longer be represented by a linear relationship between r and w.*

The case of Neoclassical Economics is a possibility among several others: it is verified only at a particular point, that is, for specific and unique values (w^* and r^*). The reswitching of the techniques applies in all the other cases, that is, when w and r differ from w^* and r^*. It is important to note that there is no mechanism that ensures convergence to the equilibrium value represented by w^* and r^*. Graphically, none of the techniques can be represented by a line, as shown in Figs. 5.8 and 5.9.

On the other hand, only one specific point is compatible with an exchange of techniques. We find a similar idea in Harcourt (1972, p. 43), when this author states that "(...) it is only at switch points that the wage and profit rate are the same for both methods so that any difference between their ks must be attributable to the productivities of the methods."

Apart from the case that corresponds to the production of a single good in the entire economy, the reswitching of techniques is the rule and simple switching cannot exist*: the substitution principle cannot be verified simultaneously at the macro level and with regard to choice of techniques, for any value of r.*

This analysis once again highlights the epistemological and methodological incompatibilities between the aggregate neoclassical model and the neo-Ricardian one: in the former, macroeconomic mechanisms are explained solely from their Marshallian microeconomic foundations, and the substitution principle is verified for any value of r. In the later, the criticism made, and the extension of this criticism, come from the macroeconomic foundations that support the microeconomic analysis concerning the choice of techniques; *the non-verification of the substitution principle is explained from these macroeconomic foundations.*

Due to the instability of the Ca/la and Cc/lc ratios, the system that represents the choice of techniques can assume different configurations. Nevertheless, each of these configurations is, by nature, unstable, and changes depending on the variations of the distributive variables, which invalidates the substitution principle.

Finally, the following paradox appears: while the neoclassical economy, in its micro and macroeconomic foundations, presents itself as an exchange economy, its mechanisms are valid only in an economy that produces a unique good, that is, in an economy that, for nature, excludes exchange from its analysis (Pasinetti 1975; Garegnani 1970; Deleplace 2007).

Proposition 6 The refutation of the law of marginal productivity and of the determination of factor prices based on their relative abundance (or scarcity) implies the refutation of the neoclassical theory of income distribution, for the following reasons: (a) as highlighted in relation (5.1), the distribution of income is determined from the quantity of factors multiplied by their prices (b) the concept of quantity is meaningless when capital is heterogeneous and (c) prices do not correspond to the marginal productivity. Consequently, the neoclassical theory of income distribution is completely refuted.

Proposition 7 The concept of quantity cannot be applied when it comes to aggregating heterogeneous capital and, consequently, the law of decreasing marginal productivity is incompatible with the reswitching of techniques: as the relative quantities of the factors determine their marginal productivity, it is logically impossible to reason in terms of quantities: the reswitching of techniques leads to the refutation of this law.

In the neoclassical economy, scarcity is conceived as the ratio between the respective quantities of the factors of production. In the neo-Ricardian approach, scarcity is essentially social, as opposed to its natural and universal dimension; social, because the capital/labor ratio is determined by the value of the distributive variables, and not by a "natural" scarcity, evaluated in physical quantities.

Here, we find the fundamentals from which neo-Ricardian economists elaborated their criticisms of Neoclassical Economics: on the one hand, the substitution principle shows that prices determine quantities. On the other hand, the law of decreasing marginal productivity indicates that relative quantities determine prices.

Relation (5.6) contains two unknowns, r and k.[9] It is not possible to solve a system in which the number of unknowns is greater than the number of equations. It is for this reason that neo-Ricardian economists consider that the distributive variables (w and r) are determined in an exogenous way. These variables determine the value of the quantities of factors of production and, consequently, wages and profits are not determined based on the existence of a labor market or a market for loanable funds (Herscovici 2019).

[9] As w depends on r, we can consider r and k as unknowns.

An Alternative Analysis

Relation (5.6) is incompatible with the substitution principle: if dr increases, for example, k increases, which is contrary to the substitution principle. The reswitching of the techniques allows refuting the relations (5.3) and (5.3′). Likewise, it is incompatible with (5.4) and (5.6). We can observe, according to the previous observations, that (5.3) is not verified: in this case, (5.4) and (5.6) cannot be verified either.

Apart from the case in which the economy produces a unique good, it is not possible to verify simultaneously the basic relations of neoclassical macroeconomics, using Eqs. (5.3′–5.6), that is, *it is not possible to verify simultaneously the perfect substitution of the factors of production, the remuneration of these factors to their marginal productivity and the law of decreasing marginal productivity* (Deleplace 2007, p. 474 and following). Neo-Ricardian analysis provides coherent elements to elaborate a radical critique of the Neoclassical Research Program, with regard to its microeconomic foundations; this criticism extends to the macroeconomic level.

In neoclassical framework, the price is determined by the interaction of supply and demand. On the other hand, supply itself is determined from the law of decreasing marginal productivity, and the factors of production are remunerated according to the prices that depend on this same law. As this law is no longer verified, supply and demand are no longer able to explain the formation of prices in the market (Sraffa 1925, p. 280).

In this case, the theory of labor value is an alternative interpretation to explain the formation of value and prices. In the tradition of Classical Economics, from Smith to Ricardo and Marx, the value is determined from the costs of direct and indirect labor; supply and demand are not explanatory, insofar as they explain only the momentary deviations between market prices and natural prices (or production prices, for Marx).

The paradox is as follows: the Neoclassical School refutes the theory of labor value, based on the fact that this theory would not be able to explain the formation of prices, when the capital/labor ratios are different in different sectors. Nevertheless, it is possible to solve this problem of transforming values into prices, based on the Marxist or neo-Ricardian matrix. In this regard, Marx (1894) shows (a) that, at the sectoral level, in the general case, prices have to be different from the values; (b) that this price/value deviation is not random, but systematic and; (c) that, on an aggregate level, all prices are equal to all values (Herscovici 2002).

On the other hand, the reswitching of the techniques shows that this same criticism applies to the neoclassical economy: in the neo-Ricardian view, the neoclassical construction is coherent only when the organic compositions of the two sectors are equal, that is, when the capital/labor ratios are the same (Samuelson 1962, p. 196). Within the scope of the thesis presented in this chapter, the neoclassical case is even more restricted: apart from an economy with a single good, the neoclassical case can only be verified for specific values of r and w, this equilibrium being unstable, by nature.

Final Remarks

The main conclusions can be summarized as follows: the law of decreasing marginal productivity of factors of production, the perfect substitution of these factors according to their prices and the remuneration of these factors at their marginal costs represent the pillars on which neoclassical macroeconomics was built. The necessary and sufficient condition to justify these hypotheses is that it is possible to conceive and evaluate a quantity of aggregate capital independently from the distributive variables, which corresponds to the substitution principle.

The refutation of these hypotheses implies the refutation of the entire architecture of the standard neoclassical macroeconomics and of its main results:

(i) The remuneration of the factors of production can no longer be explained based on their respective contributions to production (Clark 1891). As soon as the distributive variables are exogenous, there is no longer a labor market or a capital market in which factors are remunerated according to their marginal productivity: it is the whole neoclassical theory of income distribution that is being refuted.

(ii) This criticism also shows why the convergence mechanisms towards a stable equilibrium position can no longer operate, and thus allows the construction of dynamic growth models that highlight the structural instability of the system, Harrod's model being one of the first attempts (Herscovici 2006).

The neo-Ricardian criticism used in this work constitutes "(...) a pure case of refutability, in the sense defined by Lakatos" (Jorland 1995). Contrary to Popper's epistemology, ***this refutation is theoretical, not empirical***: it highlights the internal inconsistencies of the neoclassical macroeconomic model.

The Neoclassical Research Program fails to resolve its internal contradictions. Samuelson himself (1962) admitted it. Even so, he continued to use what certain economists called the "neoclassical parable" (Harris 1978, p. 240): capital is conceived, by hypothesis, as a homogeneous substance that can be measured regardless of the value of distributive variables.

This criticism highlights the epistemological fragility of the (microeconomic) bases on which the neoclassical macroeconomics was built; it also allows rejecting the law of supply and demand as a determinant of value (Sraffa 1925), and the empiric explicative power of functions built from such hypotheses (Felipe and McCombie 2005; Herscovici 2019).

References

Amadeo, Edward J., and Amitava Krisna Dutt. 1987. Os keynesianos neorricardianos e os pós-keynesianos. *Pesquisa e Planejamento* 17 (3).

Carvalho, Fernando Cardim de. 1983–1984. On the Concept of Time in Shacklean and Sraffian Economics. *Journal of Post Keynesian Economics* VI (2): 265–280.

Clark, J.B. 1891. Distribution as Determined by a Law of Rent. *Quarterly E Journal of Economics* 5 (April): 289–318.

Cohen Avi, J., and G.C. Harcourt. 2003. Whatever Happened to the Cambridge Capital Theory Controversies? *Journal of Economic Perspectives* 17 (Winter).

Deleplace, Ghislain. 2007. *Histoire de la Pensée Économique*. Paris: Dunod.

Denis, Henri. 1974. *Histoire de la Pensée Economique*. Paris: Presses Universitaires de France.

Felipe, Jesus, and J.S.L. McCombie. 2005. How Sound Are the Foundations of the Aggregate Production Function? *Eastern Economic Journal* 31 (3, Summer): 467–488.

Garegnani, Pierangelo. 1970. Heterogeneous Capital, the Production Function and the Theory of Distribution. *Review of Economic Studies* 37: 407–436.

Garegnani, Pierangelo. 1980. Sobre a teoria da distribuição e do valor em Marx e nos economistas clássicos. *Progresso técnico e teoria econômica*, 1–38. São Paulo: Hucitec-Unicamp.

Harcourt, G.C. 1972. *Some Cambridge Controversies in the Theory of Capital.* Cambridge: Cambridge University Press.
Harris, Donald. 1978. *Capital, Accumulation and Income Distribution.* Stanford, CA: Stanford University Press.
Hayek, F.H. 2009 [1950]. *The Pure Theory of Capital.* Auburn, Alabama: The Ludwig von Mises Institute.
Herscovici, Alain. 2002. *Dinâmica Macroeconômica: uma interpretação a partir de Marx e de Keynes.* São Paulo: EDUC/EDUFES.
Herscovici, Alain. 2006. O modelo de Harrod: Natureza das expectativas de longo prazo, instabilidade e não linearidade. *Economia e Sociedade* (UNICAMP). *Campinas* 15 (26): 29–55.
———. 2013. Keynes e o conceito de capital: reflexões epistemológicas a respeito das premissas sraffianas da Teoria Geral. *Revista de Economia Política* 33 (3) (132, julho–setembro): 486–504.
———. 2019. *Essays on the Historicity of Capital.* New York: Palgrave Macmillan.
Hunt, E.K. 1981. *História do Pensamento Econômico.* Rio de Janeiro: Editora Campus.
Jorland, Gérard. 1995. *Les paradoxes du capital.* Paris: Editions Odile Jacob.
Marcuzzo, Maria Cristina, and Rosselli Annalisa. 2011. Sraffa and His Arguments Against 'Marginism.' *Cambridge Journal of Economics* 35: 219–231.
Marx, Karl. 1976 [1867, 1894]. *Le Capital, Critique de l'économie politique.* Paris, Livre III: Editions Sociales.
Pasinetti, L. 1975. *Lezione di teoria della produzione.* Bologna.
Petri, Fabio. 1998. The "Sraffian" Critique of Neoclassical Economics: Some Recent Developments. *Revista da Sociedade Brasileira de Economia Política* n. 3, dezembro de 1998, Rio de Janeiro: 5–44.
Ricardo, David. 1821 [2001]. *On the Principles of Political Economy and Taxation*, 3rd ed. Kitchener, ON: Batoche Book.
Robinson, Joan. 1953–1954. The Production Function and the Theory of Capital. *Review of Economic Studies* 21 (2): 81–106.
———. 1980. *Further Contributions to Modern Economics.* Oxford: Basil Blackwell Publisher.
Samuelson, P.A. 1962. Parable and Realism in Capital Theory: The Surrogate Production Function. *Review of Economic Studies*, June.
Schefold, Bertam. 2018. Continuity and Change in the Transition from the Classical to the Neoclassical Theory of Normal Prices. In *Money, Finance and Crises in Economic History*, 9–26. Routledge.
Solow, Robert. 1956. A Contribution to the Theory of Economic Growth. *Quarterly Journal of Economics* 70: 65–94.

Sraffa, Piero. 1925. Sulle relazion ifracosto e quantitá prodotta. *Annali di Ecónomia* II (1): 277–328.

———. 1926. The Law of Return Under Competitive Conditions. *The Economic Journal* 36 (144, December): 277–328.

———. 1960. *Production of Commodities by Means of Commodities: Prelude to a Critique of Economic Theory*. Cambridge: Cambridge University Press.

CHAPTER 6

Hayek and Neoclassic Economics: Some Dangerous Liaisons?

This chapter aims to analyze the epistemological nature of the rupture between Neoclassical Economics and Hayek. For such purpose, in the first moment, I will study the epistemological choices made by Hayek, within the scope of the dialogue he maintained with Popper. In the second moment, I will study the ***modus operandi*** *from which Hayek deduces his main results; this should allow defining and characterizing the nature of the epistemological rupture represented by the framework elaborated by Hayek, in relation to the Neoclassical Economics. It will thus be possible to evaluate the commensurability, or the incommensurability, of these two paradigms.*

In the economic literature, several authors (Root 2018; Roncaglia de Carvalho 2008) conceive Hayek's writings as pioneering works whose object of study is directly linked to complexity and economic dynamics. They also recognize that, from an epistemological point of view, Hayek realized a radical rupture in regard to Neoclassical Economics; Hayek elaborated an adequate framework to propose an alternative approach, both in relation to Keynesian and Neoclassical Economics.

This chapter aims to analyze the epistemological nature of this rupture. For such purpose, in a first time, I will study the epistemological choices made by Hayek, within the scope of the dialogue he maintained with Popper. In a second time, I will analyze the *modus operandi* from which Hayek deduces his main results; this should allow defining and characterizing the nature of the epistemological rupture represented by the

A. Herscovici, *Value, Historicity, and Economic Epistemology*, https://doi.org/10.1007/978-3-031-21157-7_6

framework elaborated by Hayek, in relation to Neoclassical Economics. It will thus be possible to evaluate the commensurability or the incommensurability of these two paradigms.

This debate started with Keynes, Sraffa and Hayek, in the thirties, and continues today with Phelps. It is important from both a theoretical and empirical point of view: it allows specifying the explicit and implicit assumptions of each of these approaches and providing elements to guide the different economic and monetary policies.

Hayek's Scientific Research Program

Methodological Monism and Universalism

On one hand, Hayek claims, as Popper did,[1] that scientific laws must be universal; on the other hand, contrary to Popper, he refutes methodological monism. According to Hayek, the Physical Sciences, which represent the Sciences, by nature exact, deal with objective facts, different from ideas: "In the natural sciences the contrast between the object of study and the explanation we provide coincides with the distinction between ideas and objective facts" (Hayek 1952, p. 49). In this sense, Natural Sciences study objective facts, which are determined independently from scientists' points of view, i.e., independently from scientists' "Habitus."

In Social Sciences, including Economics, it is not possible to establish this distinction between object of study and idea: "The difficulty arises precisely from the fact that ideas appear with two qualities: as part of their object and as an idea about this object" (idem). According to Hayek, in Social Sciences, it is impossible to identify objective facts: a fact is the product of a certain idea and, consequently, it does not exist objectively.

On the other hand, Hayek affirms that, in Natural Sciences, the method to be used is the *analytical* one (ibid., p. 54): complex mechanisms that appear in aggregate level are studied from the identification of its simple elements. The starting point of this *démarche* is the complex phenomenon; it is necessary to disaggregate this phenomenon in simple elements to elaborate a scientific explanation.

We can note that standard Neoclassical Economics tried to adopt such method: within a particular view of methodological individualism, the aggregated (i.e., macroeconomic) phenomena are essentially explained

[1] Caldwell (2011, p. 43) emphasized Popper and Hayek's scientific dialogue.

by mechanisms of micro order, which refer to the micro-foundations of Neoclassical Macroeconomics. These simple elements are studied from the mathematical tool: maximization with restrictions, convergence towards a stable equilibrium position, for example: the methods employed in Classical Mechanics were imported into Economic Science (Vercelli 1991).

Contrarily to Natural Sciences, according to Hayek, the method to be used in Social Sciences is the *synthetic* one: it is necessary to start from the particular, from the individual level to reach the aggregate level. The economist can observe the individual's behaviors concretely: "For the Social Sciences, the types of conscious actions are given (...)" (Hayek 1952, p. 56). Consequently, if individual actions are objective data that can be observed, the macro-social sets are not objective facts.[2] They are just a simple projection of the human spirit, by nature, subjective (idem, p. 81), i.e., a mental and intellectual construction, historically and sociologically determined.

Thus, the synthetic method consists of starting from individual behaviors to study the concrete modalities; macrostructures emerge "(...) from the combined efforts of individuals, to produce desirable results that no one would be able to imagine or to predict" (ibid., p. 137). The "spontaneous order" realized by the competitive market corresponds exactly to this synthetic method.

Based on these elements, the methodology recommended by Hayek is incompatible with Popper's one: the methodological monism is refuted, and the falsifiability criterion cannot be applied. With regard to this last point, the Hayekian method does not allow making predictions, in the sense defined by Popper (1959, p. 44).

It is necessary to formulate the following observations: (a) these epistemological choices highlight certain incompatibilities, in relation to the postulates used by Neoclassical Economics (b) They also emphasize the limits of the use of the mathematic in Economic (c) For certain authors, they constitute a fundamental rupture in relation to the Neoclassical Economics and thus allow carrying out an evolutionary analysis (Root 2018) and (d) a priori, they refute the hypothesis of ergodicity used in Neoclassical Economics.

[2] Hayek defines these approaches as holistic: they conceive these aggregates as objective facts.

Beyond these oppositions, Hayek agrees with Popper when it comes to define the scientific laws nature: scientific laws must be, by nature, universal. This is a common point between these two authors, and a common opposition to the schools that they define as historicist.

In several works, Popper affirms that, to be scientific, a law must be universal (1959, p. 66; 1972, p. 131). This universality implies that, to be valid, a law cannot depend on certain initial conditions. A historical law is incompatible with the criterion of falsifiability proposed by Popper, and its scientificity can never be tested: when the results of the law do not correspond to the observed facts, it is always possible to invoke the fact that, during this period, some initial conditions were not verified.

History only can be explained from the combination between some initial conditions, historically determined, and a universal law. The example used by Popper is the following one (1959, pp. 62 and 63):

(1) "When a wire is brought to bear a weight that exceeds the one which characterizes its breaking strength, it will break."
(2) "Such weight is one kilo."
(3) "The weight attached to this wire was two kilos."
(4) "This wire will break."

The affirmation (1) is the expression of a universal law; (2) and (3) are the initial conditions, i.e., the causes, while (4) is the prediction, in the Popperian sense. *The specific prediction relates to some event which will be verified; the causality principle is explained from the relation between some initial conditions and this universal law.* Causes do not exist per se, but only in relation to a universal law (Popper 1959, p. 62). Popper will exclude causality principle from his investigation (idem, p. 69). The scientific law is, by nature, ahistorical, because *it does not depend on some specific initial conditions.*

From the refutation of methodological monism, Hayek arrives at the same issue:

> "(...) history can never take us beyond the level at which we can understand the functioning of the spirits of the individuals who work, because they are similar to our spirit. When we no longer understand, when we can no longer recognize categories of thoughts similar to ours, history ceases to be a human history." (1952, p. 122)

The analytical categories used by historicist approaches (society, social classes, social formation, etc.) are intellectual constructions and not facts; as such, they cannot be the object of scientific study. The object of study is constituted by the action of individual agents, and economic science aims to analyze the modalities from which these individual behaviors produce results at the aggregate (idem, p. 136).

Thus, a scientific theory must have a universal dimension; contrary to the historicist thesis, it is not possible to limit the explicative value of a theory to a specific historical period. The criticism that both Popper and Hayek do, regarding the different strands of historicism, can be summarized as follows:

(i) According to Popper, if scientific laws were historical, there would be no way to explain the transition from one period to another (1972, p. 131).
(ii) For Hayek, any theory has to be universal: a monopoly price in Egypt, four hundred years before Christ, or a monopoly price practiced today, will be explained from the same law (1952, p. 118). This price is uniquely defined from objectively identifiable individual behaviors (idem, p. 119), which thus allowed reconstructing the mechanisms that produced it; and, for Hayek, the nature of such mechanism does not change over time.

The divergences between Popper and Hayek appear with respect to the characteristics of the universe and the criterion of scientificity. Popper adopts the principle of falsifiability: a law can be considered scientific while it is not refuted by the different observations (Popper 1959, p. 72). Thus, a scientific law allows forecasting and such predictions must be verified by the observations. Ultimately, this method can be applied if the universe is ergodic. In this case, the forecasts verify a probabilistic distribution, and there is no discontinuity between the past, the future and the present (Herscovici 2002, 2019); it is a deterministic approach.

On the contrary, Hayek's approach is characterized, a priori, by *methodological indeterminism*: a given cause can generate different effects, depending on the historical components:

"The advance of science will thus have to proceed in two different directions: while it is certainly desirable to make our theories as falsifiable as possible, we must also push forward into fields where, as we advance, the degree of falsiability necessarily decreases. This is the price we have to pay for an advance into the field of complex phenomena." (Hayek, Theory of Complex Phenomenon, p. 29, apud Caldwell 2011)

The falsifiability criterion is intrinsically linked to methodological determinism and, consequently, incompatible with the study of complexity (Herscovici 2002). On the other hand, the falsifiability criterion comes from a binary logic: either a theory is falsifiable, or it is not. The fragmentation of this criterion to different degrees does not make sense.

It is interesting to note that an author like Milton Friedman, who claims his affiliation with the Neoclassical School, has epistemological positions similar to those of Hayek:

(a) in his famous article that deals with the unrealism of hypotheses, he states that Economic Science is essentially positive, as not normative (1966, p. 4).
(b) Likewise, he claims that Economic Science cannot use the criterion of falsifiability as a criterion of scientificity. He "relaxes" this criterion: in this respect, he states that "(…) predictions that manifest at an 'acceptable frequency' in light of factual evidences (…)" (idem, p. 9) can substitute the falsifiability criterion.

Complexity is characterized by its non-ergodicity, that is, by the impossibility of producing reliable forecasts based on the mechanisms that allow the construction of probabilistic functions; it is the reason why some authors affirm that Hayek's analyses dealt with complexity. As I will demonstrate later, from this, Hayek refutes the modus operandi of the neoclassical program: maximization, stable and predetermined equilibrium, social efficiency assessed using the Pareto criterion.

Hayek's method is much closer to Dray's conception than Hempel's (respectively 1942 and 1957). He points out that the future is indeterminate, and can be conceived as one of the various possibilities; the future is not determined from a deterministic calculation:

"In particular, sciences that study complex phenomena are only able to provide a range of predicted values rather than make specific predictions of particular events. (…). Because they forbid certain type of outcomes, such theories are weakly testable, so they are still scientific. But precise predictions, often seen as the hallmark of science, are impossible." (Caldwell 2011, p. 23)

With regard to this epistemological dimension, I want to highlight certain limits and certain contradictions:

(i) Hayek rejects holistic approaches because they do not study objective facts. This thesis demonstrates a naive positivism: a fact is not objective per se, but it is an interpretation made in light of a theory. Facts are intellectual constructions, whether directly or indirectly identifiable (Popper 1972, p. 99).

(ii) For Hayek, theories that apply universally allow "explaining" how "(…) different configurations of the same elements can produce entirely different complexes (…)" (Hayek 1952, p. 120).

Here, we can establish a parallel with Poincaré: "*What remains is that such antecedent, accompanied by such incidental circumstance, produces such consequence; and that the same antecedent, accompanied by such other accessory circumstance, produces such another consequent. Time doesn't matter*" (1908, p. 167).

In this sense, we can argue that Hayek's approach is non-deterministic. Notwithstanding, Poincaré argues that scientific laws are provisional (idem, p. 64) and that "(…) the true nature of the things" does not exist, from a scientific point of view (ibid., p. 173). Consequently, such approach is incompatible with Hayek's universalism; such universalism means that the object of science is to reveal such "true nature."

(iii) Hayek's methodology is linked to methodological indeterminism; in this case, how scientific laws can be universal? If they are, they must be verified at any time and in any place; but if, as Hayek claims, they depend on certain initial conditions, they are no longer universal. In Popperian terminology, this is *an immunization strategy*.

(iv) Finally, all works related to complexity emphasize *the historicity of scientific laws* and the irreversibility of the studied processes (Israël 1992; Prigogine 1996). These works were initially developed in Mathematics, Physics and Natural Sciences: thus, the opposition established by Hayek between Social Sciences and Natural Sciences is not pertinent: today, *epistemological monism translates the omnipresence of historicity, and not of universality* (Herscovici 2019).

The Hayekian Individualism

Before studying the concept of methodological individualism adopted by Hayek, I want to define the following typology, with regard to the methods used in Sciences. We can establish the following distinction: atomism, radical individualism and radical holism (Herscovici 2002).

Radical holism, which Popper and Hayek assimilate to different forms of historicism, explains movements based on macrostructures, ignoring, hypothetically, microstructures. Reductionism consists in denying the explanatory power of these microstructures.

Atomism studies only the autonomous individual, and ignores interindividual relationships. Such hypothesis may be justified from the following arguments:

(a) recognizing the explanatory value of individual psychology, and this form of reductionism consists of studying macro-social and macroeconomic developments based on individual psychologies.
(b) It is also possible to consider that individual preferences are exogenous, as Neoclassical Economic does. The *methodological individualism*[3] *employed by Neoclassical Economics* is different in nature: as neoclassical economists do, Hayek considers that individual psychological elements are exogenous and "objective" data[4] (Hayek 1952, p. 57); preferences are exogenous, by hypothesis. It is also Popper's position that, in the context of methodological individualism, rejects "psychologism" (1959, p. 199).

This type of individualism ignores interindividual relationships. The representative agent method characterizes perfectly this choice. Macroeconomic structures are studied according to their microeconomic foundations. For example, aggregate production functions are based on

[3] Certain authors describe it as ontological individualism (Roconglia 2008, p. 99).

[4] In this regard, it is interesting to note that some results formulated by recent developments linked to behavioral economics are incompatible with Neoclassical hard core (Da Silva and Wallmann 2017).

purely microeconomic mechanisms: constant returns scale and decreasing marginal productivity, in the Marshallian tradition. Reductionism consists of reducing macroeconomic analysis to its microeconomic foundations.

Hayekian individualism is different: Hayek defines his method by subjectivism and individualism (1952, p. 52). Subjectivism is directly related to the "objective" observation of the subjective individual's behavior: it is the starting point of Hayek's analysis. The individual level is recognized as being the objective "fact" to be studied, just as, in the Natural Sciences, the facts would be constituted by macroscopic entities, complex, by nature.

On the other hand, Hayek's synthetic method does not start from the principle that the decentralized actions of a multitude of agents consciously and voluntarily produce a macroeconomic equilibrium. The competitive process is, by nature, "imperfect," its effects are not predictable, but it allows the best adjustments to be made by the different economic agents:

> "Fundamentally, in a system where the Knowledge of the relevant fact is dispersed among many people, prices act to coordinate the separate action of different people in the same way as subjective values help the individual to coordinate part of his plant." (Hayek 1945, p. 526)

It is also important to note that there is a feedback effect between the aggregate mechanism and the individual agents: the market aggregates the information necessary to the individual agents, thus coordinating decentralized decisions and allowing the adjustments to be made to carry out the most efficient allocation of resources (Hayek 1935, p. 323).

Hayek's *démarche* can be presented as follows: from a formal point of view, it is possible to write the following equations: let's assume two individual agents, X and Y: a_1 and b_1 represent interindividual relationships, and a_2 and b_2 the retroactive effects implemented by the aggregate process.

System I

$$Z = X^* + Y^* \tag{6.1}$$

System II

$$X^* = X + a_1Y + a_2Z \tag{6.2}$$

$$Y^* = Y + b_1X + b_2Z \tag{6.3}$$

Equations (6.2) and (6.3) ⇒

$$Z = X^* + Y^* = (X + Y) + (b_1Y + b_1X) + Z\,(a_2 + b_2) \tag{6.4}$$

Equation (6.4) represents another formulation of the totality, where Z is the sum of the parts. Only, in this case, each part contains the three dimensions: the atomist, the "relational" and that linked to the relations of each element with the totality.

A microanalysis, done at the individual level, can cover these three dimensions; individual behavior can "internalize" the relational component as well as the feedback effects.

The Nature of Capital

From Bohm-Bawerk's works, Hayek conceives capital as a *roundabout method of production* (Hayek 2009, p. 59). Part of labor is used to produce capital goods: this translates into a reduction of current consumption and in an increase in future consumption. Capital is conceived as an *advance* that allows labor productivity (idem, p. 139) and output to be increased: such advance depends on the entrepreneurs' expectations, and the interest rate represents the compensation for parting with current consumption; consequently, it is logically impossible to consider a quantum of capital and to evaluate it independently from the interest rate:

> "But the relative values of the different kinds of input will inevitably depend on the rate of interest, so that such an aggregate cannot be regarded as something that is independent of, or as a datum determining the rate of interest." (Hayek 1935, p. 143)

This result is incompatible with the neoclassical conception of capital and is similar to the Cambridge controversy: an aggregate quantity of capital cannot be conceived as a constant value (Steele 2006, p. 7). In Hayek's system, the capital is heterogeneous (Dostaler 1989, p. 35), and such conception is contrary to the neoclassical one; we can observe similarities with the Ricardian analysis regarding the concept of dated labor.

(i) In so far as it is not possible to consider the value of an aggregate quantity of capital as constant, convergence towards equilibrium, or steady-state, is not systematically verified (Harris 1978, p. 219). This result is fully consistent with the fact that Hayek refuses to use the equilibrium concept in his analysis.
(ii) From the same perspective, with regard to the loanable funds theory, equilibrium is not systematically reached (cf. p. 165 and following).

Notwithstanding, for Hayek, investment is an intertemporal decision of consumption, a concept used in Solow's neoclassical growth model (1956), and the interest rate is the compensation for postponing consumption. In such real economy, investment depends on previous savings, and the natural interest rate, called the equilibrium rate by Hayek (1935, p. 23), allows knowing previously the "real" variables and to realizing an efficient allocation of resources.

According to Hayek, investment is financed by credit money; if the interest rate is lower than the equilibrium interest rate, the situation will be characterized by over-investment (Deblock and Gislain 1989, p. 122; Steele 2006, p. 10), considering the conditions of the real economics. Such gap between the real interest rate and equilibrium interest rate will translate into inefficient resource allocation, an excess of current demand and an excess of future supply. This is a way to avoid momentary scarcity and to ignore the trade-off between current and future consumption. Crisis must be interpreted as the inevitable manifestation of real scarcity (Parguez 1989, p. 144).

Regarding Keynes, Hayek writes that:

> "(...) he has given us a system of economics which is based on the assumption that no real scarcity exists, and that the only scarcity with which we need concern ourselves is the artificial scarcity created by the determination of people not to sell their services and products below certain arbitrarily fixed prices." (1945, p. 374)

But what does the real scarcity represent for Hayek, if not a reference, ultimately, to the regulatory role assumed by the real sector? In this case, contrary to the interpretation of several authors, it is not possible to argue that the Hayek's analysis is a monetary one. In this regard, Phelps (2011) states that "(...) the theoretical perspective of Hayek, which is non-monetary at its core and more structural, does apply!". *This primacy of the real sphere, in relation to the monetary one, allows questioning the pertinence of Hayek's concept of monetary economics, as well as the importance and the existence of the epistemological rupture carried out by Hayek, in relation to the Neoclassical Economics.*

In various parts of the General Theory, Keynes states that the scarcity of factors of production is essentially social, and does not relate to the relative physical quantities, as this is done in standard neoclassical production functions.[5]

The Nature of the Rupture Between Hayek and the Neoclassical Economics

Equilibrium and Adjustment Mechanisms

I will follow Hayek's *démarche*; at first, in *The Pure Theory of Capital*, he voluntarily ignores the incidence of money, to dedicate himself to the analysis of the concept of equilibrium (1950, p. 30). In this work, he first studies the general equilibrium, based on the interdependence between the different markets. The concept of stationary equilibrium does not allow studying the dynamics of competition, for the following reasons: once the initial equilibrium is disturbed, what is the adjustment process that allows reaching another state of equilibrium?

> "This would involve explaining how, once the more mobile elements have been adjusted, a temporary state of rest is arrived at which will last until the slower changes in the more permanent part of the productive equipment are effected." (Hayek 1945, p. 19)

This statement allows highlighting a series of methodological problems: what is the nature of the adjustment process, and how to explain, once the initial equilibrium is disturbed, the constitution of a new equilibrium position and the fact that the system converges towards this position? Hayek will criticize the neoclassical approach and focalize his analysis on such adjustment process: his approach can be compared with Schumpeter's analysis with regard to innovation and the process of creative

[5] We can make the same kind of observations in regard to Ricardo's analysis (Sraffa 1932; Herscovici 2019).

destruction: Schumpeter essentially analyzes the modalities of rupture of the initial equilibrium and the modalities proper to the progressive adjustment mechanism towards another equilibrium position. Nevertheless, Hayek questions and refutes the existence of a convergence towards equilibrium (1948, p. 94).

This analysis is reminiscent of Arrow's famous paradox (1986): in a situation of disequilibrium, "(...) what does rational behavior mean? Do individuals speculate about the balancing process (...)?" (Idem, p. 236).

Hayek responds as follows: as explained in the concept of spontaneous order, individuals act without being able to predict or evaluate the macroeconomic implications resulting from their actions. Thus, individual behavior is not rational because his actuation is not based on a conscious process of maximization, be it micro or macroeconomic. On the other hand, *the spontaneous order implemented from the competitive market is a process similar to Adam Smith's invisible hand*: a multitude of relatively independent individual decisions would be able to produce *a superior and socially efficient order*; Hayek adds that each individual has partial and imperfect knowledge, and that the price system aggregates the necessary information to realize the best global adjustment.

The main differences between Hayek and the mainstream are as follows: if, as Arrow states (1985, p. 63), "The two pillars of neoclassical doctrine are the principle of optimization by economic agents and the coordination of their activities by the market," in the name of the synthetic method, *Hayek refutes the former, but adopts the latter*.

Even if this regulation is not implemented from a substantive rationality, if the efficiency of the competitive system is not evaluated using the Pareto criterion, even if, as Hayek himself acknowledges (1948, p. 94), this competition cannot be assimilated to pure and perfect Walrasian competition, we find in Hayek's Scientific Program fundamental characteristics of the neoclassical PPC: a normative approach in which the competitive market constitutes a norm to be preserved or restored (Phelps 2011).

It is paradoxical to note that, regarding the concept of pure and perfect competition used by the Neoclassical School, Hayek criticizes and refutes the normative dimension of this type of approach:

> "It appears to be generally held that the so called theory of 'perfect competition' provides the appropriate model for judging the effectiveness of

> competition in real life and that, to the extent that real competition differs from that model, it is undesirable and even harmful." (1948, p. 92)

Hayek just substitutes the standard pure and perfect competition (PPC) by another concept of competition, similar to Schumpeter's concept. But his approach remains normative, even though it is another type of competition, based on the adjustments made by the competitive market and on the consumer sovereignty (assimilated to the citizen's freedom in his works linked to Political Sociology [Hayek 1944]). But what is the "competitive order" (1948, Chapter VI), what is the *real competition* he opposes to the neoclassical scientific program, an objective fact, as preconized by the synthetic method?

> "The basis of comparison, on the grounds of which the achievement of competition ought to be judged, cannot be a situation which is different from the objective facts and which cannot be brought about by any known means. It ought to be the situation as it would exist if competition were prevented from operating." (1948, p. 100)

Hayek uses the null hypothesis method (Popper 1972, p. 177): "reality" is analyzed in terms of the deviations it presents in relation to a given norm. While the standard used by Neoclassical Economics is Pure and Perfect Competition, the standard used by Hayek is the competitive order. The numerous criticisms that Hayek addresses to the neoclassical approach are linked to the fact that this analysis denies the competitive dynamics and the adjustment processes proper to this dynamics.

The pertinent question is the following: *is the rupture thus operated at the level of the modus operandi, or is it possible to consider that the hard core of the Research Program developed by Hayek constitutes an alternative to the standard Neoclassical Economics?* It is also important to note, in this regard, that the economic and monetary policies advocated by these two schools of thought present, in concrete terms, several similarities (Phelps 2011).

The Hayekian Modus Operandi

Capital Scarcity and Economic Cycle

For both Hayek and Keynes (and this observation can also be applied to Smith, Ricardo, Marx and Kalecki), over-investment is the cause of a crisis, but divergences appear when considering the cause of such over-investment.

From Hayek's perspective, abundance of capital is explained by the distortion produced in the relative prices by credit money: such distortion modifies the relative price and does not allow for an efficient resource allocation. *Hayek's analysis is dichotomous and normative*: dichotomous because it is possible to separate real and monetary mechanisms, and normative because it requires the restoration of the conditions that allow the ideal competitive situation to emerge (Deblock and Ghislain 1989, p. 122).

Such a demarche is used by most mainstream economists: for example, the rational expectations theory considers that the gap in relation to the equilibrium position and the effective one is explained by a monetary shock (Phelps 2011) and that the economic policy must be based on rules, and not on discretionary decisions (Mankiw 1990). Fluctuations and inefficient allocation of resources are due to exogenous variables, i.e., a shock: monetary, related to productivity or to expectations.

On the contrary, Keynes's analysis is not normative and not dichotomous: not normative because the purpose is not to realize the most efficient allocation of resources, but to reduce fluctuation and unemployment; and not dichotomous because it is impossible to study a real economy independently from monetary (and financial) variables.

For Keynes, as well as for Marx and Kalecki, over-investment occurs due to the market's very "failures," independently of external shocks. From Hayek's perspective, fluctuations are caused by an exogenous variable, i.e., by the specific actions of banks that produce a monetary shock. That result is also stated by rational expectations theory. In Keynes's analysis, fluctuations are produced endogenously, by the system itself (Herscovici 2019).

Savings, Business Cycle and Money Nature

Several authors claim that Hayek provides a monetary analysis of the cycle (for example, Soromenho 1998, p. 51). Nevertheless, Hayek studies the deviations produced by the credit money in relation to the real sector; as monetary phenomena are conceived as "disturbances" in relation to real variables, to what extent is it possible to speak of monetary analysis of the cycle, to what extent does this analysis differs, in essence, from standard Neoclassical Economics, or Rational Expectations Theory?

It is necessary to analyze the characteristics of what Hayek calls money. Contrary to Keynes' conception, in the face of uncertainty, money does not fulfill any value reserve function, but only provides the liquidity necessary to finance investment.

The universe defined by Hayek is characterized by the existence of uncertainty (1935, p. 93), in the sense defined by Knight. From a Keynesian point of view, part of the demand for money is conceived as a means of preventing against uncertainty. In Hayek's analysis, the preference for liquidity, i.e., the demand for money, is limited to real variables, that is, investment. Sraffa's criticism goes exactly in this direction:

> "That is to say, that money is not only the medium of exchange, but also a store of value, and the standard in terms of which debts, and other legal obligations, habits, opinions, conventions, in short all kinds of relations between men, are more or less rigidly fixed." (Sraffa 1932, p. 43)

The Hayekian conception of money is ambiguous: on the one hand, he argues that money is not neutral, as it produces distortions in relative prices, which translates into an inefficient allocation of scarce resources. On the other hand, the adjustment mechanisms are conceived in regard to real processes, and not monetary ones. Finally, it is necessary to have previous savings to finance "real capital." As Sraffa (1932) pointed out, Hayek is unable to detach himself from an analysis in real terms, *which constitutes a negation of the very concept of monetary economics*:

> "The fundamental fact which guides production, and in which the scarcity of capital expresses itself, is the price of input in terms of output, and this in turn depends on the proportion of income spent on consumers' goods compared with the proportion of income earned from the current production of consumers' goods. These proportions cannot be altered at will by adjustments in the money stream, since they depend on the one hand on the real quantities of the various types of goods in existence, and on the other hand on the way in which people will distribute their income between expenditure on consumers' goods and saving. Neither of these factors can be deliberately altered by monetary policy." (Hayek 1941, p. 393)

One more time, Hayek invokes the primacy of the real sphere over the monetary one. In the same line of thought, *savings is a real mechanism* that determines investment: the natural interest rate corresponds to the efficient allocation of scarce resources. This natural interest rate is determined endogenously, based on the supply and demand for funds, in the same way as in the theory of loan funds. Savings represents a roundabout method of production, that is, at the aggregate level, an intertemporal choice of consumption.

We must note that the rupture implemented by Keynes, in relation to the Economics that he describes as classical, occurs essentially in Chapter XIV of the General Theory: he demonstrates the logical inconsistencies of the "classical" conception of the interest rate, as well as the fact that this rate must be determined exogenously. His conception of savings and interest rate determinants allows refuting the entire architecture of the neoclassical aggregate model (Herscovici 2019). Consequently, the rupture initiated by Hayek, if it is possible to speak of rupture, is much less "radical" as it appears.

In this sense, the only difference between Hayek's conception and the neoclassical one he intends to refute consists in affirming that the optimal allocation is not achieved through a long-term static equilibrium, but through a continuous process of dynamic adjustment. On the other hand, several authors consider that the Walrasian General Equilibrium is, by nature, notional (Catephore and Morishima 1980); as such, it will never be achieved, and does not constitute a description of the reality of the markets.

I can argue that, in the Hayekian construction, there is a primacy of the real variables and that the monetary variables only serve to produce the distortions of the relative prices, which deviate *temporarily* the system from its desirable trajectory. The money supply growth necessarily generates, from the Cantillon effect, a change in relative prices, notably between consumer and production goods:

> "Hayek proposes that monetary theory no longer has as its object of study the general price level (a concept that he strongly criticizes) and starts to investigate how money affects the determination of relative prices, regardless of changes in its 'purchasing power', a theme that he develops in another work (Hayek, 1931)." (Boianovsky 1992, p. 80)

In summary, the methodological and epistemological divergences between Hayekian Economics and standard Neoclassical Economics (including the theory of rational expectations) are related to their modus operandi: the basic axioms linked to the regulatory character of the market game and to the rooting in real variables are common to these two approaches. From such perspective, I agree with Phelps when he recognizes that, in contrast to Keynes, Hayek's cycle theory is not monetary (2011); ultimately, the monetary disturbance disappears in the long term, and the adjustment is implemented in regard to real variables.

Finances, Expectations and Auctioneer

Notwithstanding, there is a difference between the Hayekian theory and the theory of rational expectations: in the former, due to subjective individualism, the agents do not elaborate a mental representation of the set from a given theoretical model and, by definition, there is no homogeneity of expectations. However, beyond this divergence, several convergences remain.

In the Hayekian analysis, the sole function of finance is to finance "real" investment. It is one more common point between Hayek and the Neoclassical Economics, and an irreconcilable divergence with the Keynesian economics (GT, Chapter 8). In the theory of rational expectations, for example, speculation, by hypothesis, does not exist: (a) the price system instantly provides information to all participants, which means that there are no information asymmetries (b) The role of the banking system consists uniquely in financing investment and (c) fluctuations in bond prices are regulated from their fundamental value, that is, from their "real" value (Fama 1988; Tirole 2016).

We find again this determinism of real variables in relation to monetary variables: the credit money provided by the banking system is neutral. The adjustment mechanism, as it is conceived by Hayek, is just a Walrasian *tâtonnement*, in which prices determine quantities:

> "In many small changes he [the individual] will have to consider only these quantitative indices (or 'values') in which all the relevant information is concentrated: and by adjusting the quantities one by one, he can appropriately rearrange his dispositions (...)." (Hayek 1945, p. 85)

Real Cycle Theory or Monetary Cycle Theory?

Ultimately, we can question the monetary nature of the cycle, in Hayekian analysis: on the one hand, Hayek explains the economic cycle from the deviations introduced by money in the price system, but on the other hand, the real sector constitutes the regulatory element from which the system returns to the equilibrium position, even if this equilibrium is dynamic.

The procedure adopted is the same as that used by the theory of rational expectations, and generates the same type of internal contradictions:

(a) the real sector fulfills the regulatory function in the following sense: when the distortion caused by money in the price system causes the deviation that exceeds a certain critical value, an adjustment process operates in such a way that the monetary variables become again compatible with the real variables: in the long run, the system gravitates from the position determined by the real variables. In this sense, I fully agree with the following statement by Hicks, with regard to Hayek "(…) where I do not walk with him is in the view that the disturbances in question have a monetary origin. He did not emancipate himself from the illusion (common to many economists, even the greatest economists) that with money removed 'in a state of exchange' everything would somehow fit" (Hicks 1973, p. 133).

(b) But, in this case, it is not possible to speak of a monetary cycle, nor of money neutrality, at least in the short run.

(c) From a perspective that intends to be dynamic, it is not possible to ignore the mechanisms of path dependence, neither the influence of short-term fluctuations on the long-term position.

In summary, I can say that the Hayekian analysis of the business cycle is elaborated in real terms, not in monetary terms: the long-term regulator is constituted by real variables, money does not even have a function of its own, it is neutral, and it does not affect the long-term position. The criticism formulated by Hicks (1967, p. 61) is fully justified: Hayek elaborates a theory of capital, not a theory of money.

It is a capital theory because the analysis is focused on the real variables: investment and savings; these real variables correspond to the long-term equilibrium position. Capital theory because savings is conceived as a real mechanism, which corresponds to the efficient allocation of capital compatible with the long-term position.

It is not a monetary theory for the following reasons: in the equilibrium position, agents' forecasts are perfect, that is, they are carried out systematically (Boianovsky 1992, p. 79): in this case, there is no uncertainty and, consequently, the agents do not retain money as a store of value. If, on the contrary, there is uncertainty, as Hayek states, this uncertainty is incompatible with the existence and stability of this equilibrium (Herscovici 2002), money is no longer neutral and it assumes a store of wealth function: "(...) monetary theory, in the strict sense, falls outside equilibrium theory" (Hicks 1933, p. 35).

Information and Prices: The Competitive Order

Hayek defines neoclassical perfect competition based on the following characteristics: the homogeneity of goods, the fact that agents are price takers, free entry and exit in the industry, and the fact that agents benefit from complete knowledge about the different components of the markets (1948, p. 95). I will focus my analysis on the first and third points.

According to Hayek, homogeneity is incompatible with his conception of competition:

> "The function of competition is here precisely to teach us who will serve us well: which grocer or travel agency, which department store or hotel, which doctor or solicitor, we can expect to provide the most satisfactory solution for whatever particular personal problem we may have to face." (idem, p. 97)

Contrarly to homogeneity, competition corresponds to a differentiation of the goods offered, and thus allows satisfying consumers with diversified preferences; standardization, that is, homogeneous goods, would translate into a decrease in competition and in consumer freedom of choice.

It is important to note that for Akerlof (1970), Grossman and Stiglitz (1976, 1980), for example, the refutation of the postulate of homogeneity leads to the conclusion that markets are not socially efficient, whereas, under these conditions, according to Hayek, they would be. However, what mechanism allows disclosing information for all agents, and what is the nature of this information?

Each individual has a partial and intrinsically limited knowledge, with respect to the aggregate set. Here, it is not a question of scientific knowledge, but of tacit knowledge and specific events (Polanyi 2002); this kind of knowledge allows carrying out continuous adjustments in the markets, and implementing flexible and efficient coordination:

> "And the problem of what is the best way of utilizing knowledge initially dispersed among all the people is at least one of the main problems of economic policy or of designing an efficient economic system." (Hayek 1948, p. 520)

Theoretically, there are two possible modes of coordination: the first one is decentralized, and operated by the market, the other one is centralized and implemented from a central institution (state, planning institution, etc.). Hayek argues that the market is the only viable solution for the following reasons:

(a) a centralizing mechanism, operated by a restricted group of individuals, is unable to collect and process all the information necessary to implement this coordination.
(b) such mechanism obligatorily does not correspond to the preferences of more part of individual. Bearing in mind the particularities of each individual, any decision taken in this way is necessarily against the willingness of most part; in the scope of Hayekian subjectivism, the consumer is best able to define his choices, in terms of consumption.

Hayek states that a competitive market is able to implement this coordination: it does not interfere in the preferences of individuals and transmits all the necessary information for agents to make the decision that suits them.

However, due to several works related to the information economics elaborated later, it is necessary to emphasize the informational limits of the competitive price system; to what extent is this system able to aggregate and disseminate information, without "distortions"?

Hayek starts from the implicit hypothesis of *self-enforcement*: the price system can be used freely by agents: transaction costs, in their most general definition, are nil. The different concrete ways of accessing the market do not imply costs. Coase's (1960), and more specifically Williamson's (2002) works, on the contrary, demystify the role of the market:

(i) Access to the market, and to the information necessary to operate in this market, translates into positive transaction costs.[6] Market is no more, *systematically*, the most efficient governance modality: depending on the specificity of assets and the level of transaction costs, there are other alternatives, in terms of social efficiency (Herscovici 2012).
(ii) Information Economics, as developed by Akerlof (1970) and Grossman and Stiglitz (1976, 1980), highlights the fact that market prices do not disclose information on quality and on individuals' behaviors; in such cases, markets are rationed (Stiglitz 2000) and do not satisfy the Pareto optimality conditions, or in the Hayekian terminology, market does not efficiently allocates resources.

Hayek recognizes that, in some situations, the price system is bounded: the state ought to intervene to ensure "the prevention of frauds (including the exploration of ignorance)" (1946, p. 35).

Prices do not disclose all the pertinent information for all individuals in multiple situations. The distortion of competitive prices may be caused by the following elements: state intervention with public subsides, oligopolistic or monopolistic market structures, monetary creation, as argued by Hayek; however, free rider behaviors or information asymmetries produced by the market itself may also cause price opacity (Akerlof 1970; Grossman and Stiglitz 1976). In other words, *such distortions may be produced by exogenous variables (e.g., institutions), or by endogenous variables (i.e., by the competitive market itself)*.

Some authors argue that the specificities of the Austrian school, regarding the neoclassical ones, consist in studying the information imperfections (Egger 1978). But Neoclassical School study information too: Friedman (1966), Stigler (1961), the Rational Expectations Theory and Mankiw (1985) incorporate these imperfections in the neoclassical framework; notwithstanding, as demonstrated by Grossman and Stiglitz (1980), such imperfections produce asymmetries that are incompatible with market efficiency.

Hayek resolves the paradox of efficient markets (Grossman and Stiglitz 1976) from the spontaneous order that characterizes the competitive

[6] Stiglitz highlights the importance of Coase's and Williamson's works in regard to Information Economics (Stiglitz 2000, p. 1440).

market: despite recognizing the existence of intrinsic information asymmetries, he concludes that markets are efficient.

Final Observations

This chapter allows arguing that the epistemological rupture that Hayek intends to elaborate, in relation to the Neoclassical Economics, is partial and particularly ambiguous. The hard core of the Hayekian Research Program is largely similar to the hard core of standard Neoclassical Economics, including the theory of rational expectations: *linking economic movements to real variables, normative approach and refuting the role of money as a specific asset*.

The differences appear at the level of the auxiliary hypotheses, that is, the modus operandi. Neoclassical and Hayekian approaches share the same hard core, but develop different auxiliary hypotheses. These are not two different and incompatible Research Programs, but simply two different developments of most part of the same hard core. In both cases, neither of these programs reveals how "black boxes" work: pure and perfect competition or spontaneous order by the markets represents a Deus ex machina that solves the problems of economic coordination and macroeconomic adjustment:

> "Hayek did no better than those he opposed in explaining precisely how the system self-organizes into a satisfactorily coordinated state. So, curiously, Hayek's premonitory vision of a complex system ran into exactly the same problem as that which blocked the progress of general equilibrium—the lack of any mechanism that would bring it into (in his case) a coordinated state and, in the case of general equilibrium theory, an equilibrium state." (Kirman 2016, p. 556)

On purpose, the title of this chapter is an allusion to the book of the Laclos, author of the XVIII century; these *liaisons* are dangerous, because they want to appear for what they are not, emphasizing divergences, and voluntarily occulting epistemological convergences. These differences come much more from a sociological strategy of differentiation than from Epistemology.

Finally, Hayek's approach is not without contradictions: how is it possible to speak of monetary economics if all economic movements are conceived in real terms? How to reconcile the active role of money and the primacy of real variables? How can we say that this approach constitutes an analysis of complexity, from an evolutionary perspective, if economic processes are reversible and universal?

References

Akerlof, G. 1970. The Market for "Lemons": Qualitative Uncertainty and the Market Mechanism. *Quarterly Journal of Economics*, August, 89.

Arrow, Kenneth J. 1985. The Potential and Limits of the Market in Resource Allocation. In *Issues in Contemporary Microeconomics and Welfare*, ed. G.R. Feiwel, 107–124. London: Macmillan.

———. 1986. Rationality of Self and Others in an Economic System. *The Journal of Business* 59 (4): 385–390.

Boianovsky, Mauro. 1992. Hicks, Hayek e a dinâmica monetária wicksElliana. *Revista Brasileira de Economia*, Rio de Janeiro 46 (1): 77–95.

Caldwell, Bruce. 2011. *The Collected Works of F.A. Hayek*, vol. 15. Chicago: The University of Chicago Press.

Catephore, George, and Michio Morishima. 1980. *Valeur, Exploitation et Croissance*. Paris: Economica.

Coase, R.H. 1960. The Problem of Social Cost. *Journal of Law and Economics* 3: 1–44.

Da Silva, Sérgio, and Daniel Wallmann. 2017. *Mind Nudgers. The Methodological Shuffle of Behavioral Economics*. Seattle: KDP Amazon

Deblock, G., and J.J. Gislain. 1989. Le crédit et la théorie du cycle économique chez Hayek. *Friedrich Hayek. Philosophie, économie et politique*, sous la direction de Gilles Dostaler et Diane Ethier. Paris: Economica.

Dostaler, Gilles. 1989. Friedrich Hayek sa vie son œuvre. *Friedrich Hayek. Philosophie, économie et politique*, sous la direction de Gilles Dostaler et Diane Ethier. Paris: Economica.

Dray, W. 1957. *Laws and Explanations in History*. Oxford University Press.

Egger, J. 1978. The Austrian Method, 1976. In *New Directions in Austrian Economics*, org. Louis Spadaro. Kansas City: Sheed Andrews and McMeel.

Fama, E. 1988. Market Efficiency, Long Term Returns and Behavioral Finance. *Journal of Financial Economics* 49 (3, September): 283–306.

Friedman, Milton. 1966. *The Methodology of Positive Economic*. Cambridge: Cambridge University Press.

Grossman, S.J., and J.E. Stiglitz. 1976. Information and Competitive Price System. *The American Economic Review* 66 (2, May): 76.

———. 1980. On the Impossibility of Informationally Efficient Markets. *The American Economic Review* 70 (3, June): 393–408.

Harris, Donald. 1978. *Capital, Accumulation and Income Distribution*. Stanford, CA: Stanford University Press.

Hayek, F.A. 1944. *The Road to Serfdom*. UK: Routledge Press.
———. 2009 [1950]. *The Pure Theory of Capital*. Auburn, Alabama: The Ludwig von Mises Institute.
Hayek, Friedrich von. 1935. *Prices and Production*. New York: Augustus M. Kelly Publishers.
———. 1945. The Use of Knowledge in Society. *The American Economic Review* 35 (4): 519–530.
———. 1948. *Individualism and Economic Order*. London, UK: The University of Chicago Press, George Routledge & Sons.
———. 1952. *Scientism and the Study of Society*. Glencoe, Illinois: The Free Press.
———. 1985 [1946]. *La route de la servitude* (The Road to Serfdom). Presses Universitaires de France.
Hempel, C.G. 1942. The Function of General Laws in History. *The Journal of Philosophy* 39 (2, January 15): 35–48.
Herscovici, Alain. 2002. *Dinâmica Macroeconômica: uma interpretação a partir de Marx e de Keynes*. São Paulo: EDUC/EDUFES.
———. 2012. Informação, conhecimento e Direitos de Propriedade Intelectual:os limites dos mecanismos de mercado e das modalidades de negociação privada. A contribuição de Williamson à análise dos Direitos de Propriedade Intelectual. *Economia e Sociedade, Campinas* 21 (3, 46): 667–694.
———. 2019. *Essays on the Historicity of Capital*. New York: Palgrave Macmillan.
Hicks, John. 1967. The Hayek Story. In *Critical Essays in Monetary Theory*, 201–215. Glagow: Oxford University Press.
———. 1973. *Capital and Time*. Oxford: Clarendon Press.
———. 1982. *Money, Interest & Wages Collected Essays on Economics Theory*, vol. II. Harvard University Press.
———. 1982 [1933]. Equilibrium and the Trade Cycle. In *Collected Essays on Economic Theory*, 2. Oxford: Blackwell.
Israël, Giorgio. 1992. L'histoire du déterminisme et ses rencontres avec les mathématiques. *Chaos et déterminisme*, op. cit.
Kirman, A. 2016. Complexity and Economic Policy: A Paradigm Shift or a Change in Perspective? A Review Essay on David Colander and Roland Kupers's Complexity and the Art of Public Policy. *Journal of Economic Literature* 54 (2): 534–572.
Mankiw, Gregory. 1985. Small Menu Costs and Large Business Cycles: A Macroeconomic Model of Monopoly. *The Quarterly Journal of Economics* 100 (2, May): 529–537.
Mankiw, N.G. 1990. A Quick Refresher Course in Macroeconomics. *Journal of Economic Literature* XXVIII (December): 1645–1660.
Parguez, Alain. 1989. Hayek et Keynes face ´à l´austérité. In *Friedrich Hayek. Philosophie, économie et politique*, op. cit.

Phelps, Edmund. 2011. *Keynes vs. Hayek: Stumbling Blocks to Spending Our Way to Prosperity*. Produced by Reuters, 8 November.
Poincaré, Henri. 1908. *La valeur de la Science*. Paris: Ernest Flammarion, Editeur, 278 pp. Collection: "Bibliothequede philosophie scientifique".
Polanyi, M. 2002. *Personal Knowledge: Towards a Post-Critical Philosophy*. London: Routledge.
Popper, K.R. 1959. *The Logic of Scientific Discovery*. London: Hutchinson & Co.
———. 1972. *The Poverty of Historicism*, 2nd ed. London: Routledge & Kegan Paul.
Prigogine, Ilya. 1996. *La fin des certitudes*. Paris: Editions Odile Jacob.
Roncaglia de Carvalho, André. 2008. O conceito de individualismo metodológico em Hayek revisitado. *Revista Análise Econômica* 26 (50): 83–109.
Root, Hilton L. 2018. Keynes, Hayek, and the Roots of Complexity, Theory in Economics. *Policy and Complex Systems* 4 (1, Spring).
Solow, Robert. 1956. A Contribution to the Theory of Economic Growth. *Quarterly Journal of Economics* 70: 65–94.
Soromenho, Jorge Eduardo de Castro. 1998. Os novos-clássicos e a teoria dos ciclos de Hayek. *Revista de Economia Política* 18 nº 3 (71, julho–setembro): 38–543.
Sraffa, Piero. 1932. Dr. Hayek on Money and Capital. *The Economic Journal* 42.
Steele, G. 2006. Hayek's the Pure Theory of Capital. In *The Elgar Companion to Hayekian Economics*, ed. Norman Barry. Edward Elgar Publishing.
Stigler, George J. 1961. The Economics of Information. *The Journal of Political Economy* 69 (3, June): 213–225.
Stiglitz, Joseph. 2000. The Contribution to the Economics of Information to Twentieth Century Economics. *The Quarterly Journal of Economics*, November.
Tirole, Jean. 2016. *Economie du bien commun*, 629 p. Paris: PUF.
Vercelli, Alessandro. 1991. *Methodological Foundations of Macroeconomics: Keynes and Lucas*. Cambridge University Press.
Williamson, O. 2002. The Theory of the Firm as Governance Structure: From Choice to Contract. *Journal of Economic Perspectives* 16 (3, Summer): 171–195.

CHAPTER 7

Money, Finance and Real Economy

From the non-neutrality of money to the non-neutrality of finance.

Cardim wrote that "A monetary economy cannot be reducible, even in the long run, to a real economy" (1992a, *p. 171). In his 2016 book, he again states that, according to Keynes, "Real variables were not sufficient to describe, neither short or long term equilibrium positions (…)" (p. 3). This characteristic constitutes one of the main foundations of the "Keynesian revolution," that is, of the epistemological rupture to which the General Theory (GT) corresponds.*

In this chapter, I will only add that this differentiation between the real economy and the monetary (production) economy makes it necessary to redefine the economic nature of activities related to finance, as well as the role played by the banking system: in this sense, after having defined the main characteristics of the post-Keynesian approach, I will study the spillover effects that finance can exert on the productive sector and the interest rate.

In Cardim's works, this theme appears in several papers:

i. "Again, the debate allowed Keynes to refine his analysis by making clear the financial side of his principle of effective demand" (Cardim de Carvalho 1996, pp. 325–326). Just as money is not neutral, finance is not neutral either: these two assets influence Effective Demand, that is, the "real" variables.

A. Herscovici, *Value, Historicity, and Economic Epistemology*, https://doi.org/10.1007/978-3-031-21157-7_7

ii. The emergence of new financial products for the financialization of the economy "(...) reduces the horizon of expectations in the financial markets with some impact on the financing of longer-term activities, as argued below" (Cardim de Carvalho 1997, p. 481). Speculative finance harms productive investment, linked by nature to the long term, weakens the finance/funding circuit and translates into financial fragility, in the Minskian sense. It is necessary to redefine the role of the banking system, as well as question its supposed "neutrality":

> "The same financial structures that allow productive investment and capital accumulation, and economic growth, to reach the levels characteristic of modern capitalist economies are also those where fragilities are accumulated that ultimately cause deep crises, such as the one that began in the US economy in 2007 and has since spread throughout most of the world." (Cardim de Carvalho 2016, p. 306)

This non-neutrality of finance broadens the critique of Neoclassical Economics: it denies the existence of information asymmetries and, consequently, the existence of financial speculation (Fama 1988; Malkiel 2003), trying to maintain the primacy of the real economy based on the hypothesis of the fundamental value of financial bonds.

Since, in the post-Keynesian approach, the role of agents is conceived as a theory of asset choice, it is not possible, as the neoclassical analysis does, to reduce financial activity to a simple intermediation whose function consists only of implement productive investment from savings. The thesis defended in this chapter can be formulated as follows: just as the post-Keynesian analysis recognizes that money influences the real sector, finance also exerts its effects on this sector. This constitutes one more convergence between Neoclassical Economics and Hayekian economics: they refute the existence of speculative finance and information asymmetries, to assert *the primacy of the real sector over monetary and financial ones*.

In the first part, I will study the elements that underlie the rupture introduced by Keynes, with regard to the interest rate, its nature and the different components of the demand for money. I will show, from a simple formalization, why Keynes refutes the Loanable Funds Theory (LFT) and, consequently, the whole architecture of neoclassical macroeconomics. In the second part, I will define speculative finance and show how it exerts its effects on the productive sectors of the economy; I will emphasize the importance of the role of the banking system in this speculative dynamics, and show the extent to which this analysis is incompatible with the hypotheses and results of the Neoclassical School, regarding the role of banks and the economic nature of finance.

Keynes and the LFT: The Fundamentals of Criticism and the Affirmation of the Non-Neutrality of Money

Keynes's Critique

In Chapter 14 of the GT, Keynes highlights the limits, that is, the problems of internal coherence, of classical theory, with regard to LFT. The criticism made by Keynes is directly linked to the modalities for determining the interest rate and, consequently, to the nature of savings. For the classics, the demand for funds (or for resources) is assimilated to investment; symmetrically, the supply of funds corresponds to savings (GT, p. 143). The "natural" rate is the rate that corresponds to the equalization between demand and supply of funds, for a situation of full employment.

This reasoning is based on the following assumptions: (i) At the aggregate level, the interest rate is determined endogenously, by the demand and supply of funds (Cardim de Carvalho 1996, p. 319). (ii) In the Marshallian tradition, investment, that is, the demand for a certain amount of capital, corresponds to the demand for funds; the interest rate is the price paid for the use of capital in any market (GT, p. 143). It is conceived as the rate of rent on capital and is obligatorily equal to the rate of profit. (iii) In this perspective, by definition, savings finances investment. Thus, *savings is conceived as a real mechanism*, i.e., a non-monetary mechanism.

The interest rate represents the premium for waiting, for giving up present consumption; finally, this natural interest rate represents the rate that allows equaling investment and savings to a level that corresponds to full employment, in the sense that there is no involuntary unemployment. Within the scope, I will show how, and why, Keynes refutes these results.

For Keynes, the demand and supply of funds determine the interest rate from the moment that income is constant (GT, p. 145); only under these conditions, it is possible to endogenously determine the interest rate from the LFT. However, a variation in investment is incompatible with the fact that income remains constant (GT, p. 145 and 146): from the moment that there is a multiplier effect, any variation in investment corresponds to a variation in income: in GT, "Income, thus, was the variable adjustment charged with the task of balancing investment and savings decisions of individuals, and the way it was only called the multiplier" (Cardim de Carvalho 1996, p. 314).

In (neo)classical theory, the interest rate is the reward for waiting, as far as consumption is concerned. In the tradition of Mills and Jevons, the rational being would be endowed with a preference for present consumption: the interest rate would be the reward for him to postpone present consumption. Saving is an intertemporal consumption choice: in the neoclassical growth models deriving from Solow's canonical model (1956), saving represents an increase in future consumption. In fact, only if income remains constant, an increase in current savings correspond to a decrease in current consumption, an increase in investment and, consequently, an increase in future consumption.

Within the neoclassical construction, the LFT fulfills a triple function: (a) it is another way of expressing Say's law (Petri 1998); the fact that savings finances investment means that, at the aggregate level, all the income distributed in production activities corresponds, directly or indirectly, to the expenses made in the entire economy (b) it assumes that there is a monotonic relationship between the interest rate and the investment. This relationship allows explaining the adjustment modalities for the equilibrium position and directly refers to the problem of the nature of capital (Herscovici 2013) (c) it allows justifying the automatic adjustment of the system to the stable equilibrium position, in the long run.

In fact, in the neoclassical model, Investment and Savings are endogenously determined from real variables: "Thus, the equilibrium rate of interest depended, for orthodox theory, on thrift (that determined the propensity to save) and productivity (that limited the interest that could be paid by the marginal investment project)" (Cardim de Carvalho 1996, p. 314).

The divergences between the two models (the one exposed in GT and the neoclassical model) can be formalized as follows:

$$\begin{aligned} I &= \varphi 1[e - r] \\ \text{with} \quad & \varphi_1^{'} > 0 \end{aligned} \tag{7.1}$$

$$\begin{aligned} S &= \phi 3(Y) \\ \text{with} \quad & \varphi_3^{'} > 0 \end{aligned} \tag{7.2}$$

(*e* as the marginal efficiency of capital, *r* as the interest rate, I and S, respectively, as investment and savings and Y as the income).

There are two equations and three unknowns, *e*, *r* and *Y*[1]; it is not possible to solve this system. As Keynes states, it is not possible to determine simultaneously the interest rate, the marginal efficiency of capital and income.

The classic solution is to exogenize income; in this case, income is determined in the real sphere, from a well-behaved aggregate production function, in which there is perfect substitutability of the factors of production. The interest rate is determined by the LFT; in the classical tradition, the interest rate is equal to the rate of profit and the marginal productivity of capital.

In the Keynesian system, on the contrary, there is an exogenous determination of the interest rate (Vercelli 1991, p. 184, Pasinetti 1997, p. 212). The implications are as follows:

i. The LFT is no longer explanatory, as it does not allow determining the equilibrium interest rate.
ii. The exogeneity of the *interest rate is explained from its monetary and financial determination*, that is, from the money store of wealth function and from financial speculation.
iii. From this simple system of equations, it is possible to deduce that *product is determined by the interest rate, that is, by a monetary variable*, in the sense defined above; this is synonymous with money non-neutrality.

The adjustment mechanisms that make it possible to move from an unbalanced position to the equilibrium position are also different. Within

[1] This formalization is inspired by Vercelli (1991, p. 184).

the scope of Keynes' analysis, in GT, the adjustment is implemented from a variation in income, through the bias of the multiplier effect: ex post, global savings and investment are equal. The variation in income produced by the initial variation in investment corresponds to a variation in savings, in such a way that the increase in savings is equal to the increase in investment: "Savings are created by investment since they are allocations of income generated by the investment activity itself" (Cardim de Carvalho 1996, p. 315).

Savings cannot finance investment, because savings are the result of income variation produced by the initial investment variation: *it is impossible to finance this initial investment from a value that does not exist when this investment is realized.* Thus, investment cannot depend on previous savings (Chick 1991, p. 192; Cardim de Carvalho 1997, p. 468).

In the classical tradition, on the contrary, the adjustment takes place from a variation in the interest rate, this movement explaining the systematic convergence to the natural interest rate. It is equally important to note that, in LFT, investment and savings are determined from the same variable (the interest rate), and that this interest rate is itself determined by savings and investment.

Interest Rate and Liquidity Preference

The Interest Rate Determination

In GT, *the interest rate is determined exogenously by the liquidity preference* (LP), from the following mechanism: the LP determines the demand for money, which explains, in *a second moment*, the variations in the interest rate necessary to equal, again, demand and supply for money (GT, p. 137). There is thus a monetary determination of the interest rate, which is ultimately determined by LP.

In the neoclassical model, on the contrary, the interest rate determines the demand for money and is conceived as the opportunity cost of holding money (Friedman 1974, p. 25); the higher this cost, the lower the demand for money. On the other hand, the fact that the interest rate is equal, in the equilibrium position, to the marginal productivity of capital, which is equal to the profit rate, in the neoclassical model, does not allow me to deduce, as Jevons does, that the rate of interest is determined by the marginal productivity of capital (Denis 1974, p. 499). We find, again, Keynes' critique of LFT:

i. Interest rate and marginal productivity of capital (marginal efficiency of capital, in GT) are determined independently: the interest rate depends on uncertainty and LP, the marginal efficiency of capital, on long-term expectations of entrepreneurs and on the supply price.
ii. The equality between the interest rate and the marginal efficiency of capital characterizes only the equilibrium position, in which the expected return on the last investment made is equal to the interest rate. The interest rate is determined exogenously and without any relation to the marginal efficiency of capital,[2] based on institutional mechanisms and/or agents' assessment of uncertainty.

Keynes' analysis, in GT, denies the neoclassical causality relationship; *this denial emphasizes the monetary determination of the interest rate and the fact that money determines investment, that is, the real sphere*. In fact, the causality of the neoclassical model is as follows: investment and savings determine the interest rate (based on the LFT), which determines the demand for money. In contrast, in GT, the LP determines the demand for money and this determines the interest rate. *Thus, in neoclassical theory, the demand for money is determined by the interest rate, while in GT, the interest rate is determined by the demand for money, that is, by LP.*

Contrary to Hicks' interpretation (the IS/LM model), LP is not a simple component of demand for money, but a fundamental determinant of the interest rate (Cardim de Carvalho 1992b, p. 97).

Preference for Liquidity and Idle Money: The Ambiguities Present in GT

In the Keynesian scheme, the interest rate does not equilibrate savings and investment at the level that corresponds to full employment, but allows equating "the desire to keep wealth in liquid form" with an exogenous money supply determined, hypothetically, by the Central Bank (GT, p. 37). LP is explained by the fact that money fulfills the function of store of wealth: it provides its holders with security in the face of uncertainty, in the sense defined by Keynes.

The demand for money depends on three motives: transaction and precaution (L1), which depend on income, and speculation (L2), which

[2] I therefore fully agree with Pasinetti when he states that: "(...) if the interest rate determines the investment, the reciprocal is not verified" (Pasinetti, op. cit., p. 209).

inversely depends on the interest rate. While the demand for money that depends directly on income implies the neutrality of money, only the demand for money due to speculation would explain its relationship with uncertainty; expectations regarding interest rate fluctuations would thus be the main source of uncertainty.

Equilibrium in the money market checks the following equation:

$$L = L_1(Y) + L_2(r) \quad (7.3)$$

L as the money supply, L_1 as the money demand for transaction and precautionary motive and L_2 as the money demand for speculation motive.

The ambiguities stem from the fact that, for Keynes, the demand for money for precautionary motive depends on income and not on uncertainty. We must question this approach and explain the different modalities in which uncertainty manifests itself: (a) The transaction motive is related to the "real" sphere, and expresses the neutrality of money (Cardim de Carvalho 2010, p. 718) (b) The precautionary motive is defined as "(...) the desire for *security* in relation to the future monetary equivalent of a certain part of the total resources" (GT, p. 139, emphasis added). The definition given by Keynes is particularly ambiguous: on the one hand, the precautionary motive is defined as a function of uncertainty, but, on the other hand, the demand for money linked to this motive depends on income: "This meant minimising the more revolutionary elements of his theory, the demand for money as a defense against uncertainty" (Cardim de Carvalho 2010, p, 717).

This definition is contradictory insofar as precautionary money demand is defined in terms of income rather than uncertainty. Kahn (1972) *highlights this contradiction, and links the precautionary motive with uncertainty, and more precisely with the uncertainty linked to the demand for money due to speculation.*

This component of the demand for money works through the following mechanism: if, at *t*, speculators expect, at *t + 1*, an increase in the interest rate, they expect a decrease in the value of the financial security at *t + 1*. At *t*, the demand for money due to speculation (L_2) will decrease because they want to buy the security at *t + 1*. Liquidity preference will increase at *t*: as speculators have to make a choice between buying a bond and holding money, they will choose the money at *t*. The precautionary motive is defined in terms of the uncertainty related to interest rate variations. *Agents build up an idle money stock that allows them to postpone the purchase of financial securities.*

The speculation motive is defined from the concept of degree of confidence. Speculators' expectations are more "reliable": they allow them to know before other agents, the future variations of the interest rate (GT, p. 129). Speculators will take profits by buying the security when its value is low, and selling it when its value is high (Herscovici 2019).

"In other words, the precautionary demand has to do with the possibility of change, while the speculative motive is a bet on a certain direction of change. Kahn's own approach was to make the speculative demand for money a definite bet on the direction of change in future interest rates, to be affected by the confidence with which the wealth-holder entertains this expectation of change" (Cardim de Carvalho 2010, p. 175).

The dynamics of speculation can be explained from the information asymmetries that exist between the different groups of agents: speculators are those who are able to "(…) predict the bases of conventional valuation a few months in advance (…)" (GT, 129). This is explained by the fact that they are able to predict future changes in the interest rate before other agents.

The probability of less informed agents predicting these evolutions is lower. Based on mimetic behavior, they will imitate, *with some time lags*, the choice of informed agents; the gains made by speculators are explained exactly from this time lag.

This difference in trust between speculators (that is, the informed) and the "general public" (the uninformed or uninformed agents in the terminology used by Grossman and Stigitz [1980]) accounts for the mechanism highlighted by Kahn (1972): by nature, the error made by speculators, with regard to the realization of their expectations, will always be smaller than that made by the "general public."[3]

Both speculators and the "general public" want to save money to buy, "later," financial bonds. However, speculators bought the title before the general public; in other words, the demand for money, on the part of speculators, has as its objective the purchase of bonds within a period shorter than the period foreseen by the general public.

The two motives (precaution and speculation) are interlinked, in the speculative dynamics: money can be demanded as a store of value, or on

[3] Keynes makes this distinction: regarding agents who are little or not informed, he speaks of "(…) mass psychology of ignorant individuals (…)" (GT, p. 128).

the contrary, to buy assets. The choice will be made based on the degree of confidence of each agents group in their expectations. As stated by Kahn (1972), in a given period, it is impossible to determine which part of the idle money corresponds to the precautionary motive and the speculation motive. As the reason for speculation is explained by the fact that it demands a quantity of money due to the purchase (immediate, or almost immediate) of a certain asset, the part of the demand for money that, depending on agents' expectations, is allocated the purchase of assets, in the more distant future, will be conserved, in view of its function as a store of value. In all cases, it is an "idle" money whose purpose is not to purchase goods and services immediately.

On the other hand, I do not believe that LP can be defined solely in terms of activities linked to speculation; LP is also determined from productive investment. For Keynes, productive investment is a decision that is related to the long term. Keynes uses a Marshallian conception, in which the short term is characterized by a constant capital stock, and the long term by the variation of this capital stock (Cardim de Carvalho 1990). Short-term expectations can be revised in the short term, and "(...) replaced by realized results" (GT, p. 56): Keynes disregards uncertainty in the short term and, consequently, uncertainty manifests itself essentially in the long-run deadline.

The costs that relate to the short term are reversible, while the investment costs relate to the long term are irreversible; it is the reason why uncertainty manifests itself essentially in the long run. On the other hand, Keynes states that "(...) it is not part of the nature of long-term expectations that they can be revised at short intervals of time in light of the results achieved" (Idem). Once the investment is made on the basis of some long-term expectations, it constitutes *an irreversible cost for the entrepreneur*, even if these expectations are not fulfilled in the future.

The concept of strong uncertainty, as defined by Keynes (1935) *directly depends on the irreversible character of investment*. In the universe defined by Neoclassical Economics, there is no uncertainty. This absence of uncertainty is justified by the absence of irreversible costs: in the Marshallian tradition, in pure and perfect competition markets, there is free entry and free exit in the industry—in the theory of contestable markets by Baumol (1982), for example, one of the conditions for markets to be contestable is that there are no barriers to exit, i.e., that investment decisions are irreversible.

On the contrary, with regard to speculative finance, speculative investment is considered reversible, as it relates to the short term. In this regard, Keynes states that the speculator has "(…) the opportunity to review his decisions and modify the investment before there is time for major changes to occur"; those investments that are "fixed" for the community become "liquid" for the "individual" (GT, p. 127). Thus, LP cannot be limited to speculative activities; it is also related to the productive sectors, and to the relations between such sector, money and finance. The choice of assets is made between productive assets, money and finance.

Speculative Finance, Spillover Effect and Non-neutrality of Finance

Productive Versus Speculative Finance

Keynes explicitly differentiates two financial logics: the entrepreneur one that I will call productive finance, and the speculative one (GT, p. 131).

A specific financial security (in this case, a bond) is issued on the primary market. The return arising from the interest rate is calculated based on the issue value, for a fixed duration. It is *productive finance*: (a) its return is certain, and determined ex ante by the interest rate applied to the issue value of the financial security (b) It is a financial mechanism that operates in the long term and (c) this mechanism is directly connected with productive activities (GT, p. 131, Herscovici 2017; Orléan 2011, p. 267).

On the contrary, the return of *speculative finance* comes mainly from fluctuations in the value of this bond in secondary markets. Speculation consists of buying the security when its value is low, and selling it when that value is high. The return comes mainly from the financial surplus realized by the speculator: the speculator "(…) only in the expectation of a capital gain is willing to acquire a security" (GT, p. 131). Speculative finance has the following characteristics: (a) *its return depends directly on the variation in the security's value* (b) it is a short-term mechanism that is explained by the information asymmetries existing between different groups of agents (Herscovici 2019) and (c) it is totally disconnected from the productive sector.

According to Keynes himself, equilibrium is reached when we can verify the following relationship (GT, p. 177 and following):

$$q_1 + a_1 = a_2 = l_3 \tag{7.4}$$

(q as the return on the asset, a as the change in its value during the period considered and l as the liquidity premium).

Relation (7.4) establishes a comparison between the return of three assets, the first being a productive asset, the second a speculative one and the third money. If one of these assets has a higher return than the others, there will be a transfer to the asset with the highest return, until it is checked again (7.4). *These propagation effects translate into a portfolio adjustment mechanism, which makes it impossible to determine the part of bank credits destined to financial circulation and that destined to industrial circulation* (Cardim de Carvalho 2005, pp. 328 and 330): the banking system is no longer neutral in relation to the productive sector and thus assumes an active role in financial speculation. Contrarily to what is stated by orthodox theory, the role of banks does not consist solely of financing the activities of the productive sector.

The intensification of financialization, that is, of the activities that are related to what I defined as speculative finance, has the effect of equalizing the return on each investment, in order to verify (7.4). This translates into an increase in the rate of return (r^*) used to be able to carry out the productive investment and, consequently, into a "rejection" of productive investments whose marginal efficiencies are lower than this rate of return.

The investment function used by Keynes can be written as follows:

$$\begin{aligned} &I = \phi(e - r^*) \\ &\text{with} \quad \phi' > 0 \end{aligned} \tag{7.5}$$

(e as the marginal efficiency of capital and r^* as the minimum required rate of return).

As financialization translates into an increase in r^*, many investments that could be carried out with a lower return are not carried out (Pasinetti 1997). The transfer of productive to speculative assets translates into a fall in production and in the level of employment; the production elasticities of these speculative assets being particularly weak, the employment lost in the productive sector is not compensated by the employment created in the sector linked to speculation.

Liquidity Preference and Idle Money

The demand for money is composed of active money and idle money: active money is directly related to the purchase and/or financing of assets, whether productive or financial. The "idle" money consists of retaining money to postpone the purchase, considering that the money allows it to conserve its value over time. LP is directly related to the uncertainty linked to productive ("real") investment and speculative investment.

Based on these observations, it is necessary to rewrite the relationship that expresses the balance in the money market as follows:

$$L = L_1(Y) + L_2(r) + L_3(\Omega_3) + L_4(\Omega_4) \tag{7.6}$$

Ω_3 represents the uncertainty linked to productive investment and Ω_4 the uncertainty inherent to speculative investment. L_1 and L_2 represent the active money components, as they represent a demand for money that corresponds to expenditures made "today"; L_3 and L_4 represent the idle money, destined to postpone the purchase of productive and financial assets, due to the uncertainty and expectations regarding the evolution of the rate of profit.

Based on the previously constructed relationships, it is possible to state that these components are interdependent. For example, an exogenous decrease in r has the following implications: an increase in L_2 as a function of expectations regarding the value of securities, and an increase in L_1 as a function of the increase in investment and the resulting increase in output and employment.

An increase in money supply will have a positive effect on output only if it exceeds the increase in demand: as a function of (7.6), this condition will be verified only if the effects of the increase in money supply are not neutralized by the increase in L_1 and L_2 and by decreasing L_3: "While it is to be expected that, *ceteris paribus*, an increase in the quantity of money will reduce the interest rate, this will not occur if the public's preference increases more than the quantity of money" (GT, p. 141, emphasis added). Intuitively, when there is a fall in the interest rate, a greater amount of capital becomes profitable, which can be interpreted as a decrease in uncertainty linked to productive investment, and consequently, as a decrease in L_3.

The development of financial speculation implies an intensification of the uncertainty that weighs on productive investment: while the liquidity of this type of investment is, by nature, limited, the liquidity relative to speculative investment is high. From this liquidity, it is possible to explain their returns. *Thus, the greater the liquidity of speculative investments, the greater the variations in the value of securities, and the greater the uncertainty regarding productive investments.*

This mechanism is implicit in the definition of the offer price:

$$P_o = \Sigma Q_i/(1+e)^n \tag{7.7}$$

(P_0 as the supply price, Q_i as the investment return at each period, an e as the marginal efficiency of capital.)
Relation (7.7) clearly shows that an increase in the chosen update rate corresponds to a decrease in Po, for constant ΣQi. The offer price is related to "(...) the rate of return expected to be obtained from the money invested in a *newly* produced good; and not the historical result obtained by an investment in relation to its original cost, when examined retrospectively at the end of its life" (GT, p. 115, original emphasis).

On the other hand, the liquidity of a given asset is defined by the fact that its value is guaranteed over time (Cardim de Carvalho 1992a, p. 184). Thus, the greater the instability of the chosen update rate, as highlighted in relation (7.7), the greater the uncertainty regarding the determination of the asset's supply price; its liquidity varies, its irreversibility is accentuated, which corresponds to an intensification of the uncertainty linked to this type of asset. Consequently, L_3 increases.

The beginning of a crisis is usually characterized by an increase in the interest rate, which initially causes a financial crisis and a cumulative process of falling value of the bonds (Herscovici 2019). This translates into a drop in L_1 and L_2 and an increase in L_3 and L_4. The propagation effects develop when the increase in L_3 and L_4 becomes greater than the decrease in L_1 and L_2.

Propagation Effects and Nature of the Banking System

There is thus a propagation mechanism with regard to the increase in the rate of return caused by the intensification of financialization. As, by nature, speculation is characterized by strong instability[4] and strong

[4] In this regard, Cardim de Carvalho (2009) states that the post-Keynesian approach, "(...) takes instability as a process, a normal feature of the workings of the financial system."

uncertainty, this instability will have repercussions on investments made in the productive sector. *This financial instability corresponds to an instability in the minimum rate of return that productive investments have to achieve.*

Consequently, this analysis allows us to highlight the nature of these propagation mechanisms: *the short-term instability inherent to speculative activities determines the conditions for the economic viability of investments made, in the long term, in the productive sector.*[5] The entire economic system is subject to financial fragility à la Minsky: the development of financial activities linked to speculation implies that a growing part of long-term productive investments is financed by capital whose value is particularly unstable, and whose permanence is relatively short (Cardim de Carvalho 1997, p. 484).

This propagation effect depends directly on the degree of development of speculative finance:

> "(…) in the absence of an organized market, liquidity preference due to the precautionary motive would greatly increase, whereas the existence of an organized market would provide the opportunity for wide fluctuations in liquidity preference due to the motive of speculation." (GT, p. 139)

An organized market is made up of secondary markets in which financial securities are traded, after having been issued on the primary market. The more developed these secondary markets, the greater the opportunities for speculation, that is, for the sale and purchase of these securities, and the greater the possibilities of realizing gains as a result of changes in the value of these securities; consequently, the greater the LP fluctuations due to speculation.

In Keynes's perspective, the development of finance takes place at the expense of productive investment, as it "pulls" r^* up, and thus eliminates investments whose marginal efficiency is lower than this same rate of return "A collapse in the price of equities (…) has a disastrous reactions on the marginal efficiency of capital (…)" (GT, p. 131). *There is*

[5] It is necessary to emphasize the fact that short-term expectations determine, at least partially, long-term expectations: it is a path dependence, which implies (a) that the system does not converge towards a predetermined long-term equilibrium and (b) that there is an endogenous determination of long-term expectations (Herscovici 2019). On the other hand, this corresponds to the fact that "What matters is the long-term expectations rather than long-period values (…)" (Cardim de Carvalho 1990, p. 288).

obviously a propagation mechanism from the speculative sphere to the real one; the speculation motive determines a certain LP, the latter determines the level of the interest rate and, consequently, the level of investment and employment.

Keynes considers different situations to which different propagation effects correspond: when speculation is poorly developed, the demand for money due to speculation is weak. In this case, an increase in the money supply translates into a fall in the interest rate, and an increase in investment and employment (GT, p. 140). If, on the contrary, speculation is important, the increase in money supply will be absorbed by the increase in speculators' demand, and will have no impact on output and the level of employment.[6] The elasticity of the interest rate, in relation to changes in the money supply and, consequently, the effects caused by the increase in money supply, depend on the relative weight of speculation in the economy: the greater this weight, the smaller the effects in terms of income variation and of employment.

Finally, within a post-Keynesian perspective, it is possible to show that the development of speculation translates into an intensification of income inequalities (Dávila-Fernández et al. 2017; Herscovici, 2019); this necessarily implies a decrease in the investment multiplier and, consequently, a decrease in the effects of a fiscal policy.

i. As the stock exchange carries out daily revaluations of the value of companies, the short-term expectations of speculators "(…) exert a decisive influence on the amount of current investment" (GT, p. 126). We are in the presence of a *financial governance* in which the expectations of return on productive investment are determined "(…) by the average expectation of those who trade on the stock exchange" (Idem, p. 126). In the case of a financial bubble, return expectations are particularly high, which translates into a shift in demand for financial assets and a rejection of investments that are unable to earn a return that corresponds to these expectations.
ii. On the other hand, financial markets are particularly unstable, which means that uncertainty is high; this translates into an increase in liquidity preference, in the interest rate and, consequently, in a fall in productive investment.

[6] This corresponds to the liquidity trap in the neoclassical synthesis.

iii. The development of speculative finance has the effect of reducing the efficiency of monetary policies: as the increase in money supply is absorbed by the demand for money due to speculation, it does not translate into an increase in output or employment. The effects of this policy will directly depend on the structure of the demand for money, that is, on the components linked to financial circulation and those linked to industrial circulation (Cardim de Carvalho 2005, pp. 330–331).
iv. Finally, as the elasticity of production of financial bonds and money is close to zero, a transfer of demand to these assets has the direct consequence of a fall in the employment. From a Keynesian perspective, it is thus possible to state that, as a result of this transfer of demand, *the development of financial markets decreases the value of the expenditure multiplier and thus reduces the positive effects of economic policies.*

Regarding the employment function, Keynes differentiates industries in regard to their employment elasticities and their production elasticities (GT, p. 220 and 221). These elasticities measure the variation in employment and the variations in production that result from an initial variation in Effective Demand. Employment elasticity can be defined by the following equation:

$$e_{er} = \frac{dNr}{Nr} / \frac{dDwr}{Dwr} = \frac{dNr}{dWr} . \frac{Dwr}{Nr} \tag{7.8}$$

Producton elasticity by:

$$e_{or} = \frac{dOr}{Or} / \frac{dDwr}{Dwr} = \frac{dOr}{dWr} . \frac{Dwr}{Or} \tag{7.9}$$

Nr as employment, Dwr as demand and *Or* as supply: *d* is relative to variations.

Keynes states that "(…) if the additional demand is directed to products that have a relatively low elasticity of employment, a greater proportion of this demand will increase the income of entrepreneurs (…)" (GT, p. 225); the development of these markets has a limited effect, in terms of the level of employment.

Activities linked to speculative finance have the following characteristics: their employment and production elasticities are low. The adjustment carried out in these markets is implemented mainly from a variation in prices, and not in the quantities produced. *The supply of this type of assets is, by nature, limited* (Tirole 2016, p. 407): otherwise, the increase in demand would imply an increase in prices, which would imply an increase in supply and a subsequent decrease prices, which would strongly limit changes in the value of bonds and, consequently, speculation. Limitation of supply is one of the conditions under which speculative finance can develop; this rigidity of supply is one of the characteristics of markets in which goods and capital are highly heterogeneous (Herscovici 2017), and adjustments are made mainly from a variation in prices rather than quantities.

This analysis leads us to define the function and nature of the banking system. Just as neoclassical analysis adopts the money neutrality hypothesis, *it implicitly adopts the finance neutrality hypothesis*. The credit system is a simple intermediary between savers and investors, and only corresponds to the realization of the LFT, as it allows the concrete implementation of the market in which the demand for funds meets the supply for funds.

"Banks further complicated the relationship between saving and investment but again they were not allowed to change its ultimate nature. Bank deposits and loans dealt with the means to purchase the goods that are going to be accumulated. The possibility of accumulation continued to depend on the desire of income earners to save and of investors to invest" (Cardim de Carvalho 2012, p. 201).

This neutrality manifests itself as follows: from analyses in terms of rational expectations, speculative bubbles are conceived as a deviation from the fundamental value of these securities; the bubble bursts when this deviation exceeds a certain threshold value (Fama 1988; Malkiel 2003; Tirole 2016). This fundamental value is defined in the real sector, based on the profit expectations of the firm that launched these bonds on the market: this fundamental value is defined as "(…) the updated value of dividends, interest and rents that the bond will provide today and in the future" (Tirole 2016, pp. 404–405).

This approach maintains the postulates of neoclassical analysis: (a) the analysis is carried out in real terms, which means that, in the long run, money and finance do not influence real movements. (b) The existence of speculative finance is, by principle, denied, as there are no information asymmetries between the different agents operating in these markets and that, consequently, the only gain realized in these markets is the one corresponding to dividends and interest. The competitive pricing system is "transparent," in that it *instantly* transmits pertinent information to the set of agents present in the market. (c) The ergodicity postulate is adopted, because agents can predict the returns of bonds throughout their existence: there is no strong uncertainty (Cardim de Carvalho 1988b).

Post-Keynesian analysis is incompatible with these results: from the parable of the beauty contest (GT, p. 129), Keynes refutes the existence of a fundamental value of titles. He shows, on the contrary, that this value is determined from a self-fulfilling prophecies (Orléan 2011). On the other hand, the dynamics of this mechanism is explained by the existence of information asymmetries. It should be added that the existence of uncertainty, which justifies the PL, directly conflicts with the ergodicity postulate.

On an empirical level, it is not possible to consider that deposits made within the banking system are solely intended for the purchase of productive investments, as presupposed by the neoclassical analysis: "it is difficult to separate the precautionary from the speculative reasons since both deal with inactive balances, where money is held as an asset instead of a means of payment held in anticipation of planned expenditure" (Cardim de Carvalho 2010, p. 778).

Symmetrically, this implies that credit granted by banks is not solely intended to finance productive investment; they can serve to finance a speculative investment, or to guard against uncertainty, in the form of the constitution of idle money: "(…) one may plan to take credit for the purchase of old assets, i.e. for financial investment. This has nothing to do with the new investment of the industrial sphere, which is related to savings" (Cardim de Carvalho 2012, p. 202).

In the same way that, in the Keynesian system, there is no money neutrality, it is possible to affirm that, also, there is no neutrality of the banking system. The money retained in the banking system is not only related to transactional activities (traditional conception of transaction and precautionary motives), but also to idle money and to money linked to speculative activities.

Final Remarks

It is important to emphasize the differences that exist between this interpretation and that proposed by the neoclassical synthesis: in the interpretation I designed here, I incorporated the fundamental elements that characterize the hard core of the post-Keynesian theory, mainly the strong uncertainty, the refutation of the LFT and the asset choices theory in a universe characterized by strong uncertainty. These elements are absent in the neoclassical synthesis: (a) the demand for money due to speculation is not determined as a function of uncertainty (b) as highlighted by *the eviction effect*, for example, the interest rate is determined endogenously, based on the demand and supply funds (c) savings finances the investment, which is totally incompatible with the mechanisms highlighted in the GT.

Due to the methodological convergences between the neoclassical and the Hayekian matrix, the Keynesian critiques addressed to neoclassical theory are, for the most part, the same as those addressed to Hayekian economics: the absence of monetary analysis, a primacy of the real setor in regard to the financial and monetary ones, and some ambiguities regarding the pseudo-monetary explanation of the economic cycle.

The analysis elaborated here is totally coherent with the universe described in GT: (a) there is no dichotomy between the real sphere, the monetary sphere and the financial sphere (b) money plays a role as a store of value and (c) the interest rate is determined by the money supply, by expectations linked to speculative finance and by the uncertainty that characterizes productive investment, that is, by global LP. Thus, the limitations of the different ways of integrating Keynesian results into the neoclassical matrix appear.

The fundamental rupture between Keynes and classical economics is realized in GT Chapters XIII and XIV: in these chapters, Keynes emphasizes *the monetary and financial nature of the interest rate, as opposed to its real nature*, in classical economics. After having redefined, due to the ambiguities present in the GT, the different components of the LP, it is possible to study the propagation mechanisms that highlight *the organic relationships of interdependence between the monetary, financial and real spheres*. To the non-neutrality of money, the non-neutrality of the financial system must be added; it is one of the main conclusions, drawn from a redefinition of the demand for money in regard to the precautionary motive.

References

Baumol, W.J. 1982. Contestable Markets: An Uprising in the Theory of Industry Structure. *American Economic Review* 72 (1) (March): 1–15.

Cardim de Carvalho, Fernando J. 1988a. Da síntese neoclássica à redescoberta de Keynes. *Análise Econômica, ano* 6 (9): 3–21.

———. 1988b. Keynes on Probability, Uncertainty, and Decision-Making. *Journal of Post Keynesian Economics* 11 (1): 66–180.

———. 1990. Keynes and the Long Period. *Cambridge Journal of Economics* 14 (3): 277–290.

———. 1992a. Moeda, produção e acumulação: uma perspectiva keynesiana. *Moeda e Produção: teorias comparadas, Maria Luiza Falcão Silva org, Editora*, 113–127. Brasília: Universidade de Brasília.

———. 1992b. *Mr Keynes and the Post-Keynesians. Principles of Macroeconomics for a Monetary Production Economy*, 233. London: Edward Elgar.

———. 1996. Sorting Out the Issues: The Two Debates (1936/37; 1983–86) on Keynes's Finance Motive Revisited. *Revista Brasileira De Economia* 50 (3): 312–327.

———. 1997. Financial Innovation and the Post Keynesian Approach to the 'Process of Capital Formation.' *Journal of Post Keynesian Economics* 19 (3): 461–487.

———. 2005. Uma Contribuição ao Debate em torno da Eficácia da Política Monetária e Algumas Implicações para o Caso do Brasil. *Revista De Economia Política* 25 (4): 323–336.

———. 2009. *Systemic Crisis, Systemic Risk and the Financial Instability Hypothesis*, draft, without editor.

———. 2010. Uncertainty and Money: Keynes, Tobin and Kahn and the Disappearance of the Precautionary Demand for Money from Liquidity Preference Theory. *Cambridge Journal of Economics* 34 (4): 709–725.

———. 2012. Aggregate Savings, Finance and Investment. *Intervention* 9 (2): 197–213.

———. 2015. *Liquidity Preference and Monetary Economics*, 154. London: Routledge.

———. 2016. On the Nature and Role of Financial Systems in Keynes's Entrepreneurial Economies. *Journal of Post Keynesian Economics* 39 (3): 287–307.

Chick, Victoria. 1991. *Macroeconomics After Keynes: A Reconsideration of the General Theory*, 374. Oxford: MIT Press Edition.

Dávila-Fernández, M.J., J.L. Oreiro, L.F. Punzo, and S. Bimonte. 2017. Capital in the Twenty First Century: Reinterpreting the Fundamental Contradiction of Capitalism. *Journal of Post Keynesian Economics* 40 (2): 168–182.

Denis, Henri. 1974. *Histoire de la Pensée Economique*, 774. Paris: Presses Universitaires de France.

Fama, E. 1988. Market Efficiency, Long Term Returns and Behavioral Finance. *Journal of Financial Economics* 49 (3): 283–306.
Friedman, M. 1974. A Theoretical Framework for Monetary Analysis. In *Milton Friedman's Monetary Framework: A Debate with His Critics*, ed. R.J. Gordon, 1–62. Chicago: University of Chicago Press.
Grossman, S.J., and J.E. Stiglitz. 1980. On the Impossibility of Informationally Efficient Markets. *The American Economic Review* 70 (3) (June 1980): 393–408.
Herscovici, A. 2013. Keynes e o conceito de capital: reflexões epistemológicas a respeito daspremissas sraffianas da Teoria Geral. *Revista de Economia Política* 33 (3) (julho–setembro): 486–504.
———. 2017. Nature and Implications of Financialization: From Quasi-Competitive Equilibrium to Speculative Dynamic. *Anais International Conference on Economic Theory and Policy*. Meiji University, Tokyo, Japan.
———. 2019. *Essays on the Historicity of Capital*. New York: Palgrave Macmillan.
Kahn, Richard. 1972. *Selected Essays on Employment ad Growth*, 72–96. Cambridge: Cambridge University Press.
Keynes, John Maynard. 1935. Treatise on Probabilities. In *Collected Writtings of J.M. Keynes, Vol. VIII*, 513 p. London, Mac Millan and Cambridge University Press.
———. 2009 [1936]. *The General Theory of Employment, Interest and Money*. New York: Classic Books America.
Malkiel, B.G. 2003. The Efficient Market Hypothesis and Its Critics. *Journal of Economic Perspectives* 17 (1): 59–82.
Orléan, André. 2011. *L'empire de la valeur. Refonder l'Économie*, 339 p. Paris: Éditions du Seuil
Pasinetti, Luigi L. 1997. The Marginal Efficiency of Investment. In *A "Second Edition" of the General Theory*, vol. 1, ed. G.C. Harcourt and P.A. Riach, 185–197. London: Rouledge.
Petri, Fabio. 1998. The "Sraffian" Critique of Neoclassical Economics: Some Recent Developments. *Revista Da Sociedade Brasileira De Economia Política* 3: 5–44.
Solow, R.M. 1956. A Contribution to the Theory of Economic Growth. *Quartely Journal of Economics* 70: 65–94.
Tirole, J. 2016. *Economie du bien commun*, 629 p. Paris: PUF.
Vercelli, Allessandro. 1991. *Methodological Foundations of Macroeconomics: Keynes and Lucas*, 269 p. Cambridge: Cambridge Universitry Press.

CHAPTER 8

Beyond Episteme: The Concept of Order

In this chapter, I carry out the following synthesis. It is about answering the following question: to what extent can these three controversies be explained from the analysis made by Foucault? After having identified the explanatory limits of the concept of episteme, I propose to substitute the concept of episteme for the concept of order.

i. Initially, I will show why, theoretically and empirically, microeconomic rationality is unable to ensure the macroeconomic and macro-social regulation of the collectivity. In addition to exercising individual rationality, the different strands of liberalism need to invoke a superior order to justify the social efficiency of the competitive market: the invisible hand, the first welfare theorem, the spontaneous order of the market, are mechanisms that belong to an order different from individual rationality and that emphasize its limits: such rationality is, in essence, limited, by the fact that agents cannot assess all the aggregate effects resulting from their individual decisions.

The economic order is, by nature, an emergent property: it manifests itself only at the aggregate level. The paradox is as follows: if, on the one hand, capitalist societies are characterized by individualism (Dumont 1985), they necessarily contain holistic elements.

A. Herscovici, *Value, Historicity, and Economic Epistemology*,
https://doi.org/10.1007/978-3-031-21157-7_8

ii. I propose to analyze the different economic currents from the nature of the orders they use, implicitly or explicitly, and the way they articulate the micro and macroeconomic levels. While "liberal" orders, based on different modus operandi, attribute to the microeconomic competitive order the ability to act as the regulator of society, the different heterodoxies, on the contrary, refute the self-regulatory character of the competitive market, and emphasize the necessity to implement other regulatory variables: state, institutions, etc.

In fact, each school of thought is characterized by specific combinations that make it possible to articulate, and reconcile, individual rationality and global regulation of the collectivity. The welfare economics, based on the works of Pigou, or the Social Choice school, in line with the works of Arrow and Sen, represent different modes of articulation between individual rationalities and collective rationality.

iii. Finally, the concept of order seems to me more adequate than the concept of episteme to study the long-term evolutions of Economic Science, and this for the following reasons:

   a. Contrary to the concept of episteme, the concept of order, in its historical and "concrete" dimension, is a hybrid concept. In Adam Smith's works, for example, we find simultaneously elements that come from the divine order, proper to the preclassical episteme, from the natural order proper to the classical episteme, and from modernity, from the elements linked to individualism. In the same way, Neoclassical Economics implicitly uses elements linked to the classical order (the natural and ahistorical character of capital, for example), to preclassical order and to modernity, based on the microeconomic foundations linked to methodological individualism.
   b. the endogenous forces that explain long-term evolutions are the product of such heterogeneity.

The concept of order thus defined is broader than the concept of episteme: each period is the product of heterogeneous components,[1] this heterogeneity being the engine of evolutions. It is not possible to affirm,

[1] Dow (2020, p. 13) speaks in theoretical fragmentation progress.

as Foucault does, that each epoch is characterized by a single episteme; similarly, it is not possible to characterize an author, or a school of thought, from a single episteme and a single order.

In this sense, the concept of order makes it possible to broaden Foucault's analysis, with regard to Economic Science, and notably explains the dynamics inherent to the long-term evolution of this Science.

Individualism, Individual Rationality Limits and the Concept of Order

The Modernity Paradoxes

The Holistic Dimension

The paradox of modernity, which constitutes the foundations of capitalist societies, can be stated as follows: on the one hand, the individual, in its economic, political and ideological dimensions, constitutes a fundamental component. Individual economic, political and religious freedoms are attributes of the individual and must be preserved. The individual is endowed with a rationality which determines his different choices; in the more specific case of Economics, this rationality is substantive. But, on the other hand, the existence of an order is incompatible with the full and unlimited exercise of (a) individual freedom and (b) substantive rationality.

Regarding individual freedom, it must be limited in such a way that the conditions of reproduction of that collectivity are ensured: Adam Smith (1776), for example, recognizes the necessity to maintain the general conditions that allow the reproduction of capitalist society: legitimation and respect for private property, based on the establishment of legal and state structures. Economic freedom can only be effective once these general conditions are realized.

As far as economic rationality is concerned, its limits as regulation variables appear soon. The existence of externalities, whether negative or positive, is incompatible with the exercise of substantive rationality. By nature, the existence of externalities implies that the individual agent, when making decisions, does not evaluate all the implications linked to those decisions.

Rational calculation is the result "(…) of a rigorous evaluation of prospective costs and benefits (…)" (Hirschman 1986, p. 8). The rational individual can evaluate, ex ante, all linked effects of his choices.

Concretely, this individual can only assess individual costs, but he does not know the social cost or social benefit. Consequently, his rationality is intrinsically limited. Public Economics, based on the seminal works of Pigou, Musgrave and Samuelson, studies this type of situation.

Coase (1960) showed that all economic activity (these results can extend to other areas) consists of producing externalities that, for certain social groups, are negative; In the sixteenth century, Montaigne already formulated a similar conclusion: "The profit of one is the loss of the other" (1588, p. 89). The existence of an order translates into the fact that it sets limits regarding these negative externalities. These limits vary in space and time and are the product of certain collective choices[2]: in this sense, the collective choices necessary for the survival of the collectivity, by nature, cannot be exempt from ethical and moral values (Bova 2021). *There is no neutrality of these choices: any type of individual rationality is bounded, and the collective choices translate the moral and ethical values that characterize a specific order.*

The following example, chosen by Bova (2021), highlights this characteristic: let us suppose that, in a prison, certain prisoners are sentenced to death; let us also assume that, driven by morbid and/or sadistic instincts, certain people would pay to kill these prisoners. From the point of view of a neutral, purely instrumental rationality, devoid of any moral value, the prison administration would have to adopt this solution: the utility of those who enjoy killing would increase without decreasing the utility of prisoners who, in any case, will die. Nevertheless, from a moral point of view, such collective decision is unacceptable and violates the inalienable rights of the individual, rights that constitute the foundations of modern democracies. In the concentration camps, the Nazi regime applied an instrumental rationality to its extermination activities, which reveals the values that this system wanted to impose on society.

Consequently, the regulation of the collectivity cannot be based solely on the individual rationalities of its members: the existence of a certain order is necessary to implement this regulation. Certain mechanisms will act to limit individual choices. *Any human collectivity is thus characterized by a holistic dimension, that is, by the fact that it imposes limits on the exercise of individual rationalities.*

[2] For example, the definition of pollution rights, or the ban on smoking in public places.

Beyond Episteme Concept

With regard to Economics, the analyses of different schools of thought, and the nature of the ruptures between these different currents, are directly related to the nature of the economic order, that is, to the different conceptions of that order. For example, contrary to what certain economists have stated (Marshall, Blaug), it is not possible to see in Ricardo the precursor of marginalist economics: the nature of the Ricardian order is different from the standard neoclassical conception: (a) Macroeconomic mechanisms are not limited to its own microeconomic fundamentals and (b) the nature of the macroeconomic order is also entirely different.

Unlike Foucault's analysis, my problematic is directly related to the differences that exist, implicitly or explicitly, in the characteristics that different schools of thought attribute to the economic order. Modernity, if it incorporates individual action, does not eliminate the concept of order, as defined in the preclassical and classical episteme. On the other hand, the economic order is not limited to an instrumental rationality, but incorporates certain moral and ethical values; *this economic order "imports" components that come from the orders proper to previous epistemes, that is, to the divine or natural order.*

The hybrid character of a concrete order is justified from a sociological analysis of the production field (in the sense defined by Bourdieu) of Economic Science:

i. A field of production is a space of legitimacy that evolves and changes over time; it is characterized by a temporality, temporality that results from changes in the positions of power within the field (Herscovici 1994). Each episteme corresponds to a certain field of production, that is, to a certain symbolic power structure.
ii. Each episteme, as defined by Foucault, is characterized by the coexistence of different schools of thought, each represented by different combinations of various orders, and by a hierarchy between these different schools. From the sociological perspective developed by Bourdieu, it is possible to affirm that, within the field of academic production, different schools of thought coexist and present incompatible methodologies and results, with a different degree of legitimacy. Contrary to Foucault's analysis, this highlights the epistemological non-homogeneity of episteme, that is, its intrinsically hybrid character.

Due to the intrinsic historicity of this social space, the shifts in power relations, within the field of production of Economic Science, highlight the hybrid character of episteme, and allow the explanation of long-term evolutions, that is, the shift from an order to another. This analysis makes it possible to "flexibilize" the concept of episteme, and explains the endogenous mechanisms that work in regard to long-term evolutions.

Again, it is necessary to establish a parallel between the cultural field and the scientific field: the temporality of the cultural field (Idem) is explained by the struggle between different artistic schools to reach a dominant position in the field; the same mechanism works in the scientific field.

Finally, with regard to Economic Science, due to the hidden interests behind the different theories, I could invoke the Gramscian concept of the organic intellectual: if, for example, the Physiocracy represented the interests of rural producers, the Ricardian economy represented, in part, the interests of the nineteenth-century industrial bourgeoisie.

The Different Orders

In Economics, two theses coexist: the one that, for different reasons, states that the market is able to implement the social order, and the one that shows, on the contrary, that the role of institutions is a fundamental element to implement this social order: in a first approximation, the first can be described as "liberal," and the second as *institutionalist*.

The liberal order, whether in the neoclassical or Hayekian version, is an *ex ante order*: the mechanisms that, from an initial position of disequilibrium, allow explaining how this order is carried out, are voluntarily ignored. The system spontaneously carries out this order: a Deus ex machina. This applies both to General Equilibrium, in conditions of CPP, and to the spontaneous order of the Hayekian market.

On the contrary, the institutional order is carried out ex post: as institutions correspond to "social pacts" that allow for the temporary conciliation of antagonistic interests (Boyer 1987), it is through the mediation of these institutions that order is being achieved. *Institutions constitute the tools from which a given order is implemented*: even the liberal order presupposes a series of institutions to exist concretely, notably the "general conditions" evoked by Smith. On the other hand, these institutions are not universal but intrinsically historical.

Neoclassical Economics intends to carry out a "neutral" analysis, as it does not incorporate the historical dimension linked to institutions (Tsoulfidis 2017, p. 4); the different heterodoxies, on the contrary, endogenize institutions, in their historical and social dimensions: as the individual is not conceived as given, that is, as "immutable," or as his preferences are not exogenous, historicity is reintroduced into the analysis. It is the reason (a) why the old institutionalism is intrinsically historicist and (b) why evolution and change are explained from endogenous variables (Hodgson 1988, p. 171).

The "Liberal" Order

The liberal order uses the implicit hypothesis according to which the market system generates positive externalities. The tradition, from Mandeville (1732) to Smith (1776) and Hayek (1945), adopts this hypothesis: private vices are metamorphosed into public virtues, the individual interest works for the general interest, the increase of an agent's utility does not harm other agents, or the spontaneous order of the market provides all the necessary information to agents operating in the market.

This order, since it generates positive externalities, or, at least, does not gernerate negative externalities, allows for making individual and collective interests compatible. Nevertheless, the existence of an order is incompatible with the implementation of a substantive individual rationality. In the Wealth of Nations, Smith defines the natural rate of profit, which constitutes one of the components of the natural price, as "(…) profit that [the capitalist] can reasonably expect to obtain from the sale of his products" (Smith 1776, vol. I, p. 160). Here, profit is not the product of maximizing a microeconomic function, but simply corresponds to an average judged satisfactory. According to Marx, in the same sector, individual profit rates can be different (Herscovici 2002).

Hayek recognizes that the individual agent is unable to process the information available to maximize its utility or profit functions: "(…) prices act to coordinate the separate action of different people in the same way as subjective values help the individual to coordinate part of his plant" (Hayek 1945, p. 526) in such a way that an efficient allocation of resources is carried out. Nevertheless, he refutes the idea of maximization since it was elaborated by marginalist economics. An independent mechanism, which translates into a "superior" order, compensates for the failures that result from the limits of individual rationality[3]: the "spontaneous order of the market".

Pareto's optimum is based on a similar logic, but on another *modus operandi*: beyond the theoretical limits that characterize it (Sen 1982), it reconciles private and collective interests, while increasing the utility of certain agents without decreasing the utility of others: *the first welfare theorem* formally demonstrates that any general equilibrium carried out in a situation of pure and perfect competition corresponds to a Pareto optimum. Thus, in the absence of externalities, the market perfectly aggregates individual preferences.

More precisely, within the scope of the neoclassical matrix, the Pareto optimum is characterized by the absence of externality: the action of the agent that increases his utility does not translate into a decrease in the utility of other agents: *the microeconomic rationaliy is conceived as a mechanism that can provide a perfect coordination, and that does not produce negative externalities*:

i. this approach is incompatible with Coase's (1960) and with Commons'conception: "Every private business or job has, in fact, the qualities of both public utility and public disutility, depending on the current economic and human valuations" (Commons 1924, p. 326).
ii. In this particular case, the activities developed in these markets do not generate (negative or positive) externalities, which means that this analysis refutes the existence of any social cost generated by the different economic activities. This is incompatible with Pigouvian Economics or Social Choice theories.

We can observe that this concept of order does not allow explaining the problem of the transition from the micro to the macro: order is a *Deus ex machina* that coordinates a set of individual decisions, but the concrete modalities which make this coordination act are unexplained:

[3] The paradox is this: the concept of order can be described as Hegelian, insofar as it manages to impose a rationality that is not the simple sum of individual rationalities. This rationality is *an emergent property*.

a. Neoclassical Economics does not explain how, from an initial situation of disequilibrium, the system returns to equilibrium (Arrow 1986).
b. Hayek invokes the spontaneous order of the market without specifying the concrete modalities that make this coordination possible.

The nature of the economic order is comparable to the natural and/or divine order that prevailed in epistemes prior to modernity (Foucault 1966): a mechanism that acts independently of individual wills and ensures the global regulation of the collectivity. Regarding the Smithian concept of invisible hand, Veblen states that "The Creator has established the natural order to serve the ends of human welfare; and he has very nicely adjusted the efficient causes comprised in the natural order, including human aims and motives, to this work" (1899, p. 17); for this reason, he qualifies the methodology employed by Smith as animistic (idem, p. 21).

In a different way, both the Austrian school and Adam Smith, or standard Neoclassical Economics, conceive of the economic system as a self-organizing system that generates spontaneous order: "This literature on self-organization and spontaneous orders provides essential insight that institutions and other social phenomena can arise in an unconceived way through structured interactions between agents. (…) This literature shows that a social order can arise that is not itself an intention or property of any individual or group of individuals" (Hodgson 2006, p. 13).

The "Institutional" Order

Other theoretical approaches consider that the market is unable to coordinate individual decisions, and that agents do not have the operational conditions to exercise substantive rationality: on the contrary, institutions are defined as "(…) a socially constructed invariant- or emergent property- (…)" (Hodgson 1988, p. 189).

- In Keynesian Economics, due to the strong uncertainty that characterizes the economic universe, and the refutation of the ergodicity hypothesis (Davidson 1996), equating the marginal cost of capital with its effective marginal productivity is impossible; consequently, maximizing is not the point. As stated by Keynes, the expectations of entrepreneurs will fail (1936).

- Regarding the tendency of the rate of profit to fall, Marx states that the necessary devalorization of part of social capital, to temporarily maintain the rate of profit, translates into a struggle between different individual capitalists (1859, Livre III, p. 269): the invisible hand has failed one more time, and regulation operated by the market game implies a partial destruction of part of social capital (Idem).
- In Keynes' General Theory, the equilibrium represented by the Effective Demand point is an equilibrium without full employment, which constitutes a contradiction, in the terms used by Neoclassical Economics. On the other hand, Harrodian instability perfectly illustrates the market's own coordination failures (Herscovici 2006).
- The analyses by Grossman and Stiglitz (1980), based on the refutation of the homogeneity postulate and the existence of information asymmetries, highlight the paradox of the efficient market hypothesis: the stability of the competitive equilibrium is explained by positive externalities produced by the informed agents in favor of the uninformed agents. Nevertheless, the existence of the speculative cycle shows that (a) equilibrium is by nature unstable and (b) the externalities produced explain the fact that the gain of informed agents is made to the detriment of uninformed agents, which fails the conditions of Paretian optimality (Herscovici 2019).

Such analyses demonstrate that the substantive microeconomic rationality is incompatible with the maximization of social welfare: the emergence and development of free riding behaviors, do not allow the Pareto optimum conditions to be verified, and instituitions are necessary to regulate such activities.

This type of analysis leads to the following conclusions: (a) the rationality of the individual agents is, by nature, limited, since the economic universe is characterized by strong uncertainty (Keynes and Stiglitz); (b) the market does not allow aggregating individual decisions and fails to make them compatible with social well-being, which makes the intervention of institutions necessary to coordinate the set of these activities.

Besides being by nature limited, microeconomic rationalities are unable to implement macroeconomic and social regulation, in the sense of coordinating a multitude of individual and highly diversified performances:

"(…) institutionalism points to the concept of socioeconomic order, arising upon variety at the micro-level" (Hodgson 1988, p. 171).

Welfare Economics and Social Cost

Welfare Economics: Varian, Pindyck and Rubinfeld's Model

The Problem of Social Costs

Welfare Economics approach justifies individual rationality limits in regard to a divergence between individual and social costs; such limits are defined by private property rights system. *Social rules as property rights, for example, may be conceived as a public good whose consumption is mandatory* for all members of the collectivity; such public good will produce positive externalities for some social groups, and negative ones for others; they limit the individual choices. The own divergences between individual and collective choices proof that individual rationality cannot act as a social regulatory variable; a *coercion mechanism* is necessary to reestablish the optimality conditions, and, from the liberal perspective, such coercion will be implemented in the most efficient way by the private negotiation, by the private property rights system, and by the market. At this respect, the liberal solution to solve the quality problem in some markets implies creating certification markets, to certify the goods and services quality (Herscovic 2017).

On the other hand, *Welfare Economics remains a normative analysis*: social choices will be made to reestablish the competitive conditions, i.e., the equalization between marginal productivity and marginal cost.[4] The self-enforcement hypothesis is verified: the implementation of such rules does not translate into transaction costs.

Varian's analysis (2005) is designed from the following example: in a field where the cattle graze, he will compare two situations: in the first one, the access to the field is free for all members of the community; and, in the second one, the field access is regulated from a private Property Rights System. Hardin's tragedy of commons (1968, p. 1244) is interpreted in the following way: each producer will increase the number of

[4] In the case of a natural monopole, the monopolistic firm will receive a public subside to equalize marginal cost and price.

cows to maximize their profit and verify such relation:

$$\max c/f(c) - a.c \tag{8.1}$$

a as the unitary cow price, f (c) as the value of the milk produced by *c* cows and f(c)/c as the average value of milk produced.

Each producer will increase the number of cows grazing in the field until equalizing marginal product with the last cow purchased: "(....) it will be profitable to graze a cow as long as the output generated by the cow is greater than the cost of a cow" (Varian 2005, p. 642):

$$MP(c) = a \tag{8.2}$$

(MP as marginal product).

Equation 8.2 may be expressed by:

$$f(c) - ac = 0 \tag{8.3}$$

equivalent to:

$$f(c)/c = a \tag{8.4}$$

While average product is superior to *a*, rational agent will increase the number of cows grazing in the field until verifying (8.3) and (8.4); microeconomic rationality implies verifying (8.4) (Idem, p. 643). However, such increase will diminish the average milk production and *generate a negative externality concerning the whole producers*. As shown in Fig. 8.1, the commons system implies using a higher number of cows (c_2) than the one that corresponds to the social optimum (c_1).

Such mechanism is explicit in Fig. 8.1: the cows owners do not pay for the cows grazing in the field, because access is free. But c_2 is higher than the number which corresponds to the social optimum.

Pindyck and Rubinfeld's analysis is directly elaborated in terms of social cost. At the equilibrium position, c_1 in the Fig. 8.2, *the marginal social cost is equal to the marginal product*: such social optimum is typical of a competitive situation (Baumol 1969, p. 126): externalities are totally endogenized by the agents. Beside the private costs, the costs related to the decrease in productivity are embedded in the marginal social cost (Pindyck and Rubinfeld 1995, p. 646).

In the presence of commons (c_2 in the Fig. 8.2), the marginal social cost is higher than the marginal product, which translates into a negative

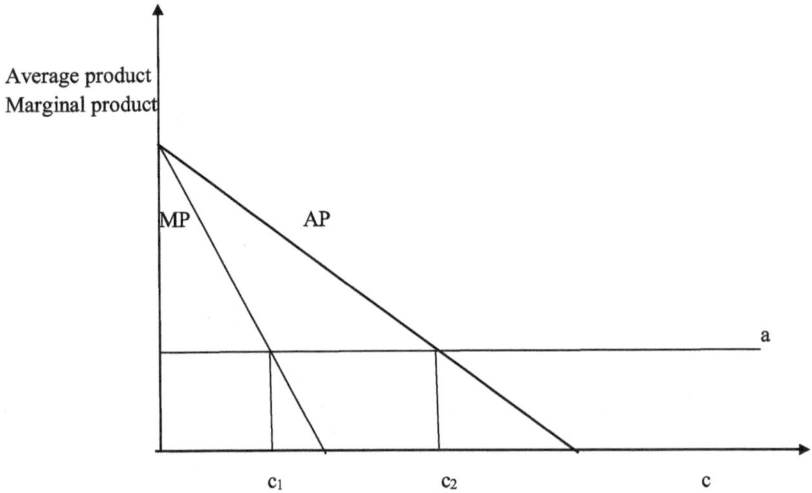

Fig. 8.1 Varian's analysis (AP: average product; MP: marginal product)

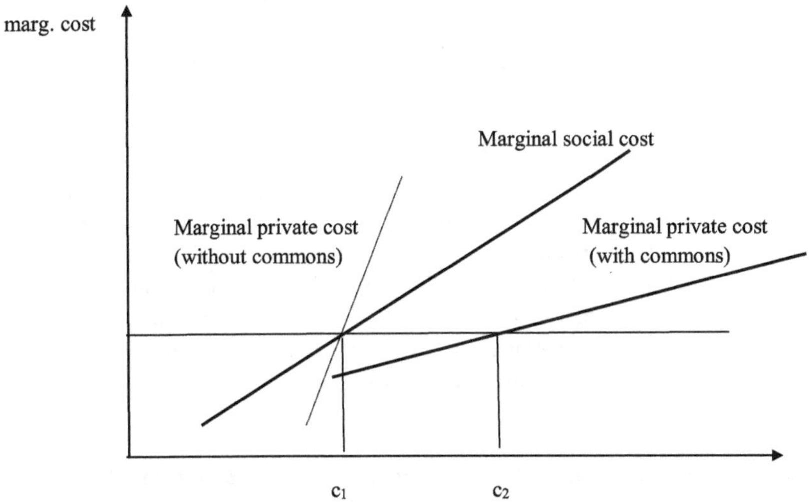

Fig. 8.2 Pindyck and Rubinfeld's analysis

externality and corresponds to a suboptimal equilibrium. This situation highlights the divergence between private interests and social welfare.

If the field is a common good, beyond some critical value, in terms of cows grazing, such common good will deteriorate; such mechanism implies in *a diminution in the average production of milk*. At this respect, Varian (2005, p. 643) considers that supply structure is competitive and that producers are price takers: in the same way that in the Cobweb theory, the different producers do not evaluate the implications of their action on the aggregate level.

The main results of this analysis are the following:

i. When the field is a private property, the owner will limit the number of cows grazing, insomuch to preserve the social optimum conditions and to equalize marginal social cost and marginal product. The number of cows will verify Eq. (8.1).
ii. If, on the contrary, there is free access to the field, the tragedy of commons will translate into the divergence between private rationality and social welfare: *the common good deterioration is explained by the fact that the marginal social costs are higher than the private marginal costs. Consequently, the average product tends to be zero* (Ibid.).

The solution is to limit the field access modalities: such limitation may be implemented by the privatization or by other coercion mechanisms. The privatization, as the New Law and Economics argues, allows avoiding the super-production and realizing an efficient resource allocation. We can note that this analysis allows formulating the same results of Stigler (1966), regarding the "Coase's Theorem": from the nil transaction costs hypothesis, private negotiation is the most efficient social mechanism to realize the allocation of scarce resources.

Some Limits

Pindyck, Rubinfeld and Varian argue that a private system of Property Rights (PR) is socially efficient as it restores the competitive conditions. Two types of limits appear: those related to the capacity of Pure and Perfect Competition to do it, and those related with the choice of such coercion system.

Are the Walrasian competition and the Pareto Optimum the norms to be adopted to design the analysis? Here, we do not want to criticize such *démarche*, but to highlight the problems of internal coherence. As Baumol affirms (1969, p. 126):

> "(....) the validity of the use of the competitive criterion as a norm becomes doubtful (....) for as we have seen, a competitive price for one commodity can be considered desirable in our present argument only if the price of every other commodity is competitive."

The economic specificities of public goods (or of commons) do not allow verifying the competitive conditions: no rivalry, no exclusion, decreasing marginal costs and increasing scale returns. As the price competitive system fails in regard to the market coordination, the choice of alternative mechanism is a fundamental issue: "consumers' wants will not guide production (...)" (Ibid., p. 133). In other words, from an intertemporal choice perspective, the competitive system does not work and leads to the exhaustion of the common good (Ibid., p. 132). At this respect, to avoid the stock exhaustion, Hardin (1968) affirms that (a) it is necessary to find a social arrangement to implement a coercion mechanism and (b) that such arrangement is not an optimal one: "Injustice is preferable to total ruin" (Idem).

For the neoclassical perspective, coercion only can be implemented from privatization. Although neoclassical authors admit other possibilities,[5] they only study the modalities related to privatization. Such choice may be justified by the following reasons: (a) transaction costs (TC) related to other modalities would be higher (Varian 2005, p. 644) (b) PR may be totally defined. At this respect, Varian speaks about "well-defined property rights in the good involving the externality" (Idem, p. 630). Under such hypothesis, private regulation may turn endogenous all externalities with nil or low TC.

Varian does not consider the existence of positive TC. On one hand, it is possible to consider that the implementation of the PR system implies positive TC. At this respect, Barzel (1997, p. 4 e 5) defines TC as "(...) the costs associated with the transfer, capture and protection of rights." Consequently, we can deduce that, in Varian's analysis, *nil TC corresponds*

[5] Varian affirms that "Of course, private property is not the only social institution that can encourage efficient use of resources" (op. cit., p. 644).

to the self-enforcement hypothesis: the PR system is totally efficient and "free."

On the other hand, as PR are well-defined, agents may negotiate such rights and achieve a Pareto optimum (Varian, op. cit., p. 630). This private negotiation reintroduces the market logic (the "missing market"): negative externalities are negotiated and totally endogenized.

These externalities are essentially *supply externalities*: the components related to demand are ignored. *We can refute this primacy of supply*: as shown by the Ricardian theory of differential rent, demand plays a fundamental role in the dynamics. It does not adapt passively to the supply variations but, at the contrary, it determines the global dynamics. The exogenous variations of the demand determine the production conditions and the costs increase.

In fact, three conditions are necessary and sufficient to verify and to generalize the neoclassical results: the absence of positive TC, i.e., the self-enforcement hypothesis, and the primacy of supply.

The results of the economic analyses of commons must be differentiated in regard to the economic characteristics of the goods. In Varian, Pindyck and Rubinfeld's analysis, the stock available is constituted by standard goods, by nature divisible and verifying the neoclassical hypothesis, i.e., decreasing marginal utility, law of decreasing marginal productivity and constant returns of scale. The self-enforcement hypothesis is systematically verified, the PR system is efficient and there is no uncertainty in regard to the quality. This last proposition implies verifying the homogeneity postulate. In such universe, the TC are nil. Efficient PR system allows implementing a negotiation which maximizes the social utility: in his interpretation of Coase's results (The "Coase's Theorem"), Stigler (1966) adopts these hypotheses.

When the goods are complex, the problem is different: complexity is not necessarily related to the technological or physical complexity, but to the institutional choices that regulate their production and social modalities of appropriation.[6] Such complexity is directly linked to the presence of externalities, and indivisibilities: when there is no congestion effect, contrary to the tragedy of commons, the increase in production or demand does not translate into a decrease in stock; when the production

[6] For example, the river navigation in the Middle Age (Heller and Eisenberg 1998), or the lighthouse (Coase 1988).

Table 8.1 Ricardo's theory of differential rent

t_1: $p_{1.1}$ as the profit in the land of best quality in period 1(1)
t_2: we need exploring land of inferior quality (2)
On the land of quality 2, the profit is $p_{2.2}$, inferior to $p_{1.1}$, and a rent (R_{12}) appears on lands of quality 1
$p_{2.2} = p_{1.1} - R_{12}$
t_3: we need exploring land of quality 3
$p_{2.3} = p_{2.2} - R_{2.3} = p_{1.1} - R_{1.3} = p_{\cdot 3.3}$
and so on

is cumulative, it translates into an increase in production, i.e., an increase in the stock level.[7]

When the assets are specific, Williamson affirms that they are characterized by "(…) weak property rights (especially intellectual property rights), and undisclosed quality (…)" (2002, p. 603). In such case, the *self-enforcement hypothesis is not verified*: contracts are incomplete and transaction costs are positive.

Ricardo's Theory of Differential Rent: An Other Order

As far as the economic role of PR is concerned, we must establish a parallel with Ricardo's analysis, regarding the exhaustion of the common stock. According to Ricardo, the increase in corn demand will turn the land of best quality scarce: (a) a differential rent appears on the lands of best quality, and (b) the average rate of profit decreases as the rent of the land owners increases (Table 8.1).

In Fig. 8.3, two mechanisms are working simultaneously:

i. The corn value is determined by the labor quantity necessary on the land of worst quality, the one whose access is free. As production increases, the price increases, as shown in Fig. 8.3.
ii. While the marginal social cost is smaller than the marginal private cost, it is socially profitable to increase the production until q_2. When the production is higher than q_2, the situation is suboptimal: the marginal social cost becomes higher than the private marginal cost.

[7] For example, the peer-to-peer networks, or some scientific or didactic platforms as Wikipedia.

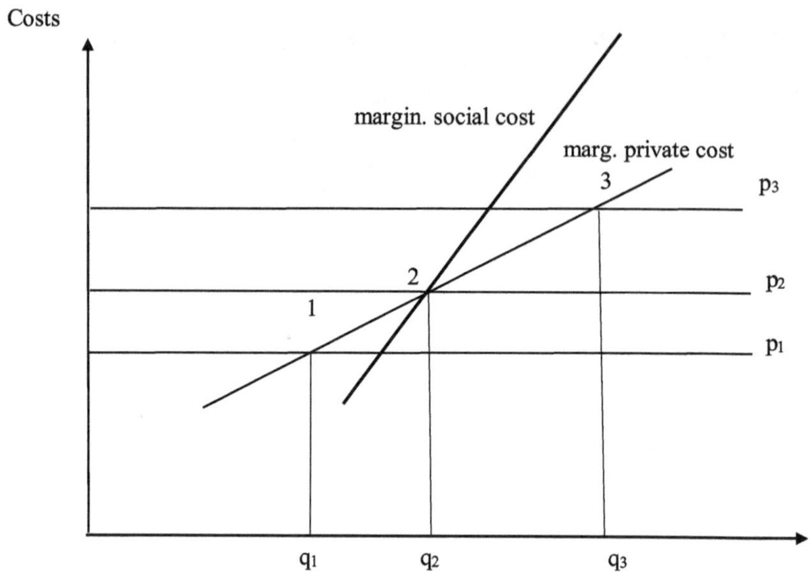

Fig. 8.3 Ricardian differential rent and social optimum

From such approach, the land rent may be conceived as a negative externality: the land rent is totally unproductive and cannot be defined as a component of value.[8] The land rent is a social cost as the corn price is higher and the average productivity lower. Points 1, 2 and 3 in Fig. 8.3 represent situations in which individual profit is maximized: the private marginal costs are equal to the private marginal product. Beyond q_2, the situation is the one characterized by the tragedy of commons, because marginal social cost is higher than the private one.

Notwithstanding, the economic mechanisms highlighted by Ricardo are different from those pointed by the Neoclassical School: according to the former, *the private PR system does not allow solving this problem.* In other words, private property will not diminish the negative externalities. On the contrary, *private property is the concrete manifestation of such negative externalities.*

[8] This represents Ricardo's main opposition to Smith.

The main differences between Ricardo's analysis and the neoclassical one are the following:

i. For Ricardo, demand increase is an *exogenous variable and the consequence of general development* (1821, p. 70). On the other hand, for Varian, the number of cows is an endogenous variable which can be regulated. It is the reason why private property is a mechanism for maintaining such quantity to its equilibrium level. While, in the Ricardian system, demand is the determining variable and supply the determined variable, the causal relationship is inverted in neoclassical analysis: such opposition reveals the incompatibilities between a demand side and supply side approaches.
ii. In Ricardo's analysis, corn price increase is explained by demand and production increase; in Varian's analysis, the cow unitary price is constant. *It is surprising that Varian does not consider the increasing marginal costs law.*

The Social Choice

Social Choice theories will provide another explanation regarding the divergences between private interests and social welfare, and thus underscore the fact that collective choices, by nature, embody the moral, social and political values that characterize the collectivity. analyzed. It is an order of a different nature from the one used by Neoclassical Economics.

The Condorcet's Paradox

This paradox (Condorcet 1785) highlights the methodological gap between the individual level and the aggregate one: collective choice cannot reflect all individual choices. Let's assume a voting system in which three individuals must choose between three candidates, from an ordinal approach. The order relationships are as follows:

Individual 1: $A > B > C$ (1)
Individual 2: $B > C > A$ (2)
Individual 3: $C > A > B$ (3)
(1) and (3) $\Rightarrow A > B$
(1) and (2) $\Rightarrow B > C$

Transitivity implies that A > C. However, at the global level, in the system as a whole, C will be chosen, since C is preferred twice to A. The choice made at the system level does not correspond to the simple sum of the individual choices; the non-transitivity of individual choices underscores the fact that collective choice does not reflect individual choices.

An order exists at the aggregate level. This order has its own mechanisms that are not the simple manifestation of individual mechanisms. This gap between the micro and the macro levels highlights the limits of rationality exercised by the individual agent; if, at best, he can assess the private costs and benefits linked to his choices, he cannot assess the social costs and benefits.

The welfare economics elaborated from Pigou's work highlights the need for public intervention when divergences between private and public costs appear. Nevertheless, defining the criteria from which these public interventions will be determined, with regard to the allocation and amount of resources, is necessary: the problem of financing production and allocation of public goods is being placed. *The criterion chosen depends on the collective values that characterize the collectivity, and cannot be defined independently of such criterion.*

Arrow's Impossibility Theorem

Arrow (1951) studied this problem from the following example: let's suppose that three individuals (1, 2 and 3) must establish an order relationship between four candidates (x, y, z and w). Let's also assume that each of these individuals assigns, respectively, the weight 4 to the first choice, the weight 3 to the second, the weight 2 to the third and the weight 1 to the fourth. (In this case, the utility is cardinal.)

Let's assume the choices are made as follows:

- Individuals 1 and 2 established the following order relationship: $x > y > z > w$.
- Individual 3, the following relationship: $z > w > x > y$.

The total utility that comes from individuals (1) and (2) can be represented by the following relationship:

$$x = 8 > y = 6 > z = 4 > w = 2$$

The utility of the individual (3):

$$z = 4 > w = 3 > x = 2 > y = 1$$

At the global level, we have $x > z$: x corresponds to a total utility of 10 and z to 8.

In a second time, let's assume that y is eliminated:

(1) and (2): $x = 8 > z = 6 > w = 4$.
(3): $z = 4 > w = 3 > x = 2$.

At the global level, x and z are equivalent in terms of total utility. The problem can be formulated as follows: *collective choice depends directly on the options initially available.* In this sense, it is up to the state, and/or institutions, to determine the range of possibilities.

The Impossibility of Defining a Purely Individual and Collective Rationality

For obvious reasons, this individual choice has to be, in one way or another, bounded. Certain norms and rules have to be respected, to allow the continuity of the collectivity and its regulation:

> "Economic theory in this, as well as in some other fields, tends to suggest that people are honest only to the extent that they have some incentives for being so (…). No society would be viable without some norm and rules of conduct. Such norms are necessary for *viability* in fields where strictly economic incentives are absent and cannot be created." (Johansen 1976, apud Sen, 1982, p. 96, emphasis added)

The purely economic rationality must be limited by rules and norms, to ensure the survival and the global regulation of that collectivity. This collective choice is made from the institutions, whose performance is exercised according to the moral and ethical values adopted by the collectivity. Consequently, this necessary limitation of individual freedoms will be determined by the collective choices, as demonstrated by Arrow's impossibility theorem.

On the other hand, the concept of rationality cannot be purely instrumental: within the scope of an individualist perspective, some relational mechanisms are embedded in individual preference. The concept of commitment elaborated by Sen (1982, pp. 105–106) gives an account of this mechanism and highlights the limits of maximizing individual utility as an explanatory element of preferences. The individual's moral values can lead to consider the relationship between his individual utility and the other members' utility: "The characteristic of commitment with which I am more concerned here is the fact that it drives a wedge between personal choice and personal welfare" (Idem, p. 94). Individual utility depends on externalities produced by individual choices, *which highlight the interdependence of individuals within the collectivity*. On the other hand, sympathy and compassion are ethical and moral values embedded in the individual utility function and mark the limits of "pure" hedonic behavior.

If affirming the neutrality of individual rationality is impossible, in the same way, affirming the neutrality of collective decisions is impossible. The choice of public goods to be provided by the state, or social rules to be applied by institutions, is not defined in terms of the technical characteristics of the goods, *it is a social and ethical choice*: social since it implements solidarity mechanisms between different members, and ethical since it is linked to certain moral values, such as respect for moral and physical integrity of each member, in a democratic perspective.

Democracy, Freedom and Law

One of the fundamental elements that allow defining Democracy are the inalienable rights of Man, as defined in the Universal Declaration of Human Rights.

Civil rights are related to the individual's specificities: freedom of thought, religion and economic freedom (Bobbio et al. 1991, vol. I, p. 354). They correspond to the private sphere and are imprescriptible, from the moment the behavior of these individuals "(...) do not violate the behavior of others" (Idem). Contrary to the previous, essentially holistic orders, these characteristics are part of an individualistic society, in the sense that it is based on the recognition of the individual and his natural rights (Dumont 1985). Political rights concern freedom of political association and electoral rights; finally, the Social rights are defined by the labor, education and health rights.

Initially, with the development of capitalism, the public space, in the sense defined by Habermas (1978), had the function of protecting the private sphere from authoritarian interference by the state. It is a manifestation of the individualism that characterizes the origins of the capitalist system: "Princes give me enough if they take nothing from me, and do me well when they do not harm me: that's all I ask of them" (Montaigne 1588). To these rights, adding political rights is necessary. These two types of rights correspond to what Rawls (2009, p. 241) calls freedom of conscience for all, and what Mill (1859) and Hayek (1960) define as a protected sphere (Sen, op. cit., p. 292). Defining these two types of rights based on their autonomy in relation to political and/or economic power is equally possible (Herscovici 2021). In this phase of capitalism, the limits of state interference are being defined based on Civil Rights and Political Rights.

In a later phase, which corresponds to Fordism, Welfare-State intervention expanded. In the context of the Welfare Economics, due to the existence of externalities, the modalities of private appropriation were limited: for example, urban law aimed to limit the modalities of private appropriation of urban space to reduce the resulting negative externalities.

Finally, starting in the early 1990s, we observe the reverse movement, that is, a return to the primacy of private rights: an extension of private property rights linked to different types of intangible capital (Intellectual Property Rights, patents, trademarks) (Herscovici 2012), an essentially private negotiation of pollution rights, etc. Again, we observe the oppositions between individual rights and collective choices (Nozick 1973, apud Sen 1982, p. 305).

Regarding the problem defined, these historical evolutions clearly show that the limits of the State's decision-making power changes over time. In the initial phase of capitalism, as a legacy of the old regime, civil rights were threatened by politics, that is, by the decision that came from an autocratic power. Today, we can observe the opposite phenomenon: the civil rights of particular social group threaten social rights. The current pandemic may be analyzed in terms of these elements: movements that claim freedom of choice regarding vaccination and the absence of limitations for those who have not been vaccinated try to limit the State space and to amplify the private one with regard to Public Health.

Final Remarks

The concept of order, as I defined it, corresponds to the theoretical issues raised by Condorcet, Arrow, Sen and Rawls: there is a distortion between individual and collective choices, in the sense that the latter do not systematically "translate" the former. Each collective choice consists in imposing a collective solution on society as a whole; both options may seem autocratic. However, the solution chosen must respect the individual's fundamental rights.

Rawls (2009, p. 255) writes that: "(...) when the constitution is not threatened, there is no reason to limit the freedom of the intolerant." Nevertheless, in respect to the current pandemic, for example, the "intolerant" threaten the constitution, as shown by the recent attempted invasion of the Capitol by pro-Trump groups, in the United States.

In order to avoid diffuse and continuous violence, the Weberian State, as an instance that holds a monopoly on violence, has to limit certain individual freedoms as they threaten the political and democratic foundations of the collectivity. Certain groups, generally minority groups, intend to assume, in place of the State, these social, political and ideological functions, and impose their values on the entire community, with regard to implemented collective decisions: it is the open door to all forms of tribal violence, symbolic and physical violence, and the progressive destruction of civil rights.

References

Arrow, Kenneth J. 1951. *Social Choice and Individual Values*. New York: Wiley.

———. 1986. Rationality of Self and Others in an Economic System. *The Journal of Business* 59 (4): 385–390.

Baumol, W. 1969. *Welfare Economics and the Theory of State*. Cambridge: Harvard University Press.

Barzel, Yoram. 1997. *Economic Analysis of Property Rights*. Cambridge University Press.

Bobbio, Norberto, Nicola Matteuci, and Gianfranco Pasquino . 1991. *Dicionário de Política*, Vol. I. Brasília: Editora da UnB.

Bova, D.M. 2021. About the Morality of Economic Policies Principles. *Academia Letters*, Article 2124. https://doi.org/10.20935/AL2124ur.

Boyer, Robert. 1987. *La Théorie de la régulation: une analyse critique*. Paris: La Découverte.

Coase, R.H. 1960. The Problem of Social Cost. *Journal of Law and Economics* 3: 1–44.

———. 1988. *The Firm, the Market and the Law*. University of Chicago Press.

Commons, J. 1924. *Legal Foundations of Capitalism*. New York: The Macmillan Company.

Condorcet, Monsieur le Marquis de. 1785. *Essai sur l'application de l'analyse à la probabilité des décisions rendues à la pluralité des voix*. Paris: Imprimerie Royale.

Davidson, Paul. 1996. Reality and Economic Theory. *Journal of Post Keynesian Economics* 18 (4): 479–508.

Dow, Sheila. 2020. *Economic Methodology, the Philosophy of Economics and the Economy: Another Turn?* Division of Economics, Stirling Management School, University of Stirling, Stirling FK9 4LA, UK.

Dumont, Louis. 1985. *Homo aequalis. Genèse et épanouissement de l'idéologie économique*, NRF. Paris: Editions Gallimard.

Foucault, Michel. 1966. *Les mots et les choses*. Paris: Tel Galimard.

Grossman, S.J., and J.E. Stiglitz. 1980. On the Impossibility of Informationally Efficient Markets. *The American Economic Review* 70 (3) (June): 393–408.

Habermas, Jürgen. 1978. *L'espace public. Archéologie de La publicité comme dimension constitutive de la société bourgeoise*. Paris: Editions Payot.

Hardin, Garret. 1968. The Tragedy of the Commons. *Science* 162: 1243–1248.

Hayek, Friedrich von. 1945. The Use of Knowledge in Society. *The American Economic Review* 35 (4): 519–530.

———. 1960. *The Constitution of Liberty*. Chicago: University of Chicago Press.

Heller, M., and Eisenberg, R. 1998. Can Patent Deter Innovation? The Anticommons Tragedy in Biomedical Research. *Science* 29: 698–701.

Herscovici, Alain. 1994. *Économie de la Culture et de la Communication*. Paris: L´Harmattan.

———. 2002. *Dinâmica Macroeconômica: uma interpretação a partir de Marx e de Keynes*. São Paulo: EDUC/EDUFES.

———. 2006. O modelo de Harrod: Natureza das expectativas de longo prazo, instabilidade e não linearidade. *Economia e Sociedade* 15 (1): 29–55.

———. 2012. Informação, conhecimento e Direitos de Propriedade Intelectual: os limites dos mecanismos de mercado e das modalidades de negociação privada. A contribuição de Williamson à análise dos Direitos de Propriedade Intelectual. *Economia e Sociedade* 21 (3): 667–694.

———. 2017. Assimetrias da Informação, qualidade e mercados da certificação: A necessidade de uma intervenção institucional. *Revista De Economia Contemporânea* 21 (3): 1–18.

———. 2019. *Essays on the Historicity of Capital*. New York: Palgrave.

———. 2021. Big Data, rastreabilidade e assimetrias de informação: Opacidade, ingerência e democracia. *Revista Nova Economia* 31 (3): 979–1008.

Hirschman, Albert. 1986. *Vers une économie politique élargie*. Paris: Les Éditions de Minuit.

Hodgson, Geoffrey M. 1988. The Approach of Institutional Economics. *Journal of Economic Literature* 36 (1): 166–192.

———. 2006. What Are Institutions? *Journal of Economic Issues* 40 (1): 1–25.

Keynes, John Maynard. 2009 (Original 1936). *The General Theory of Employment, Interest and Money*. New York: Classic Books America.

Mandeville, Bernard. 1988 [1732]. *The Fable of the Bees or Private Vices, Public Benefits*, Vol. 1. Indianapolis: Liberty Fund.

Marx, Karl. 1972 [1859]. *Contribution à la critique de l'économie politique*. Paris: Éditions Sociales.

———. 1976 [1867, 1894]. *Le Capital, Critique de l'économie politique*. Paris: Editions Sociales.

Mill, John Stuart. 1859. *On Liberty*. London: J. M. Dent & Sons.

Montaigne, Michel de. 2002 [1588]. *Les Essais*. Paris: Arléa.

Pindyck, R., and D. Rubinfeld. 1995. *Microeconomics*. Upper Saddle River, NJ: Pearson.

Rawls, John. 2009 [1971]. *Théorie de la justice*. Paris: Éditions Points.

Ricardo, David. 1821. *On the Principles of Political Economy and Taxation*, 3rd ed. Kitchener, ON: Batoche Book 2001.

Sen, Amartya. 1982. *Choice, Welfare and Measurement*. Oxford: Blackwell.

Smith, Adam. 1980. *Inquérito sobre a natureza e as causas da riqueza das nações*, Vol. I. Lisboa: Fundação Calouste Gulbenkian [Original: *An Inquiry into the Nature and Causes of the Wealth of Nations*. London: Methuen and Co Ltd., 1776).

Stigler, George J. 1966. *The Theory of Price*, 3rd ed. New York: Macmillan & CO.

Tsoulfidis, Lefteris. 2017. Economic Theory in Historical Perspective. *The Journal of Philosophical Economics: Reflections on Economic and Social Issues* 10 (2): 102–124.

Varian, Hal. 2005. *Intermediate Microeconomics*. New York: W.W. Norton.

Veblen, Thorstein. 1899. The Preconceptions of Economic Science. *The Quarterly Journal of Economics* 13 (1): 396–426.

Williamson, O. 2002. The Theory of the Firm as Governance Structure: From Choice to Contract. *Journal of Economic Perspectives* 16 (3): 171–195.

CHAPTER 9

General Conclusion

Foucault's Contribution to the History of Economic Thought: An Archaeological View

Finally, we can assess Foucault's contribution to the History of Economic Thought and, more generally, to the analysis of the ideas and concepts developed by the Economic Theory. Foucault highlights the intrinsic historicity of scientific production in general, and of Economic Science in particular. This perspective seems of first importance today:

(i) it allows refuting the mystifying discourse that presents Economic Science as an objective analysis of "facts," an analysis carried out based on a similarity with the methods used in the so-called exact Sciences, free from judgments, subjective values and ideology.

Within this perspective, Economic Science is limited to a form of economic engineering that consists in determining the conditions for an efficient allocation of resources, which are, by nature, scarce. On the other hand, the works related to complex systems clearly show that the historicity, the irreversibility of the studied processes and of time are one of the fundamental characteristics of these sciences: mathematics, physics and chemistry showed that the analyzed processes are intrinsically historical (Poincaré, Prigogine, Israël).

A. Herscovici, *Value, Historicity, and Economic Epistemology*,
https://doi.org/10.1007/978-3-031-21157-7_9

It is interesting to note that Economics, and more specifically Neoclassical Economics, imported elements from other sciences, mainly physics and mathematics (Vercelli 1991): multiplier, accelerator, elasticity and differential equations. It intended to acquire a scientific status in this way, refuting the historicity generally reclaimed by the Social Sciences, in order to construct universal laws and thus reveal the intrinsic truth of a natural order that does not depend on historical contingencies.

However, the result was the opposite of what was expected: historicity was reintroduced and its importance expanded through the importation of instruments from other disciplines. *If, today, it is possible to speak of methodological monism, this is implemented from the generalization of historicity, and not from its refutation.* It is one more irony of history, of history of ideas.

(ii) Thus, Foucault's contribution consists in demonstrating that any scientific discourse can only be considered as the product of a certain period, that is, of a certain episteme: the genesis, legitimacy and readability of a certain scientific discourse are possible only from a determined episteme. This corresponds to Marx's statement:

> "Humanity never asks itself what problems it can solve, for on closer inspection it will always be found that the problem only presents itself when the material conditions to solve it exist or at least will appear." (Marx, 1859)

As demonstrated in this work, the facts to be studied are chosen by socially and historically determined subjects: consequently, scientific analysis is, at least partially, historically determined. This methodological option is incompatible with different universalist and positivist approaches: the subject is not an impartial spectator, and scientific "truth" is not an intrinsic feature of the universe.

In this sense, Foucault designs an archeology of knowledge, as he *recontextualizes* the different scientific discourses from the episteme in which they were born. This analysis implies a historical relativism and a refutation of the Popperian concept of scientific progress, at least in the long run:

(a) historical relativism due to the fact that the scientific productions of a given episteme cannot be evaluated, or judged, based on the criteria that characterize another episteme.
(b) This historical relativism allows us to refute the Popperian thesis of the progress of Science, in the long term: the progress of Science can only be conceived within the same episteme, within the scope of what Kuhn qualifies as normal science. From one episteme to another, there are only epistemological ruptures; the evolutions of Science are discontinuous (this is the term used by Foucault) and do not follow a trajectory that, in the long run, moves toward a universal truth. The incommensurability of the paradigms, in the sense defined by Kuhn, also highlights these discontinuities.

(iii) What is the conception of the History of Economic Thought that can be sustained from Foucault's analysis? Compared with Kuhn's relativism, for example, it is possible to qualify Foucault's conception of absolute relativism: Science is essentially determined by external History, and the role of internal History is negligible.

If we define epistemology as a philosophical reflection that relates solely to the methods employed by different scientific schools, it is possible to state that Foucault's analysis is centered "on the non-epistemological-discursive elements of economic theorizing" (Kologlugil 2010, p. 2). Foucault's approach would be too reductive, since it does not recognize any degree of autonomy to Science and does not attribute any explanatory value to the content of scientific discourse.

Nevertheless, there are ambiguities and contradictions: if, on the one hand, Foucault affirms the primacy of external History, in other writings, he maintains that the study used in "*Les mots et les choses*" is essentially centered on the internal history of economics (Foucault 1980).

My position is closer to the position adopted by Kuhn, since I study the evolution of Economic Science from a double perspective, that is, partly from external history, and partly from internal history. It is from this more "moderate" conception of historical relativism that I analyzed the evolution of economic thought.

Nevertheless, Foucault's contribution allows the construction of a *meta-epistemology*, that is, an epistemological reflection applied to epistemology itself. As it is an abyss structure, it is thus possible to deduce that any form of knowledge is, by definition, limited: "There is no less science for conceiving ignorance than there is for conceiving science" (Montaigne, 1588, p. 741).

Foucault's main contribution, in relation to Economics, was to allow the demystification of the economic discourse that tries to present Economics as a Science free of ideological components, a science elaborated from the standards of Mechanical Physics; this observation applies equally to different schools of thought.

The Limits of Foucault's Analysis with Regard to Economics

The limits of Foucault's analysis, with regard to economics, come from the periodization he establishes and the very definition of the concept of episteme.

The periodization elaborated by Foucault deals with mercantilism, Physiocracy, Classical Economics, including Marx; Foucault (1966) only mentions marginalism (Gane, 2014, pp. 20, 21) and soon after studies neoliberalism, based on Mises and Hayek's works (Foucault, 2010).

This periodization seems to me inadequate, or, more precisely, incomplete, for the following reasons:

(i) from a genealogical perspective, certain elements of marginalism were already present in the mechanisms highlighted by Physiocracy and, to a certain extent, in the works of Adam Smith. The foundations of Hayek's theory aim to justify the efficiency of the market and the competitive order based on the partial refutation (cf. Chapter 6) of the neoclassical construction elaborated on the basis of Marshallian and Walrasian economics.

The evolution of ideas, in Economic Science, is discontinuous and non-linear; nevertheless, the passage from one episteme to another is explained from a relation of assimilation and distinction: assimilation, when the works are carried out within the same episteme, or the same paradigm, that is, when the works share a same hard core[1]—differentiation when the critique of a theory elaborated within a given paradigm is made from a different paradigm, already built or under construction.[2]

There are also *false differentiation strategies*, when two theories oppose each other within the same paradigm: none of them questions the foundations of the paradigm within which they are operating. Here, it is a question of a sociological strategy of differentiation that aims to produce a symbolic accumulation in the field of scientific production. In Economics, these strategies are widely used:

(a) The so-called New Keynesians, led by Mankiw,[3] present their works as "revolutionaries." However, the method used is incompatible with the foundations of the General Theory: the study is centered on the components of supply, based on exogenous variations in demand—there is no strong uncertainty, money does not fulfill a reserve of value function, and in the long run, the supply curve remains vertical.

These premises inherent to the integration of Keynesian theory in the framework of standard neoclassical theory were already present in Hicks' IS/LM interpretation, and in the works of Friedman (1974). So, I don't see any revolution, no new paradigm, but just an "improvement" of work carried out previously, within the same paradigm. I could formulate the same conclusions regarding the theory of contestable markets (Baumol, 1982), or the controversy of the 1990s between New Classicals and New Keynesians: in all these cases, the controversies occur within the scope of Normal Science, that is, they neither question nor refute the core of the neoclassical Research Program.

(b) The neoliberalism studied by Foucault does not constitute a reference matrix, in terms of Economic Theory: it incorporates both elements that come from the neoclassical Research Program and from the Austrian school: Phelps (2011) claims to recognize several

[1] At this analytical level, the concepts of paradigm and episteme are similar.

[2] At this respect, see the concept of mainstream implosion (Herscovici 2019).

[3] Despite being equally qualified as New Keynesians, Akerlof, Stiglitz and Grossman belong to a totally different theoretical line: their main results allow them to refute all standard Neoclassical Economics, and these economists build an alternative paradigm linked to a New Information Economy (Stiglitz 2000).

principles of the theory of rational expectations in the analysis of the Austrian school.

(c) Finally, it should be noted that Foucault's problematic changed when he studied neoliberalism: "I tried to analyze 'liberalism,' not as a theory or an ideology, and even less, obviously, as a way in which 'society ''represents itself,' but as a practice, that is to say, a 'way of doing things' directed toward objectives and regulating itself by continuous reflection" (Foucault 1979, p. 819). In Foucault's work, there is no epistemological continuity between his study of Classical Political Economy and the modern forms he qualifies as neoliberalism.

Based on the concept of episteme, Foucault provides the elements that allow the construction of an archeology of knowledge, by specifying the social, political and historical conditions that made possible the emergence of different modalities of knowledge. However, a genealogy is lacking to explain the evolutions and the passage from one episteme to another, which makes the analysis static: Foucault compares different epistemes, without specifying the dynamics that allow explaining these transitions. The very definition that Foucault gives of episteme explains the static character and the impossibility of carrying out a dynamic analysis: the *monolithic character of the concept of episteme* does not allow understanding the links existing between the different periods considered.

If the concept of episteme constructed by Foucault represents an ideal type, in historical and concrete reality, such an ideal type, pure by definition, does not exist: a given episteme can only be a hybrid matrix, a matrix that incorporates elements from the past, the present, and that elaborates elements that will be used in the future.

Beyond Episteme: The Hybrid Concept of Order

A Typology

Contrary to the monolithic concept of episteme, the concept of order is hybrid: a concrete order, which corresponds to a certain social formation and a specific epoch, is, in most cases, a combination of several "pure" orders. The difference between episteme and what I defined as order is the same as that established by Marxist authors, between the mode of production and social formation: the mode of production is a "pure," monolithic category, while social formation a concrete category and, by nature, hybrid (Bourdé 1983, p. 278).

Regarding modernity, Dumont (1983, p. 31) states that "(....) several value-ideas that are accepted as intrinsically modern are, in fact, the result of a history in whose course modernity and non-modernity or, more exactly, individualistic value-ideas and their opposites, combined. intimately."

We can theoretically differentiate as ideal types the following categories of orders:

(i) The holistic order is implemented at the macro-social level, and the individual plays no active role. A global mechanism corresponds to the order that governs society; the individual does not have autonomy and has to fit into this order, this "social totality" (Dumont 1983, p. 21). Society is only conceived as a totality, to which the individual has to be subsumed.

This subsumption appears in two forms (Idem, p. 22): (a) subordination is characterized by the individual's agreement to the norms imposed by the totality. This dependency relationship, within the scope of a democratic society, is accepted and socially legitimized (b) submission, on the contrary, as it is practiced in totalitarian regimes, represents an attempt to fight individualism and to submit, from the practice of systematic violence, the individual to the social totality: Nazism or the Islamic State use this means.

(ii) The order linked to individualism is also hybrid, in that it combines individual wills with an order necessary for the regulation of society. It is in this context that Political Economy is born, autonomized and developed: it is possible to "isolate" a social activity solely aimed at satisfying needs, whether individual or collective, to define Economics. The application of an instrumental individual rationality can only be conceived in this perspective.

However, as demonstrated above with respect to the concept of order (cf. p. 188), *individual rationality is unable to implement a viable regulation of the social totality; the very existence of an economic order (evoked in the parable of the fable of the bees, the invisible hand or the spontaneous order of the market) highlights the limits of individual rationality and the necessary existence of some emergent properties.*

As a mechanism for regulating the social totality, pure individualism, in the neoclassical version, and the exercise of an instrumental rationality are not viable; it has to be accompanied by macro-social and economic regulations. The hybrid character appears as an intrinsic feature of any concrete order.

The paradoxes of the neoclassical discourse, or that linked to the Austrian school, are the following: on the one hand, this discourse intends to build a science free from ideological values and, on the other hand, it has to implement the regulation of social totality through mechanisms in which, by nature, moral and ethical values are embedded. There are two ways to solve this problem: the parable of the invisible hand intends to reconcile hedonism, that is, hedonistic individual action, with a social morality that aims to maximize social welfare. On the other hand, analyzes in terms of Social Choice, for example, show that (a) the regulation of the social totality can only be implemented on the basis of an order, and (b) the definition of this order necessarily implies adherence to certain moral values and the refutation of other values; as highlighted by recent events, with the violent actions of extremist groups, the maintenance of democracy and the functioning of their own institutions, constitute, on the part of most states, collective choices that meet the values proper to democratic ethics.

The developments of individualism, in terms of Political Sociology, are reflected in the concept of natural rights and the inalienable rights of the individual, as defined by the Declaration of Human Rights. Here too, the results in terms of Social Choice clearly show that the concrete system of social regulation is a combination of holism and individualism.

Orders and Episteme

We can analyze the different epistemes defined by Foucault from the concept of order and thus highlight its hybrid nature.

The pre-capitalist episteme is essentially holistic: the primacy of power in the Catholic Church, at least in the West, governs this order. The king is the earthly personification of God, and eternal life is the goal to be attained.

In the Renaissance, which, according to Foucault, belongs to this episteme, elements alien to the preclassical episteme already appear: a return to ancient cultures, the emergence of the individual as a social actor *à part entière*, the development of mercantile activities linked to international finance (Braudel 1985/1979), the development of Sciences and Arts based on a natural order. We can observe elements that announce both the classical episteme and modernity:

(a) The development of Sciences that aim to reveal a truth inscribed in nature, which has to be interpreted as a progressive replacement of the divine order by the natural order. This natural order is one of the main features of the classical episteme.
(b) A growing autonomy of intellectual, artistic and scientific activities, together with an individualization of the production of this type of activity. With regard to the Renaissance, Schumpeter draws a parallel between the mythical figure of the entrepreneur and the artist. This represents the archetype of the Schumpeterian entrepreneur: "The artist, who was, at the same time, an engineer and a businessman (…) provides the best illustration of my thought" (1944, p. 171). These are elements that characterize modernity and the emergence of individualism.

We observe the same characteristics with regard to the classical episteme: it replaces the divine order with the natural order and thus intensifies the autonomy of scientific production in relation to religious and political power. Nevertheless, Adam Smith tries to reconcile the moral and religious order with the economic rationality defined by hedonism. In the same way, the Physiocratic school is already developing components that will be widely used in the construction of the marginalist economy.

Finally, the episteme that corresponds to what Foucault calls modernity contains elements that come from other epistemes: the very concept of order highlights the limits of the role of homo economicus and the need for a macro-social mechanism to maintain the global coherence of society.

Classical economists (except Marx and, to some extent, Ricardo) invoke the existence of a human nature to justify certain hypotheses that occupy a central place in their analyses. Implicitly, all Neoclassical Economics conceives an aggregate amount of capital as a natural element, as its value does not depend on historically determined variables.

In summary, we can formulate the following conclusions: contrary to the concept of episteme, the concept of order, due to its hybrid character, provides elements to study the dynamics, that is, the social forces that explain the shift from one system to another. In addition to the archeology of knowledge, the concept of order allows the construction of a genealogy of this knowledge, which constitutes an indispensable complement and thus responds to the different criticisms made to Foucault's analysis.

I do not intend to underestimate Foucault's contribution, which seems to me essential, in relation to the following aspects: it allows me to demystify a discourse that, at least in the area of Economics, presents this Science as free from value judgments, and capable of providing universal solutions. This responds in part to the problem raised by Backhouse (2002, p. 23), regarding the History of Economic Thought: "Perhaps as important as what these definitions say is what they do not say.“ I just will add what they do not want to say.

As indicated by Vallois (2015, p. 3), Foucault's writings do not indicate a precise methodology, but they have to be used as tools by other researchers, due to the specificities of their research: "I do not write to a public, I write to users, not to readers" (Foucault 1974, p. 1391). These users "searched, found a chapter, a type of analysis, something that has been useful to them subsequently" (Foucault 1974, p. 1391); that's what I tried to do in this book.

References

Backhouse, Roger E. 2002. *The Penguin History of Economics*. Penguin Books.

Baumol, W.J. 1982. Contestable Markets: An Uprising in the Theory of Industry Structure. *American Economic Review* 72 (1, March): 1–15. Published by: American Economic Association.

Braudel, Fernand. 1979. *Civilisation matérielle, économie et capitalisme* XVème-XVIIIème siècle. Amand Coli Paris.

———. 1985. *La dynamique du capitalisme*. Paris: Champs Flammarion.

Bourdé, Guy. 1983. «L'école des «Annales»». In *Bourdé Guy et Hervé Martin, Les écoles historiques*, 215–244. Paris: Editions du Seuil.

Dumont, Louis. 1983. *Essais sur l'individualisme. Une prespective anthropologique sur l'idéologie modern*. Paris: Éditions du Seuil.

Foucault, Michel. 2010. *The Government of Self and Others: Lectures at the Collège de France, 1982–3*. Basingstoke: Palgrave.

———. 1980. Conversazione con Michel Foucault. In *Michel Foucault, Dits et écrits: 1954-1988, tome II, 1976-1988*, ed. Daniel Defert and François Ewald, 860–915. Paris: Gallimard.

———. 1979. Naissance de la Biopolitique. In *Michel Foucault, Dits et écrits: 1954-1988, tome II, 1976-1988*, ed. Daniel Defert and François Ewald, 818–826. Paris: Gallimard.

———. 1974. Prisons et asiles dans le mécanisme du pouvoir. In *Michel Foucault, Dits et écrits: 1954-1988, tome I, 1954-1975*, ed. Daniel Defert and François Ewald, 1389–1393. Paris: Gallimard.

———. 1966. *Les mots et les choses*. Paris: Tel Galimard.

Friedman, M. 1974. A Theoretical Framework for Monetary Analysis. In *Milton Friedman's Monetary Framework: A Debate with His Critics*, ed. R.J. Gordon, 1–62. Chicago: University of Chicago Press.

Gane, Nicholas. 2014. The Emergence of Neoliberalism: Thinking Through and Beyond Michel Foucault's Lectures on Biopolitics. *Theory, Culture & Society* 31 (4): 3–27.

Grossman, S.J., and Stiglitz, J.E. 1976. Information and Competitive Price System. *The American Economic Review* 66 (2, May): 246–253.

———. 1980, On the Impossibility of Informationally Efficient Markets. *The American Economic Review* 70 (3, June 1980): 393–408.

Kologlugil, Serhat. 2010. Michel Foucault's Archaeology of Knowledge and Economic Discourse. *Erasmus Journal for Philosophy and Economics* 3 (2, Autumn): 1–25. http://ejpe.org/pdf/3-2-art-1.pdf

Herscovici, Alain. 2019. *Essays on the Historicity of Capital.* Cham: Palgrave Macmillan.

Marx, Karl. 1972 [1859]. *Contribution à la critique de l'économie politique*. Paris: Éditions Sociales.

Montaigne, Michel de. 2002 [1588]. *Les Essais*. Paris: Arléa.

Phelps, Edmund. 2011. *Keynes vs. Hayek: Stumbling Blocks to Spending Our Way to Prosperity*, Produced by Reuters, 8 November 2011.

Schumpeter, J.A. 2003 [1944]. *Capitalism, Socialism and Democracy.* Taylor & Francis e-Library.

Stiglitz, Joseph E. 2000. The Contribution to the Economics of Information to Twentieth Century Economics. *The Quarterly Journal of Economics* (November).

Vallois, Nicola. 2015. Michel Foucault and the History of Economic Thought (Michel Foucault et l'histoire de la pensée économique), *Oeconmia* (5–4): 461–490.

Vercelli, Alessandro. 1991. *Methodological Foundations of Macroeconomics: Keynes After Lucas*. Cambridge: Cambridge University Press.

Author Index

A. Herscovici, *Value, Historicity, and Economic Epistemology*, https://doi.org/10.1007/978-3-031-21157-7

E

F

G

H

I

K

L

M

O

P

Q

Thematic Index

A. Herscovici, *Value, Historicity, and Economic Epistemology*,
https://doi.org/10.1007/978-3-031-21157-7

Kolibri 360 GmbH
Ferdinand-Jühlke-Straße 7
99095 Erfurt, Deutschland
produktsicherheit@kolibri360.de